THE NOVEL OF
MANNERS IN AMERICA

THE NOVEL OF MANNERS IN AMERICA

by James W. Tuttleton

The University of North Carolina Press
Chapel Hill

Library of Congress Catalog Card Number 70–174787
ISBN 0–8078–1188–2
Manufactured in the United States of America
Printed by Heritage Printers, Inc.
Charlotte, North Carolina

For Leslie

We know a man imperfectly until we know his society, and we but half know a society until we know its manners. This is especially true of a man of letters, for manners lie very close to literature.

—Henry James

✄ Contents

✖ Preface

The aims of *The Novel of Manners in America* are manifold, but perhaps the reader will forgive me if I set out here, at the beginning, what I have attempted to do in this study. First, I have tried to define, broadly, a significant form of American fiction about which there is at present much confusion and disagreement. The phrase "novel of manners" means so much in the criticism of the American novel that it means hardly anything. Howard Mumford Jones recently observed in *Jeffersonianism and the American Novel*, for example, that "all novels are in some sense novels of manners."[1] And so, in some sense, they are. I have tried to be flexible and inclusive in illustrating this form, but I have also sought to limit the definition of what it might be.

I have also sought to describe the form—to elucidate its typical themes, styles, structures, character types, ideological postures, and the characteristic strategies by which the form is brought to life by our novelists. I must confess at the outset that the mode of analysis in this study is not solely aesthetic. I recognize the novel as an autonomous artifact, and I have a deep and abiding sympathy with the modes of intrinsic criticism by which the novel may be discussed as such. But I have been governed, to a large extent, by the terms of the argument that usually attend the discussion of this form. And these terms have tended to be sociological, political, philosophical, economic, and historical as well as aesthetic. At all times I have tried to keep the discussion of these disciplines within the general domain of literary criticism. It will doubtless be said that I have not always succeeded in doing so. But even if I have not, I have tried to keep from prostituting the work of art by putting it to uses which are not within the proper field of imaginative literature. I believe, with Ralph Ellison, that a novel is a novel and not a piece of disguised sociology. But I also recognize, as he does, that a novel is in some sense a public gesture and that it may have the highest relevance to social, political, or psychological issues.

The necessity of arguing for the viability of the form—against the notion that the novel (and particularly the novel of manners) is dead—has led me to defend the proposition that America as a nation is marked by significant cultural diversity. To some extent, we are certainly a homogeneous nation: many of us shop at similar supermarkets, drive competing high-powered chromium-plated automobiles, and see well-nigh indistinguishable mass-produced movies and television programs. But our sociologists tell a somewhat different story about our alleged homogeneity, and the stratification of social groups and the complexity of customs they describe are reinforced by the conclusions of the social anthropologists, the political scientists, the economic historians, and students of American social history. The notion of American homogeneity is a myth virtually impossible to dispel—partly because of its durable grain of truth, partly because it supports the myth of our political egalitarianism.

I have tried to explore some of these problems, and their effects on our literary criticism, in the process of examining the work of some of the more representative and important American novelists of manners. Since, as Professor Jones suggests, nearly all novels are in some sense novels of manners, nearly every American novelist could be examined within the general framework I have here set up. Irving Howe, for example, has observed that "the encounter between Ishmael and Queequeg tells us as much about manners (American manners), and through manners about the moral condition of humanity, as we are likely to find in a novel by Jane Austen or Balzac."[2] But Balzac and Austen are more centrally concerned about how manners reflect the moral condition of humanity than, say, Melville, and it is with writers who are thus more centrally concerned that I have chosen to deal. The problem of selection has been most vexing. In excluding the fiction of writers like George Washington Cable, Hamlin Garland, Zona Gale, Thomas Nelson Page, Robert Grant, Arlo Bates, Francis Marion Crawford, and Henry Blake Fuller, I have invoked the principle that their work does not add anything—materially and in terms of literary quality—to the general argument I have proposed. Writers of the modern South—Flannery O'Connor, Warren, and Faulkner, for example—and writers of the modern Jewish and Negro social worlds—Malamud and Bellow, Baldwin and Ellison—I have omitted because their novels raise issues that transcend the question of manners and are thus more intelligently discussed within other critical frameworks. Only three substantial novelists of manners have I excluded from this study—Theodore Dreiser, Ellen Glasgow, and John Updike. The omission of these writers is a purely arbitrary one, dictated by reasons of space. But many of the generalizations presented herein may be usefully tested by their fiction.

Because I have tried to explore as fully as possible the question of America's cultural diversity and the question of whether there could be a novel of manners in America, each chapter takes up and develops the argument. Although most of the writers here dealt with are well known, I have not hesitated to appeal to biographical fact in trying to make clear the impulses that lead a novelist to write the kind of fiction some of our critics have dismissed as alien to America. I have tried to make each chapter an analysis which will stand on its own and which, though thesis-oriented, does not falsify the general character of the writer's work. I do not believe that I argue for any one of them a significantly higher place than he currently enjoys. But I have argued that the novel of manners itself deserves higher esteem than recent critics—particularly those ideologically committed to avant-garde experimentalism in literature and to radicalism in politics—have accorded it. It may be that the stance I have taken will seem unnecessarily argumentative. If so, let me say that I have a deep and passionate love for the fiction of writers who are not novelists of manners—symbolists, for example, like Melville, Faulkner, and Nabokov. But I believe seriously in the importance of correct literary judgments. And I believe that the reputations of a number of our writers have suffered because of errors of fact and judgment which sometimes attend descriptions of the American social scene and because of the arbitrariness with which genres of fiction are sometimes evaluated. In any event, the issues I discuss are inherently worth the argument they arouse. As Henry James observed, "Art lives upon discussion . . . upon the exchange of views and the comparison of standpoints. . . ."[3]

JAMES W. TUTTLETON
New York City
May 1972

℀ Acknowledgments

I would like especially to thank those who have given me support, advice, and encouragement—particularly C. Hugh Holman, C. Carroll Hollis, Walter B. Rideout, Henry A. Pochmann, and Edwin Haviland Miller. Thanks are also due to the National Endowment for the Arts and Humanities and the research councils of the graduate schools of the University of Wisconsin and New York University, which generously provided research grants for the completion of this study. I am indebted to the staff of The University of North Carolina Press for patient guidance and counsel in the preparation of this book.

Portions of this book have been previously published under the following titles: "The New England Character in Cooper's Social Novels," *Bulletin of the New York Public Library* (1966); "Henry James and Edith Wharton: Fiction as the House of Fame," *Midcontinent American Studies Journal* (1966); "Leisure, Wealth, and Luxury: Edith Wharton's Old New York," *Midwest Quarterly* (1966); "Edith Wharton: Form and the Epistemology of Artistic Creation," *Criticism* (1968); "Howells and the Manners of the Good Heart," *Modern Fiction Studies* (1970); "Edith Wharton: The Archeological Motive," *Yale Review* (1972); and "Louis Auchincloss: The Image of Lost Elegance and Virtue," *American Literature* (1972).

THE NOVEL OF
MANNERS IN AMERICA

*The novel, then, is a perpetual quest
for reality, the field of its research being
always the social world, the material of its
analysis being always manners as the
indication of the direction of man's soul. . . .
Now the novel as I have described it
has never really established itself in America.
Not that we have not had very great novels
but that the novel in America diverges from
its classic intention, which, as I have said, is
the investigation of the problem of reality
beginning in the social field. The fact is that
American writers of genius have not turned
their minds to society.*
                    —Lionel Trilling

*For one thing . . . there are no manners in
America to observe, compared, that is, with
Europe. And what manners there are are
nearly uniform among all Americans. This is
of course not literally true. . . . But the novelist
needs a more vivid variety of manners than, so
far, he has discovered in this country. Also,
there is the persistent distrust of or simple lack
of interest in the idea of society itself, so that
it seems unnatural to most American writers
to suppose that social conventions and laws
are beneficial to the individual.*
                    —Richard Chase

These remarks suggest that the matrix
of form for the American novel is not manners
or society. . . . There was that in the American
ethos which gave an emotional primacy to
ideas, which made them the proper subject-
matter of the novelist's art, while at the same
time the novelist was deprived of that richness
of nuance and tone which a traditional society
alone can provide. . . .

This should not surprise us, given the
condition under which the American writer
had to create. . . . For the traditional novelist,
the universal and the particular come together
in the world of manners; but for the American
artist there was no social surface responsive
to his touch.

—Marius Bewley

There are only two cultural pockets left in
America; and they are the Deep South and
that area of northeastern United States whose
moral capital is Boston, Massachusetts. This

*is to say that these are the only places in the
country which could possibly produce
novelists of manners because they are the
only places where there are any manners. In
all the other parts of the country people live in
a kind of vastly standardized cultural prairie,
a sort of infinite Middle West, and that means
that they don't really live and they don't
really do anything.*
                    —John W. Aldridge

---

*My suggestion is that the exact
opposite is true. The job of the novelist of
manners has simply become more complex,
more challenging, and more important. . . .
    Not the least of the jobs of the
contemporary novelist is that of rescuing
American society from the charge that it
doesn't exist.*
                    —John Brooks

Nothing seems at first sight less important than the out-ward form of human actions, yet there is nothing upon which men set more store; they grow used to everything except to living in a society which has not their own manners.
　　　　　—Alexis de Tocqueville

1

❧ The Sociological Matrix
of the Novel of Manners

Contemporary actuality may indeed be so strange that the imagination cannot compete with it. "It is now life and not art," Lionel Trilling has remarked, "that requires the willing suspension of disbelief."[1] And it is doubtless true that modern sociologists and psychologists have appropriated fields once reserved to the novelist. But it is by no means decided that the novel is dead—despite the claim of critics like F. W. Bateson and Sir Harold Nicolson that "the future of imaginative prose lies with history and biography."[2] The novel persists because still today— as Henry James observed of the American scene some sixty years ago in "The Future of the Novel"—"there are too many sources of interest neglected—whole categories of manners, whole corpuscular classes and provinces, museums of character and condition; unvisited."[3] The function of the novelist has always been, and is now, to observe and to order the social facts about us and to dramatize them in a new imaginative interpretation of human experience. The charge that the novel is dead, so often heard in the literary criticism of the 1950s, is today a dead issue.

There is one type of novel, though, which is generally held to be deader than usual—especially in this country. And when, in our recent criticism, writers have reflected on the death of the American novel, they have usually meant a certain kind of novel —the American novel of manners. The obituaries pronounced by our critics upon this kind of novel are primarily oversimplifications of a point of view expressed by Lionel Trilling in his provocative essay "Manners, Morals, and the Novel." (I have no wish to rehearse the extensive arguments this essay provoked in the 1950s and 1960s. The interested reader will find a sampling of them listed in my notes.)[4] Trilling's description of "manners" is of such interest that it deserves to be quoted in full:

> What I understand by manners, then, is a culture's hum and buzz of implication. I mean the whole evanescent context in which its explicit statements are made. It is that part of a culture which is made up of half-uttered or unutterable expressions of value. They are hinted at by small actions, sometimes by the arts of dress or decoration, sometimes by tone, gesture, emphasis, or rhythm, sometimes by the words that are used with a special frequency or a special meaning. They are the things that separate them from the people of another culture. They make the part of a culture which is not art, or religion, or morals, or politics, and yet it relates to all these highly formulated departments of culture. It is modified by them; it modifies them; it is generated by them; it generates them. In this part of culture assumption rules, which is often so much stronger than reason.[5]

I find this a brilliant observation about the content of the novels of manners considered in this study. But let me declare at the outset that I do not consider satisfactory some of the critical observations which have been inferred from it—namely, that American society has no hum and buzz; that we have never had in this country a hierarchy of social classes; that we have never had and do not now have a variety of manners and mores—those small actions, arts, gestures, emphases, and rhythms that express value; that, consequently, the novel of manners never really established itself in America; and that our best writers are therefore idea-oriented symbolic romancers. When Richard Chase claims in *The American Novel and Its Tradition* that American "novels" are inferior to our prose romances and that only second- or third-rate writers spend time on novels, he means that our novels of manners and their authors are inferior. Are we compelled to regard only our romances as great books? In view of the extraordinary achievement of *The Portrait of a Lady*, *The American*, *The House of Mirth*, and *The Great Gatsby*, it is remarkable that some of our critics have concluded that "we do not have the novel that touches significantly on society, on manners."[6]

To understand this issue of the relation of the American novel to our society—it has had a long and controversial history—requires of us assent to the proposition that, as James somewhere remarked, "kinds" are the very life of literature, and truth and strength come from the complete recognition of them. We need also to be aware of some aspects of the history of the American romance and of a special kind of American novel which is the subject of this book—the American novel of manners.

I

Dr. Johnson once observed that one of the maxims of civil law is that definitions are hazardous. This maxim holds true in the field of literary criticism. Although no "kind" or genre of literature has been more difficult to define than the novel of manners, formulating an acceptable definition of it is the first order of business. Without a satisfactory definition, misunderstanding rather than enlightenment is the result; and along with misunderstanding usually comes irrelevant arguments about whether America is capable of producing a novel of manners.

To formulate a definition of the American novel of manners, let us regard as polarities the concept of the individual and the concept of the group, of society. Neither of these extremes can of course be the focus of the novel. Yet every novel locates itself somewhere between these extremes. If the novel deals largely with the self, personal experience, or the individual consciousness, the result will be a work which gravitates toward autobiography or "lyric or informal philosophy." If the self is refined out of existence in favor of social documentations, the result is history or chronicle. As Mark Schorer puts it: "The problem of the novel has always been to distinguish between these two, the self and society, and at the same time to find suitable structures that will present them together. . . . The novel seems to exist at a point where we can recognize the intersection of the stream of social history and the stream of the soul. This intersection gives the form its dialectical field, provides the source of those generic tensions that make it possible at all."[7] Near the center of this convergence, where the streams of the self and of social history inter-

sect, is the novel of manners. It is probably not amiss to say that
the form emphasizes social history more than lyric, confessional,
or autobiographical statement.

Perhaps a useful test of the definition of the novel of manners—
to borrow a term from Irving Howe's definition of the political
novel—is its "inclusiveness," rather than its narrowness, for narrow definitions have provoked some of the controversies which
always attend a discussion of this genre. If we are inclusive, we
may define the novel of manners as a novel in which the closeness
of manners and character is of itself interesting enough to justify
an examination of their relationship. By a novel of manners I
mean a novel in which the manners, social customs, folkways,
conventions, traditions, and mores of a given social group at a
given time and place play a dominant role in the lives of fictional
characters, exert control over their thought and behavior, and
constitute a determinant upon the actions in which they are engaged, and in which these manners and customs are detailed realistically—with, in fact, a premium upon the exactness of their
representation.

The representation of manners may be without authorial prejudice, in which case the novelist merely concerns himself, without comment, with his society's hum and buzz of implication. But
more often the portrait of manners is put to the service of an ideological argument. The center of the novel of manners, that is, may
be an idea or an issue—for example, the idea of social mobility, of
class conflict, of professional ambition, of matchmaking, of divorce. But if, in the development of such "ideas," significant
attention is paid to a realistic notation of the customs and conventions of the society in which these ideas arise and are acted out,
then we are dealing with a novel of manners. That a novel is
"about" a subject does not necessarily disqualify it as a novel of
manners. Jane Austen's *Pride and Prejudice*, for example, is
"about" the problem of finding suitable husbands for a household
of girls; and Scott Fitzgerald's *The Great Gatsby* is "about" the
failure of the American dream. But enough attention is directed
to the traditions of the early nineteenth-century English middle
class, in the one, and to jazz-age manners and mores, in the other,

to justify our examination of both of them as novels of manners. A useful extension of this definition, therefore, would be to say that the analysis of manners yields, from the point of view of this definition, profitable insights into the meaning of the novel without any distortion of its total significance.

Since the novel of manners inclines more toward social history than toward subjective psychologies or autobiography, it is, in a fundamental sense, sociologically oriented. That is, the novelist of manners is in some sense a "sociologist" who manipulates his data in terms of a narrative rather than a scientific or "logical" framework. This fact need not prejudice our attitude toward the novelist of manners or the genre created by his observation and notation. Many good novels survive the freight of social documentation intrinsic to the form. The influence of Comte's positivism is clearly evident in George Eliot's best studies of manners in midland England, yet we are never bothered by it. With the rise of sociology as a "science," in fact, novelists discovered a new set of tools for dissecting man in society. Many worthwhile novels have in fact major characters who are sociologists, anthropologists, or students of these disciplines—for example, Edith Wharton's Ralph Marvell of *The Custom of the Country*; Sinclair Lewis's Carol Kennicott of *Main Street*, who studied sociology at college; William Dean Howells's protagonist in *The Vacation of the Kelwyns*, a professor of historical sociology at Harvard; and Marquand's Malcolm Bryant, a sociologist in *Point of No Return* who has come to Clyde, Massachusetts, to analyze its social structure.

If we look to sociology for a systematic analysis of society, we soon find ourselves dealing with five areas of social experience which may be described as follows: "Firstly, a set of social conventions and taboos regarding relations between the sexes, between parents and children, as well as people's behavior in the company of their fellowmen. Secondly, a set of commonly, or at any rate widely accepted ethical standards. Thirdly, a set of religious and philosophical beliefs, or more often a miscellany of such beliefs, concerning the position and role of man in the universe. Fourthly, a given type of economic organization, with a greater or lesser emphasis on the importance of material possessions. Lastly, the political structure of a given community, embodying certain conceptions of government, of the individual's position in the state, and of international relations."[8]

The first category, "a set of social conventions and taboos," is of course the most important area of human experience for the novel of manners. For manners represent the expression, in positive and negative form, of the assumptions of society at a given time and place. Dramatic violations of commonly held ethical values are also endemic to the novel of manners. (Sometimes morals and manners are so inextricably mixed that we cannot tell whether characters act as they do because they think it is morally right or because it is socially proper. And in the novels of Henry James we cannot always be sure that there is any difference.) From the sociological point of view, in fact, a system of ethics merely represents the crystallization of the folkways of a society. Religious or philosophical beliefs are less important to the novel of manners, but if religious or philosophical assumptions did not subtly affect the behavior of fictional characters, the novel of manners would be other than it is. Economic considerations also play a less significant role in the development of the novel of manners, though wealth is often a particularly useful device for the freedom it provides a novelist in dramatizing certain social values. Whenever religious, philosophical, or economic "ideas" tend to be blown up out of proportion, the novel of manners becomes something else—the propaganda novel advocating religious opinions, philosophical systems, or economic dogmas. This point also applies to political considerations in the novel: if they become obtrusive, not merely a part of the fabric of the fictive social world, the novel becomes something other than a novel of manners—it becomes a radical or political novel.

To put it another way, the novel of manners is primarily concerned with social conventions as they impinge upon character. These other concerns are less central to it, but they help to define the ethos of the society portrayed, they provide a body of assumptions about experience which underlie its social code, and they affect the thought and behavior of fictional characters. To return to the analogy offered by Mark Schorer, as long as the impulse of the novelist does not push him too far toward propaganda or the extreme of chronicle or history, I see him as writing the novel of manners. I assume throughout this study, incidentally, that the novel of manners is a novel and not another thing—not, for example, as Ralph Ellison puts it, disguised sociology.

"Society," as used in this study, ordinarily refers to the structure of "classes," cliques, or groups by which specific American communities are organized. More particularly, "society" may refer to whatever group is presumed by the author to constitute the class defining itself through "polite manners," such as the commercial aristocracy of Edith Wharton's Old New York or the Brahmin patriciate of Marquand's New England. In a novel of manners, the illusion of society may be generated in two ways. First, the sense of society may be created by a vast number of characters who sprawl and swarm across the printed page and who, by very mass and number, give the novel the illusion of social density, of that "substantiality" characteristic of actual society. Novelists like Balzac, Proust, Thackeray, and O'Hara develop the illusion of society by this documentary technique. On the other hand, society may be merely felt as an abstract force; that is, the novel may deal with only a few individuals who embody various social attitudes. Howells was this kind of novelist—he liked to focus on three or four characters whose conflicting manners stand for the values of the social classes to which they belong.

What is important to this genre is that there be for analysis groups with recognizable and differentiable manners and conventions. These groups need not be stable, in the sense of enduring for centuries (e.g., the English or French hereditary aristocracy). They need not even be typical of the general culture of a particular country (e.g., James's American colony in Rome). For the novel of manners it is necessary only that there be groups large enough to have developed a set of differing conventions which express their values and permanent enough for the writer's notation of their manners. Frequently the most successful novels of manners treat classes which have existed briefly or during transitional periods when one group is in the process of decay while another is rising to supplant it. Hence it need not be assumed that the novel of manners features only an aristocratic class in conflict with the bourgeoisie; any stratified groups will do. In America, Cable found such groups in New Orleans; Ellen Glasgow in Richmond; J. P. Marquand in New England; Louis Auchincloss in New York; John O'Hara in the mid-Pennsylvania coal district; and Edith Wharton in New York. To deny the reality of these distinctive groups as "social classes" is largely to miss the point of the social analysis contained in the fiction of these writers. Their fiction suggests that, once and for all, the criterion for distinguishing the novel of manners is execution—what James would have called "treatment"—rather than subject matter.

II

The novel of manners in America has not always been a popular genre with our writers. And any discussion of this form must deal with two objections which frequently attend it. One has to do with the alleged superiority of symbolic romances over the realistic novel. In part, this objection, which I shall discuss later on, is an extension of the old theory of a hierarchy of literary genres. The other objection is based on the claim that America lacks the social differences which are the sine qua non of the novel of manners. Can the novel of manners flourish in a democratic country which supposedly lacks adequate social density and a clearly stratified and stable class structure? A surprisingly large number of serious novelists and critics of the past century and a half have contended that American social experience is and has been too meager and limited to nourish a fiction that portrays men involved in the social world and perhaps even establishing through it their personal identities. A concomitant argument is often put this way: The absence of clear and stable class lines prohibits a meaningful portrayal of American manners—everybody has middle-class manners; without a diversity of manners based on class distinctions there can be no contrasts in the values, customs, or traditions of fictional characters; and without such contrasts, there can be no intrinsic interest, conflict, or "solidity of specification" in the portrait of American society. As W. M. Frohock has ironically phrased it: "At first glance the syllogism seems unattackable: only a firmly (but not too firmly) stratified society can furnish the materials of which novels are made; the society of the United States is not firmly stratified; therefore the novel in the United States is out of the question. And the corollary is that the best we can hope for is romances."[9]

Both of these objections, in their earliest form, appear as a general criticism of what was once called "the poverty for the artist of native American materials." This issue is no longer as relevant as it was a century ago, but if we know what some of our writers and critics have felt about American society, we may be better able to understand the dilemma they saw themselves as confronting.

James Fenimore Cooper was the first major novelist to indict America on the grounds of its cultural poverty. His observation is my point of departure because he first isolated the issue, and he articulated it so fully that most subsequent references to America's social thinness are mere repetitions, mostly thoughtless, of views Cooper presented in 1828:

The second obstacle against which American literature has to contend [the first was the pirating and copyright problem], is in the poverty of materials. There is scarcely an ore which contributes to the wealth of the author, that is found, here, in veins as rich as in Europe. There are no annals for the historian; no follies (beyond the most vulgar and commonplace) for the satirist; no manners for the dramatist; no obscure fictions for the writer of romance; no gross and hardy offences against decorum for the moralist; nor any of the rich artificial auxiliaries of poetry. The weakest hand can extract a spark from the flint, but it would baffle the strength of a giant to attempt kindling a flame with a pudding-stone. I very well know there are theorists who assume that the society and institutions of this country are, or ought to be, particularly favourable to novelties and variety. But the experience of one month, in these States, is sufficient to show any observant man the falsity of their position. The effect of a promiscuous assemblage any where, is to create a standard of deportment; and great liberty permits every one to aim its attainment. I have never seen a nation so much alike in my life, as the people of the United States, and what is more, they are not only like each other, but they are remarkably like that which common sense tells them they ought to resemble. No doubt, traits of character that are a little peculiar, without, however, being either very poetical, or very rich, are to be found in remote districts; but they are rare, and not always happy exceptions.[10]

This passage, expressing Cooper's characteristic ambivalence toward our "national conformity," is suspect in the very rhetorical extravagance of his description of our social dullness. The fact is that the example of his own fiction belies the assumptions here expressed. *Home As Found* and *The Pioneers*, for example, are rich in the depiction of native manners, national follies, and social offenses. But it cannot be escaped that Cooper *believed* that the character of American society prevented his writing the *roman de moeurs*, even though he wanted to. Under the inspiration of Scott, therefore, he took his characters out of the drawing room and trailed them into the woods. It should not be forgotten, however, that even in the Leatherstocking series, the real issues are sometimes social issues masked in the adventure of the romance genre. In *The Pathfinder*, for example, Cooper's real purpose is to explore the question of whether a man of the hunter class (however much a "nature's gentleman") can find settlement happiness married to a girl whose manners have been polished by real ladies—the wives of the garrison officers.

But Cooper was not alone in pointing out the deficiencies in American society for the novelist. In "Some Reflections on American Manners" in *Democracy in America*, Alexis de Tocqueville, one of the most perceptive foreign critics of American ways, remarked in 1835 that in a new democratic society, the forms of social experience are so transitory that even if a code of good breeding were formulated no one could enforce it. "Every man therefore behaves after his own fashion, and there is always a certain incoherence in the manners of such times, because they are molded upon the feelings and notions of each individual rather than upon an ideal model proposed for general imitation." The absence of an authoritative code might make for more sincerity and openness in the American character, but Tocqueville felt that "the effect of democracy is not exactly to give men any particular manners, but to prevent them from having manners at all."[11] This alleged absence of observable manners, however beneficial to the political citizen, Cooper regarded as fatal to the novelist because it deprived him of the raw material of his social portrait.

III

Some of their contemporaries, however, argued that it was an easier task to draw the portrait of American manners than Cooper and Tocqueville admitted. Social witnesses of the stature of William Cullen Bryant, John Neal, and William Hickling Prescott argued that American society, for all its apparent formlessness, still offered a rich field for fiction. As Bryant observed in his 1825 review of Catharine Maria Sedgwick's *Redwood*, American social novels do not need the European class of idle aristocrats who "have leisure for that intrigue, those plottings and counter plottings, which are necessary to give a sufficient degree of action and eventfulness to the novel of real life."[12] Though lacking a class with "polite manners," he argued, the annals of our people "are abundantly fertile in interesting occurrences, for all the purposes of the novelists." Since "distinctions of rank, and the amusements of elegant idleness, are but the surface of society," the American novelist is uniquely capable of dramatizing character through the representation of different manners. "Whoever will take the pains to pursue this subject into its particulars," Bryant observed, "will be surprised at the infinite variety of forms of character, which spring up under the institutions of our country." Bryant went on to suggest the "innumerable and diverse influences upon the manners and temper of our people": the variety of religious creeds, geographical differences (North and South, East and West, seacoast and interior, province and metropolis), diversifications in manners produced by massive immigrations, and the like. "When we consider all these innumerable differences of character, native and foreign," he concluded, "this infinite variety of pursuits and objects, this endless diversity of change of fortunes, and behold them gathered and grouped into one vast assemblage in our own country, we shall feel little pride in the sagacity or the skill of that native author, who asks for a richer or a wider field of observation."[13]

Put in this way, nineteenth-century America does seem to have been an immensely rich source of social materials for the novelist. Bryant makes us wonder seriously whether Cooper's social vision was as perspicuous as we might wish. I do not mean to say that early American novelists did not face formidable obstacles. They surely did. But the problem of the "materials" was less crucial than the artist's felt need for those "romantic associations" which these materials could not provide. By this I mean that some of our early novelists seriously resented the notion that fiction ought to deal with the actualities of American life. A strictly realistic portrait of men's ordinary lives was held inferior because it made "few demands upon the imagination." Writing novels based on everyday actualities was merely imitating, unimaginatively, what men did. And what men did in this country, in the early years of the republic, was mainly a variety of disagreeable things incident to clearing and settling the country.

More and more our writers fixated on the need for "romantic settings" to evoke aesthetic emotions. Isaac Mitchell even went to the extreme of creating a medieval castle for Long Island in his *Alonzo and Melissa* (1804). "Romance" and "novel" cannot be defined too precisely, but the differences between them were so important to early American writers that to understand the relation of the American novel of manners to American fiction, we would do well to consider them.

The basic differences, as they develop in the eighteenth and nineteenth centuries, are loosely as follows. The novel was held to be a "truthful" representation of ordinary reality; it detailed with satisfactory realism the actualities of the social world. The romance, on the other hand, less committed to the realities of ordinary life, sought to leave "the powers of fancy at liberty to expatiate through the boundless realms of invention."[14] In the romance, in other words, invention rather than observation or description was valued. The novel emphasized character as revealed in everyday life—in the religious, business, political, moral, and social relationships of people. The romance, however, was concerned very little with the interaction of men in society; in fact, in the romance social relations were often so thinly represented that the characters seem less complex, less rounded, and therefore less credible as "real people." In the romance, the representation of character often resulted in abstractions or idealizations of social types—gentlemen, heroes, villains, soldiers, aristocrats. In the novel, extremes of characterization were avoided in favor of multidimensional or rounded characters, most of them drawn from the middle class.

The novel usually did not have a complicated plot, heroic action, or improbabilities. Plotting in the romance, however, was often elaborately worked out on the basis of coincidence or chance and was, if not incredible, often implausible. In many respects, the romance extended into prose some of the characteristics of the medieval verse romance, from which it derived not only its name but its tendency toward the "poetic," the legendary, and the highly imaginative, wonderful scenes of the distant past or the strange and faraway. Since it is "less committed to the immediate rendition of reality than the novel," as Chase has observed, "the romance will more freely veer toward mythic, allegorical, and symbolic forms."[15]

Clara Reeve's early history of prose fiction, *The Progress of Romance*, defined what in 1785 was understood to be the nature of the novel: "The Novel is a picture of real life and manners, and of the time in which it is written. . . . The Novel gives a familiar relation of such things, as pass every day before our eyes, such as may happen to our friend, or to ourselves; and the perfection of it, is to represent every scene, in so easy and natural a manner, and to make them appear so probable, as to deceive us into a persuasion (at least while we are reading) that all is real, until we are affected by the joys or distresses, of the persons in the story, as if they were our own."[16] This definition will not of course do any more. It stands as a generally reliable definition of the novel of manners, though, except for the claim that the novel must deal with the time in which it is written. There is no reason why a novel of manners reflecting all of these qualities may not be laid in the past, say (like *Waverley*) "sixty years since."

To find a definition of the American romance, let us move down into the 1830s, for Scott's treatment of history gave fresh direction to the romance in this country. William Gilmore Simms, a follower of Cooper in the Scott tradition of the historical romance, provided a definitive description of the form in the preface to his *The Yemassee: A Romance of Carolina* (1835):

The question briefly is—What are the standards of the modern Romance? What is the modern Romance itself? The reply is immediate. The modern Romance is the substitute which the people of the present day offer for the ancient epic. The form is changed: the matter is very much the same; at all events it differs much more seriously from the English novel than it does from the epic and the drama, because the difference is one of material, even more of fabrication. The reader who, reading Ivanhoe, keeps Richardson and Fielding beside him, will be at fault in every step of his progress. The domestic novel of those writers, confined to the felicitous narration of common and daily occurring events, and the grouping and delineation of characters in ordinary conditions of society, is altogether a different sort of composition; and if, in a strange doggedness, or simplicity of spirit, such a reader happens to pin his faith to such writers alone, circumscribing the boundless horizon of art to the domestic circle, the Romances of Maturin, Scott, Bulwer, and others of the present day, will be little better than rhapsodical and intolerable nonsense.

When I say that our Romance is the substitute of modern times for the epic or the drama, I do not mean to say that they are exactly the same things, and yet, examined thoroughly, the differences between them are very slight. These differences depend on the material employed, rather than upon the particular mode in which it is used. The Romance is of loftier origin than the Novel. It approximates the poem. It may be described as an amalgam of the two. It is only with those who are apt to insist upon poetry as verse, and to confound rhyme with poetry that the resemblance is unapparent. The standards of the Romance—take such a story, for example, as the Ivanhoe of Scott, or the Salathiel of Croly,—are very much those of the epic. It invests individuals with an absorbing interest—it hurries them rapidly through crowding and exacting events, in a narrow space of time—it requires the same unities of plan, of purpose, and harmony of parts, and it seeks for its adventures among the wild and wonderful. It does not confine itself to what is known, or even what is probable. It grasps at the possible; and, placing a human agent in hitherto untried situations, it exercises its ingenuity in extricating him from them, while describing his feelings and his fortunes in his progress.[17]

While this definition rationalizes Simms's own practice, it is a reliable statement of what romances after Scott were conceived to be and what they aimed to do. We should note the relationship alleged between the romance and the epic poem; the indifference to actuality in favor of extravagance or improbability; the corresponding distaste for the novel of manners, which is alleged to be limited to the trivialities of the domestic circle; and the bald assertion that the romance is altogether a loftier genre than the novel. These assumptions carry over, in part, into the twentieth century, where symbol-searching critics have exhibited "an attitude of distaste toward the actuality of experience—an attitude of radical devaluation of the actual if not downright hostility to it."[18] Irving Howe has likewise remarked how "the contemporary eagerness to interpret works of literature as symbolic patterns is often due to a fear or distaste of direct experience— sometimes, of direct literary experience. . . . When hardened into critical dogma, this mode of interpretation supports the assumption that truth or reality is always 'behind' what we see and sense —that an essence lurks in the phenomenon, a ghost in the machine, a spirit in the tree."[19]

This prejudice against actuality, against the experience of the ordinary world as we know it in society, led Simms to castigate savagely the novel of manners:

In works of this class, the imagination can have little play. The exercise of the creative faculty is almost entirely denied. The field of speculation is limited; and the analysis of minute shades of character, is all the privilege which taste and philosophy possess, for lifting the narrative above the province of mere lively dialogue, and sweet and fanciful sentiment. The ordinary events of the household, or of the snug family circle, suggest the only materials; and a large gathering of the set, at ball or dinner, affords incident of which the novelist is required to make the highest use. Writers of much earnestness of mood, originality of thought, or intensity of imagination seldom engage in this class of writing. Scott attempted it in St. Ronan's Well, and failed;—rising only into the rank of Scott, in such portions of the story as, by a very violent transition, brought him once more into the bolder displays of wild and stirring romance. He consoled himself with the reflection that male writers were not good at these things. His conclusion, that such writings were best handled by the other sex, may be, or not, construed into a sarcasm."[20]

It was no sarcasm, of course. Scott's respect for novelists of manners like Edgeworth and Austen was so great that he launched his career as a writer of fiction in imitation of them. But rarely has the outworn hierarchy of literary genres—evident in Simms's praise of the romance as epic—played more havoc with the fundamental impulse of American fiction—a realistic impulse grounded in the commonplace actualities of our daily experience.

IV

The growing popularity of the romance in the nineteenth century explains in part the indifference of our novelists to American society and manners. The scope of this indifference expands as the distinction between the romance and the novel becomes more rigid. American society appears deficient not only to the novelist but also to the romancer, who demands the privilege of disengaging experience from the actualities we know. Hawthorne complained that the American character was too dully matter-of-fact, too pragmatic and commonsensical, to accord much significance to the kind of liberated experience he liked to deal with: "In the old countries, with which fiction has long been conversant, a certain conventional privilege seems to be awarded to the romancer; his work is not put exactly side by side with nature; and he is allowed a license with regard to every-day probability, in view of the improved effects which he is bound to reproduce thereby."[21] These views are expressed in the preface to *The Blithedale Romance*, a book which proved to be an extremely interesting failure. In the beautifully enclosed world of the Brook Farm community, Hawthorne had the materials for a first-rate novel. And certain scenes—for example, the search for Zenobia's body—are portrayed with masterful realism and a substantiality that we are not accustomed to find in Hawthorne. But the book is ruined for some readers by Hawthorne's addiction to the contrived mystifications of the third-rate romance.

Hawthorne's attempt to escape the representation of American society merely testifies to the eminence, if not preeminence, of society, as a factor in the creation of fiction. Even in the attempt to ignore it, Hawthorne acknowledged its fascination as a subject for fiction. Justifying the European setting of *The Marble Faun*, he remarked: "No author, without a trial, can conceive of the difficulty of writing a romance about a country where there is no shadow, no antiquity, no mystery, no picturesque and gloomy wrong, nor anything but a commonplace prosperity, in broad and simple daylight, as is happily the case with my dear native land. It will be very long, I trust, before romance-writers may find congenial and easily handled themes, either in the annals of our stalwart republic, or in any characteristic and probable events of our individual lives."[22]

This view is questionable as a description of the American scene in the 1840s and 1850s. But Henry James was quick to seize upon its implications in his biography *Hawthorne* (1879). Speaking of the preface to *The Blithedale Romance*, James remarked the thinness of Hawthorne's notebooks:

The perusal of Hawthorne's American Note-Books operates as a practical commentary upon this somewhat ominous text. It does so at least to my own mind; it would be too much perhaps to say that the effect would be the same for the usual English reader. An American reads between the lines—he completes the suggestions—he constructs a picture. I think I am not guilty of any gross injustice in saying that the picture he constructs from Hawthorne's American diaries, though by no means without charms of its own, is not, on the whole, an interesting one. It is characterised by an extraordinary blankness— a curious paleness of colour and paucity of detail. Hawthorne, as I have said, has a large and healthy appetite for detail, and one is therefore the more struck with the lightness of the diet to which his observation was condemned. For myself, as I turn the pages of his journals, I seem to see the image of the crude and simple society in which he lived. I use these epithets, of course, not invidiously, but descriptively; if one desires to enter as closely as possible into Hawthorne's situation, one must endeavour to reproduce his circumstances. We are struck with the large number of elements that were absent from them, and the coldness, the thinness, the blankness, to repeat my epithet, present themselves so vividly that our foremost feeling is that of compassion for a romancer looking for subjects in such a field. It takes so many things, as Hawthorne must have felt later in life, when he made the acquaintance of the denser, richer, warmer European spectacle—it takes such an accumulation of history

and custom, such a complexity of manners and types, to form a fund
of suggestion for a novelist.[23]

Then James continues, enumerating the characteristics of what
he calls "high civilization," qualities allegedly typical of European countries which Hawthorne as an American writer lacked
for his art; and the implication of the passage is that nothing is
left for the American novelist to work with:

The negative side of the spectacle on which Hawthorne looked out,
in his contemplative saunterings and reveries, might, indeed, with a
little ingenuity be made almost ludicrous; one might enumerate the
items of high civilization, as it exists in other countries, which are
absent from the texture of American life, until it should become a
wonder to know what was left. No State, in the European sense of
the word, and indeed barely a specific national name. No sovereign,
no court, no personal loyalty, no aristocracy, no church, no clergy,
no army, no diplomatic service, no country gentlemen, no palaces, no
castles, nor manors nor old country-houses, nor parsonages, nor
thatched cottages nor ivied ruins; no cathedrals, nor abbeys, nor
little Norman churches; no great Universities nor public schools—no
Oxford, nor Eton, nor Harrow; no literature, no novels, no museums,
no pictures, no political society, no sporting class—no Epsom nor
Ascot! Some such list as that might be drawn up of the absent things
in American life—especially in the American life of forty years ago,
—the effect of which, upon an English or a French imagination,
would probably as a general thing be appalling.[24]

Put in this way it sounds pretty appalling even to an American
imagination. And although James ascribes these deficiencies to
the America of the 1840s, he seriously believed that his own fiction suffered from the same limitations.

Howells disagreed in his review of James's biographical study
of Hawthorne. Howells complained of the attention Hawthorne
and James paid to what he called the "dreary and worn-out paraphernalia" of European novels. He argued that Hawthorne's sensibility kept him from exploiting the social world of America,
just as later critics have said of James. Howells pointed out that
The Marble Faun, which drew upon the "complex social machinery" of Europe, was inferior to Hawthorne's New England
romances. Such paraphernalia, Howells believed, needed to be
eliminated from the novel, for beneath them was the proper sub-

ject of the novelist—man and human nature: "After leaving out all those novelistic 'properties,' as sovereigns, courts, aristocracy, gentry, castles, cottages, cathedrals, abbeys, universities, museums, political class, Epsoms, and Ascots, by the absence of which Mr. James suggests our poverty to the English conception, we have the whole of human life remaining, and a social structure presenting the only fresh and novel opportunities left to fiction, opportunities manifold and inexhaustible. No man would have known less what to do with that dreary and worn-out paraphernalia than Hawthorne. . . ."[25]

Howells sent the review to James, but James was not convinced. And in a letter dated 31 January 1880, James replied:

I sympathize even less with your protest against the idea that it takes an old civilization to set a novelist in motion—a proposition that seems to me so true as to be a truism. It is on manners, customs, usages, habits, forms, upon all these things matured and established, that a novelist lives—they are the very stuff his work is made of; and in saying that in the absence of these 'dreary and worn-out paraphernalia' which I enumerate as being wanting in American society, 'we have simply the whole of human life left,' you beg (to my sense) the question. I should say we had just so much less of it as these same 'paraphernalia' represent, and I think they represent an enormous quantity of it. I shall feel refuted only when we have produced (setting the present high company—yourself and me—for obvious reasons apart) a gentleman who strikes me as a novelist—as belonging to the company of Balzac and Thackeray.[26]

This complaint underlies, in part, James's expatriation to Europe, a culture he believed to be more nourishing than America to the novelist interested in the relation between character and society. Many years later, though, James undertook to reexamine American society, and his conclusions suggest an interesting shift in attitude. The purpose of *The American Scene* as a travel work was to investigate "the great adventure of a society reaching out into the apparent void for the amenities, the consummations, after having earnestly gathered in so many of the preparations and necessities."[27] His travels in America led him to believe that it is indeed possible that new societies may be even more interesting than old societies, "especially if they are 'backed' by unlimited funds and an inexhaustible will for self-improvement."[28] These remarks tend to suggest that between the 1850s, when Hawthorne was writing the major romances, and 1907, when James published *The American Scene*, the United States had begun to assume some of the complexities and amenities of social experience that are the lifeblood of the novel of manners. Howells argued that the social complexity was available in the 1880s, and the witness of our social historians suggests that Howells was right: a limitation of James's sensibility prevented him from making fictional use of what was already there.

But Edith Wharton, the disciple of James who had the richest European experience of any of these novelists, tended to agree with the Master. Arguing that a great novel must have, in Milton's phrase, a "great argument," but that America was capable only of "the perpetual chronicling of small beer," she denied that American society offered the novelist an adequate field. She viewed Lewis's *Main Street* as an illustration of the conditions of American life which stifle the imagination:

If it be argued that the greatest novelists, both French and English, have drawn some of their richest effects from the study of narrow lives and parochial problems, the answer is that Balzac's provincial France, Jane Austen's provincial England, if limited in their external contacts compared to a Main Street linked up to the universe by telephone, motor, and wireless, nevertheless made up for what they lacked in surface by the depth of the soil in which they grew. This indeed is still true of the dense old European order, all compounded of differences and *nuances*, all interwoven with intensities and reticences, with passions and privacies, inconceivable to the millions brought up in a safe, shallow, and shadowless world. It is because we have chosen to be what Emerson called 'mixed of middle clay' that we offer, in spite of all that patriotism may protest to the contrary, so meagre a material to the imagination. It is not because we are middle-class but because we are middling that our story is so soon told.[20]

These writers have suggested in varying ways that society in America has been too shallow for the novel of manners to flourish. Even the romance, for Hawthorne, seemed too difficult of execution in this country. The conclusions of these writers, however, do not strike me as totally convincing. The element of special pleading in the tone of their remarks suggests a rationalization of obvious limitations in their talent and sensibilities. Their own novels of manners—Hawthorne excepted—surprisingly transcend conditions that seemed to them insurmountable. We have always had significant novels of manners because, despite these complaints, America has always had those variegated customs, that complexity of manners and types, that hum and buzz of implication, which forms a fund of suggestion for our writers. Still, Cooper, for example, resolutely held to the myth of our cultural homogeneity and late in his career bemoaned the absence of any "standard for opinion, manners, social maxims, or even language."[30] To overcome these felt deficiencies was a formidable task—a task to which, fortunately, Cooper at least was equal.

2

❧ JAMES FENIMORE COOPER

Worldly Manners and Christian Morals

It may seem surprising to begin a study of novelists of manners in America with James Fenimore Cooper. For most readers Cooper survives, if at all, only as the author of those Leatherstocking Tales that constitute our national epic of pioneer expansion into the virgin wilderness and the rolling prairies of the American West. But the fact is that Cooper was *first*, if not foremost, a novelist of manners—an enigma which led Cooper's biographer, James Grossman, to claim that "nothing can adequately explain how the American Scott made the mistake of beginning his career as the American Austen."[1] But if we wish to understand the genesis of Cooper's art we would do well to consider the early careers of both writers. Especially will we go astray if we think of Scott and Cooper as initially romancers.

At the beginning of his career Scott was so entranced by Maria Edgeworth's Irish novels "of that very difficult class which aspires to describe the actual current of society"[2] that, like Turgenev, he launched his writing career in an effort to imitate her. The point of *Waverley*, Scott remarked, was to attempt something "for my own country, of the same kind with that which Miss Edgeworth so fortunately achieved for Ireland!"[3] His aim was to describe the Scottish people "not by a caricatured and exaggerated use of the national dialect, but by their habits, manners and feelings; so as in some distant degree to emulate the admirable Irish portraits drawn by Miss Edgeworth."[4] The basis of

Scott's interest in the manners of his native country—which has been conveniently summarized by Nelson Bushnell in "Walter Scott's Advent as Novelist of Manners"—was "his reading of the manners novels of his predecessors and contemporaries, his critical assessment of them in preparation for editing a series of British novelists, and his avowal of the determination to record highland manners. He had also become middle-aged, a laird, and a prominent public figure; and he had lived (and was continuing to live) through critical years of egalitarian and Napoleonic threats to the status quo. These later circumstances created an added motive for affirming established manners, to which *Waverley* itself points."[5] "Inimitable" was the word Scott used to describe Jane Austen's novels. She was for him "the faithful chronicler of English manners, and English society of the middling, or what is called the genteel class."[6] He called Maria Edgeworth "one of the wonders of our age,"[7] and praised her magic in creating "those very striking pictures of manners."[8] Simms implied, as I have indicated, that Scott's admiration for these women novelists was not genuine. But Scott was unquestionably sincere. As he confessed in his private journal, perhaps with a trace of envy: "The women do this better—Edgeworth, Ferrier, Austen have all had their portraits of real society, far superior to anything Man, vain Man, has produced of the like nature."[9]

Cooper was also aware of the element of manners—not only in the women novelists, some of whom he admired, but also in Scott. It is no wonder, then, that the American Scott began by trying to imitate—if not better—the "inimitable" Austen, Ferrier, Edgeworth, and Opie. For Cooper the English novel of manners was "more true to every-day nature"[10] than gothic fantasies or cloying sentimental fiction. The English novel of manners dealt, moreover, with significant social issues—the relationship of manners and morals and the interplay of social classes, issues so urgent to Cooper that only novels of this type offered him—both in the beginning and, periodically, throughout his career, the imaginative scope to express his views.

Precaution; or, Prevention Is Better Than Cure (1820), Cooper's first novel, explores, like *Pride and Prejudice*, the hazards of matchmaking in a small English village. Full of Christian moralizing against "vicious novels," unfettered sentimentalism, and heartless villainy, *Precaution* dramatizes how young Jane Moseley errs in believing that the rascal Egerton's morals are unexceptionable because his manners are those of a gentleman. Tedious, it can be read today—although it is hardly accurate to say, as F. L. Pattee did several years ago, that *Precaution* was "the best novel written in America before 1821" and that "if republished today as a newly-discovered early work by Jane Austen it would deceive most readers."[11] But the typical Austen world *is* recreated in the novel. There are the rural gentry, the titled aristocracy, the socially ambitious tradespeople, the servants distinguished in dress and dialect, the inevitable army regiment camped in the neighborhood, the predictable ball to which all are invited, and the provincial religious bias against the modes and mores of the *haute monde* in London, "where the influence of fashion has supplanted the laws of God."[12] Even the Napoleonic campaign (in which the hero serves with distinction and the villain is conveniently killed) is briefly treated—though, as in Austen, it is the small world of the village, not the chaos of modern Europe, that interests the novelist. Exploring the mores of past and present, province and metropolis, Cooper demonstrates that, given the imperfection of the human heart, men are the same from age to age: only Christian principle survives the changing fashions, modes, and manners. *Precaution*, although an inferior novel, was not a totally inept performance for an amateur novelist whose experience of England in 1820 consisted of only a few days of shore leave in London while he was a common sailor in the American navy. In many ways, it was the unequal but "spirited performance" the *Gentleman's Magazine* made it out to be. At least, it excited no suspicions in England that an American had dissected her manners.

I

The English setting of *Precaution* doubtless reflects Cooper's complaint to his publisher Goodrich that "the task of making American Manners and American scenes interesting to an American reader is an arduous one...."[13] But in *The Pioneers* Cooper succeeded in the task by memorializing the scenes of his boyhood in Cooperstown and celebrating the venture of civilization in the New World. In *The Pioneers* he imitated neither Austen nor Scott, though he applied the approach of one to the material of the other. *The Pioneers* is thus "a semihistorical novel of manners on the American border, an examination of American life in its most distinctive and peculiar aspects, a story of the pioneers of the new world."[14] It blended the examination of manners characteristic of *Precaution* and the border romance of *The Spy*. It looked backward to the form of his first two books and forward to that persistent dichotomy in his art between the sea and forest romance and the drawing-room novel of manners.

The Pioneers, like *Precaution*, presents a truthful, realistic representation of the literal details of the world of Cooper's childhood. Set in 1793–94 in the wilderness surrounding Lake Otsego, *The Pioneers* dramatizes the clash between chaos and order, between the wilderness and civilization, between the individual will and the restraints imposed by society. When Leatherstocking breaks a newly passed law against deer-hunting in the "teeming" months, Judge Temple, as the agent of society, must punish him. Leatherstocking claims that his right to hunt is of older date than society's right to forbid him, but as the judge observes, "Society cannot exist without wholesome restraints," and "the sanctity of the laws must be respected."[15] At the end of the novel, punished and pardoned, Leatherstocking strikes deeper into the wilderness leaving civilization and its law behind.

The civilization Natty Bumppo leaves behind Cooper describes with a mixture of criticism and affection, for though it was crude, it was the world of his childhood in Cooperstown. Perhaps no other condition of American society at that time offered the novelist a greater range of character and manners than could be found in villages like Templeton on the frontier. As the title-page quotation from Paulding suggests:

> Extremes of habits, manners, time and space,
> Brought close together, here stood face to face,
> And gave at once a contrast to the view,
> That other lands and ages never knew.

Through differentiations in racial and national origin, in dialect variants, in occupations and village pastimes, Cooper records the transformations in the wilderness—clearing the forest, building the houses, schools, jails, and churches—that produce civilization, and the transformations in the people—the acculturation to the New World—that produced Americans out of diverse European nationalities. Although Cooper never lets us forget that a necessary hierarchy of social relations obtains in old civilizations, thanks to "the freedom of manners that prevailed in the new settlements" (*P*, 436), almost all of the inhabitants socially intermingle in the enterprise of founding the community. The result is a celebration of democratic possibility richly particularized in those frontier manners Cooper cherished—the turkey shoots, the fishing expeditions, the sap collecting and deer hunts, and winter nights at the village inn. Like a Currier and Ives print, *The Pioneers* brings to life a charming vision of early American settlement life.

II

Though frontier society was fluid in its manners, rudimentary social "classes" freely intermingling, Cooper struggled throughout the 1820s and 1830s to refute "the very prevalent notion of Europe, that society must, by necessity, exist, in a pure democracy, on terms of promiscuous association...."[16] This struggle gave rise in 1838 to *The American Democrat*, an exploration of American social and civic relations, and to *Homeward Bound* and *Home As Found*, both novels of manners. Arguing that "the celebrated proposition contained in the declaration of independence is not to be understood literally," Cooper held that equality of social condition is rendered impossible by the rights of property guaranteed in the Constitution. Class divisions (and thus differing manners) arise in a democracy owing to inequalities in education, intelligence, physical abilities, moral values, and cultivated taste. At the summit of the social structure is the class of democratic gentlemen—"the repository of the manners, tastes, tone, and, to a certain extent, of the principles of a country."[17]

To dramatize the existence, even the necessity, of social classes and the sanctity of the rights of property, Cooper composed *Homeward Bound* and *Home As Found*. The composition of these two novels thus reflects that recurrent dichotomy in Cooper between the attractions of the romance and the novel. The essential issues in *Homeward Bound* are two: cosmopolitanism vs. provincialism and the necessary inequalities in a democratic state. Both are dramatized in the clash of manners, attitudes, and actions between Paul Blunt-Powis and the Effinghams vs. the American newspaperman Dodge, who steadfastly believes that he is as good as anybody and that New York is the social and political capital of the world. The Effinghams, descended of Judge Temple in *The Pioneers* and now the proprietors of Templeton, and Paul have been broadened by travel, their judgments have been deepened, and their narrow nationalistic pride has been abolished. Advancing the idea that America as a culture is neither at the head of civilization, as so many nationalists like Dodge proclaim, nor at the bottom, as so many arrogant Europeans like Sir George believe, Cooper locates the mean in Paul Blunt-Powis, who conceals his nationality in order to love the excellence of every nation and to criticize national imperfections with detachment.

These issues are developed largely in dialogue because of the limitations of the shipboard setting. Yet this setting offers precisely the kind of closed society in which the clash of manners can be generated and dramatized. Much of the novel is given over to defining the manners of the gentlemanly class. Dodge is envious when the Effinghams reserve a private cabin instead of sharing a double berth. Persons of gentlemanly feeling, Cooper observes, "when circumstances will at all permit, prefer economizing in other things in order to live by themselves for the month usually consumed in the passage, since in nothing is refinement more plainly exhibited than in the reserve of personal habits."[18] Cooper satirizes the egalitarian view that everyone aboard ship must be intimate with the others. When Captain Truck makes it a point to introduce each passenger to the group, Cooper complains that while Captain Truck

was perfectly acquainted with a ship, and knew the etiquette of the quarterdeck to a hair, he got into blue water the moment he approached the finesse of deportment. He was exactly of that school of *élégants* who fancy drinking a glass of wine with another, and introducing, are touches of breeding; it being altogether beyond his com-

prehension that both have especial uses, and are only to be resorted
to on especial occasions. Still, the worthy master, who had begun
life on the forecastle, without any previous knowledge of usages,
and who had imbibed the notion that 'manners make the man,' taken
in the narrow sense of the axiom, was a devotee of what he fancied to
be good breeding, and one of his especial duties, as he imagined, in
order to put his passengers at their ease, was to introduce them to
each other; a proceeding which, it is hardly necessary to say, had
just a contrary effect with the better class of them. [*HB*, 25–26]

Most readers will doubtless find these attitudes snobbish; the
passengers certainly do, resenting the reserve of the Effinghams.
As the chief mate observes, "If a man chooses to keep his hands
in the beckets, why let him, say I; but I take it as a slight to the
company to sheer out of the usual track in such matters." The
captain agrees—decorum requires at least a handshake: "One
would do as much to a Turk for manners' sake" (*HB*, 27). But
such was Cooper's resentment of vulgar familiarity, such was his
appreciation for "aristocratic reserve," that the privacy, exclusiveness, and snobbishness of the Effinghams are affirmed.

Home As Found was written to illustrate the principle that
"the governing social evil of America is provincialism," a vice
created by the absence of a "standard for opinion, manners, social
maxims, or even language. Every man, as a matter of course, refers
to his own particular experience, and praises or condemns agree-
ably to notions contracted in the circle of his own habits, however narrow, provincial, or erroneous they may happen to be."[19]
As a consequence of this provincialism, Cooper felt the country
"in its ordinary aspects, probably presents as barren a field to the
writer of fiction . . . as any other on earth; we are not certain that
we might not say the most barren. We believe that no attempt
to delineate ordinary American life, either on the stage or on the
pages of a novel, has been rewarded with much success" (*HAF*,
vi).

Whether or not Cooper could portray American society, and
he could, he at least believed that it was "a desperate undertaking,
to think of making anything interesting in the way of a *Roman
de Société* in this country." Still—and this is his justification for
presenting America with yet another novel of manners while dis-
claiming the possibility of doing it—"useful glances may possibly

be made even in this direction, and we trust the fidelity of one or two of our portraits will be recognized by the looker-on, although they will very likely be denied by the sitters themselves" (*HAF*, vi).

Home As Found satisfies more than its predecessor one's sense of what is meant by the *roman de société* or the novel of manners. Lewis Leary has in fact called the book "America's first extensive novel of manners, its formlessness itself anticipatory of a native trend."[20] It opens with a six-chapter introduction to New York "society" with Eve Effingham as mistress of one of the largest establishments in New York. To convey his social analysis Cooper's personae explain to Sir George Templemore the character of American society and correct his misconceptions about it. Society exists in New York by virtue of distinctions and differences which inevitably arise in large groups, Cooper explains. From these differences coteries develop which are ranked by enlightened opinion, custom, and usage. " 'All the old families, for instance, keep more together than the others,' " Sir George is told, " 'though it is the subject of regret that they are not more particular than they are' " (*HAF*, 45). Distinction in America, he learns, is conferred by wealth and merit, though usually several generations of distinction are necessary to produce "old families," a period so short that Sir George thinks it ridiculous. To illustrate the relative status of several "classes" or coteries in New York society, Cooper takes the Effinghams and Sir George on a round of visits.

Their first stop is the home of Mr. and Mrs. Jarvis, whose social station, though not that of a leader in New York, is sufficiently high to warrant a visit from the Effinghams. As country neighbors they are very sociable people; "their town associations, however, were as distinct as if they dwelt in different hemispheres, with the exception of an occasional morning call, and now and then a family dinner given by Mr. Effingham" (*HAF*, 54). These dinners are never repaid by the Jarvises for a reason too subtle for Mrs. Jarvis's comprehension. As her husband explains it to her: " 'I dined with Mr. Effingham because I like him; because he was an old neighbor; because he asked me, and because I found a pleasure in the quiet elegance of his table and society;

and I did not ask him to dine with me, because I was satisfied he would be better pleased with such a tacit acknowledgement of his superiority in this respect, than by any bustling and ungraceful efforts to pay him in kind" (*HAF*, 57). Mr. Jarvis, in other words, knows how to keep his place—a deference to rank that always charmed Cooper.

The Jarvis "at home" is intended to represent American society —or at least American "company"—in a simple but wholesome form. Mrs. Jarvis, for all her goodness at heart, stands in happy ignorance of many usages "essential to the much-coveted social *éclat* at which she aimed." She had no servant to announce guests at the door and knew no better than to lionize the journalist Dodge. Most readers will find the smugness with which Cooper treats her offensive, but his intention—to make of the novel a guidebook to correct social usage—is not without its interest.

After considerable satire on newly arrived Yankees who fancy themselves "*au fait* of all the niceties of breeding and social tact" (*HAF*, 59), Cooper takes the party to the Hudson Square house of Mrs. Hawker, who is "as near the head of fashion in New York as it is possible to be . . ." (*HAF*, 58). Known only to a select few, Mrs. Hawker comes of an established family, yet so exclusive is she that, like the van der Luydens in Wharton's *The Age of Innocence*, her name is not even known to the *arrivistes*. Her reception for the party is conservative, dignified, simple, and gracious. Though the evening is full of interminable talk about the differences between Europe and America, it is clear that Cooper intends Mrs. Hawker's circle to represent the acme of society in New York. "Mrs. Hawker is a lady," Eve remarks, "and there can be no higher term" (*HAF*, 73). Hers is real society; Mrs. Jarvis's is just company, a crowd. Thereafter, the Effinghams and their guests go on to Mrs. Houston's dance, a large affair open to a promiscuous society, a bad imitation of balls the Effinghams had attended in Europe.

Having surveyed society in the city, Cooper then transports his company to "The Wigwam" at Lake Otsego—the residence of Judge Temple earlier described in *The Pioneers*. And some of Cooper's most effective scenes are laid there. Moreover, his analysis of what he calls the three stages of society, based on the more complex social analysis of Condorcet, throws light on Cooper's changing judgment of Templeton, or Cooperstown, as it passed from a frontier village into a town. When a new settlement is established, he observes, men have a kindly feeling toward each other because they are engaged in a mutual enterprise. "The distance that is unavoidably inseparable from education, habits, and manners is lessened by mutual wants and mutual efforts; and the gentleman, even while he may maintain his character and station, maintains them with that species of good fellowship and familiarity, that marks the intercourse between the officer and the soldier in an arduous campaign" (P, 187). In this happy period "good will abounds; neighbor comes cheerfully to the aid of neighbor; and life has much of the reckless gayety, careless association, and buoyant merriment of childhood. It is found that they who have passed through this probation," Cooper went on, doubtless thinking of his own childhood, "usually look back to it with regret, and are fond of dwelling on the rude scenes and ridiculous events that distinguish the history of a new settlement, as the hunter is known to pine for the forest" (P, 188). It is this stage in the social evolution of Cooperstown, during the novelist's childhood, that induced such nostalgia in *The Pioneers*. By 1838, however, Cooper was so irritated at some of the residents of Cooperstown that his nostalgia had evaporated.

In the second stage in the development of society, "tastes are too uncultivated to exercise any essential influence, and when they do exist, it is usually with the pretension and effort that so commonly accompany infant knowledge" (P, 188–89). In this stage, "manners suffer the most" as we see "the struggles for place, the heartburnings and jealousies of contending families, and the influence of mere money." Gradually, "those gradations of social station" which mark every civilization develop; an aristocracy of wealth and merit emerges from this struggle. Even greater disparities in class status develop during this period because the immigrants, who introduce new manners into the community, cannot compete equally with the established.

In the third phase, the gradations of class crystallize, and men and things come within what Cooper calls "the control of more general and regular laws." In this state the civilization of the community "conforms to that of the whole region, be it higher or be it lower," and there are developed "castes that are more or less rigidly maintained, according to circumstances" (*P*, 189). We have no doubt that the more rigidly they were maintained, the better Cooper liked them.

Templeton of *The Pioneers* was located in the first phase. In *Home As Found* the village has reached the second phase. Rudiments of a community have developed, but tensions have been created by the large number of new men, some of them transients heading westward, who neutralize the influence of "time and the natural order of things" (*P*, 190). Their provincialism is illustrated in Aristabulus Bragg, the land agent for the Templeton estate, and Steadfast Dodge. Because of the narrow-minded egalitarianism of these transients, the central crisis of *Home As Found* is provoked—the Three Mile Point controversy.

The Three Mile Point, a picnic ground near Cooperstown, was customarily used by the villagers. When he returned from several years in Europe, Cooper claimed exclusive use of this point as owner of the land. Some of the "newer" townspeople protested that it was public property. Their claim to public use of the "Fishing Point," as it is called in the novel, leads Edward Effingham to observe this of the manners of the new people: "That unequalled pecuniary prosperity should sensibly impair the manners of what is termed the world, by introducing suddenly large bodies of uninstructed and untrained men and women into society, is a natural consequence of obvious causes; that it should corrupt morals even, we have a right to expect, for we are taught to believe it the most corrupting influence under which men can live; but I confess I did not expect to see the day when a body of strangers, birds of passage, creatures of an hour, should assume a right to call on the old and long-established inhabitants of a country to prove their claims to their possessions, and this, too, in an unusual and unheard-of manner, under the penalty of being violently deprived of them!" (*HAF*, 256).

The solution to the unpleasant consequences of rapid social mobility is clearly the instruction of the new people in the rights of others and a respect for wealth and merit wherever they are established. For gentlemen like Effingham, "of all tyranny, a vulgar tyranny is . . . the most odious" (*HAF*, 258). It can be offset, Cooper held, only when the manners of public life are leavened by the influence of the gentlemanly class. For Eve, even the European aristocrat is not the equal of gentlemen of her father's class. "Rich, and possessing all the habits that properly mark refinement, of gentle extraction, of liberal attainments, walking abroad in the dignity of manhood, and with none between them and the Deity, Eve had learned to regard the gentlemen of her race as the equals in station of any of their European associates, and as the superiors of most, in everything that is essential to true distinction" (*HAF*, 209–10). For Eve, and Cooper, "the position of an American gentleman might readily become, nay . . . ought to be, the highest of all human stations, short of that of sovereign. Such a man," Eve believed, "had no social superior, with the exception of those who actually ruled, in her eyes; and this fact, she conceived, rendered him more than noble, as nobility is usually graduated" (*HAF*, 209).

The rest of the novel confirms her view. The Effinghams defeat the newcomers on the Fishing Point issue, Dodge gets his comeuppance, and Paul Blunt-Powis turns out to be John Effingham's long-lost son—in a tangle of confused identities and relationships that seals rather than prevents Paul's marriage to Eve. Eve's cousin Grace marries Sir George, and all turns out well.

But this customary love plot, with stock romantic leads who conclude the novel in marriage, is not the real center of the book. Exposing narrow provincialism, pointing out the social advantages and necessities of a gentry based on wealth and merit, defending the rights of property, exposing and defeating Jack Cade-ism in the Fishing Point controversy—these are the important issues of the novel. And they are conveyed in part by Cooper's detailed notation of society in New York and Templeton—the *soirées*, salons, balls, Fourth of July celebrations, even the first baseball game, and by Cooper's treatment of the distinctions in class signaled by religion, dialect, architecture, dress, and manners. These social notations constitute the means by which Cooper's readers were spared the fate of "those English who form their notions of society from novels written by men and women who have no access to it, and from the records of the court journal" (*HAF*, 313).

III

In the 1840s the political agitation which developed on the baronial estates in upper New York State monopolized Cooper's attention and provoked a trilogy of "antirent" novels sometimes called the Littlepage Manuscripts. These three novels grew out of Cooper's study of the early history of the colony of New York, when tracts of land were offered to Dutch patroons who guaranteed to settle on their patents fifty or more immigrants. The patroons attracted tenants by offering them generous lease terms, some properties being leased in perpetuity, some for the duration of three lives, and others for varying shorter periods. The relationship between tenant and landlord is too complex to explore fully here.[21] But it may be noted that between 1839 and 1846 hostilities arose between them because some of the tenants did not like the conditions of their leases and the landlords were unwilling to alter them or to sell the land. Because the lease terms were so generous in the early years when the estates were developing, landlords did not begin to profit from them until the properties were fully productive. This meant that the proprietors of large estates often made investments only to provide for their children and grandchildren. By the time their descendants were beginning to enjoy the profit of ownership, the tenants were attacking the system of leaseholds as antiquated and demanding the right to buy into lands which they and their forefathers had farmed and improved for perhaps a century or more. In these years political agitation was sometimes violent, and many of the renters refused to pay rents owed. In the midst of this controversy, Cooper's antirent trilogy—*Satanstoe* (1845), *The Chainbearer* (1845), and *The Redskins* (1846)—made its appearance.

Like *Homeward Bound* and *Home As Found*, these three novels are both novels of purpose and novels of manners. Robert E. Spiller has in fact called *Satanstoe* not merely "a novel of manners in an American setting," but "the best of this type that Cooper ever wrote."[22] Unlike the former pair of novels which are set in the present, though, *Satanstoe* and *The Chainbearer* are novels of manners set in the past. Historical novels in the tradition of Scott, they record manners faithfully in the tradition of the English realists. Cooper's purpose in this trilogy is to defend the rights of property by showing how property leases originated, to demonstrate how false principles have corrupted the tenants who wished to break the leases and have the property parceled out for sale.

To demonstrate the legitimacy of the leases and the decay of principle, Cooper was obliged to trace in three volumes the history of the settlement of New York from early colonial times down to the 1840s. "Each of these three books has its own hero, its own heroine, and its own picture of manners, complete," Cooper assures us, "though the latter may be, and is, more or less thrown into relief by its pendants."[23] *Satanstoe*, the first volume in the series, set in the 1750s, narrates the granting of the two patents (called Ravensnest and Mooseridge) to the Mordaunt and Littlepage families. These estates are united at the end of the novel by the marriage of Cornelius Littlepage and Anneke Mordaunt, a pair of Dutch-English New Yorkers. *The Chainbearer*, set shortly after the Peace of 1783, deals with the troubles caused by squatters on the estates, now owned by Mordaunt Littlepage, son of Corny and Anneke. *The Redskins*, which brings the history of the estates and the family down into the 1840s, deals with the opposition of the tenants to the terms of their leases and with the violence they inflict upon the person and property of Hugh Roger Littlepage, Mordaunt's grandson.

Satanstoe is the best of the three, probably because in this first novel Cooper was less motivated by political propaganda than by the task of combining in one tale a notation of colonial American manners and the lore of the forest. Although "every chronicle of manners has a certain value," as Cooper observes in the preface, *Satanstoe* is doubly important because it reveals how the customs and usages of nineteenth-century New York originated and developed. The method of Cornelius Littlepage in composing his manuscript is that of the social historian: ". . . there is little hope that any traces of American society, in its more familiar aspects, will be preserved among us, through any of the agencies usually employed for such purposes. Without a state, in a national point of view at least, with scarcely such a thing as a book of memoirs that relates to a life passed within our own limits, and totally without light literature, to give us simulated pictures of our manners and the opinions of the day, I see scarcely a mode by which the next generation can preserve any memorials of the distinctive usages and thoughts of this" (*S*, 9). *Satanstoe* is intended to remedy this desideratum by recreating the daily life of colonial New York as Cooper had learned it from history and from the records of his family.

Satanstoe dramatizes with winsome verisimilitude the conditions, usages, and attitudes of genteel colonial life in the mid-eighteenth century. Cooper's notations of domestic customs are thorough and realistic. The ladies dress for dinner ("that no lady ever neglects, even though she dines on a cold dumpling"), they dine at a fashionable hour ("at half-past eight, my aunt being fond of town hours, both dining and supping a little later than my mother, as being more fashionable and genteel"), are toasted in their presence ("the customs of New York allowed a lady who is present to be toasted"), provide entertainment by singing, and afterwards enjoy an evening promenade ("no one presumed to promenade the Mall, who was not of a certain stamp of respectability"). Cooper records the street cries of colonial New York, discriminates between proper and improper forms of address and distinguishes precisely, but often at intolerable length, all the dialects of the region—Yankee, Dutch, Indian, and Negro.

Cooper's device for portraying the provincialism of the colonial New Yorkers is to contrast their manners with those of a British officer serving in the colonies—a university man, heir to a baronetcy, one familiar with the world. In the rivalry between Corny Littlepage and Major Bulstrode for the hand of Anneke Mordaunt, Corny finally wins out because Major Bulstrode comes to see Anneke as superior to "the great vulgar world, which includes all but the very best in taste, principles, and manners, whether it be in a capital or in a country." Anneke belongs to "the great *respectable* world," as Cooper calls it, which, though less numerous, "contains the judicious, the instructed, the intelligent, and on some questions, the good." Higher than "what fashion can make her" (*S*, 499), Anneke is not meant for London life; consequently, Bulstrode surrenders her to Corny.

As in *Afloat and Ashore; or, The Adventures of Miles Wallingford*, Cooper also contrasts the manners of the English and those of the Dutch. His Dutch New Yorkers are represented as ponderous of mind and body, ill-educated, given to excesses at table and bottle, fun-loving, sterling, brave, honest, and true. The hero of *The Chainbearer*, in fact, is a Dutch surveyor, Andries Coejemans. Though uneducated and unfamiliar with the cultivated usages of polite English society, old Andries is given heroic stature because he realizes that "the column of society must have its capital as well as its base" (*C*, 8–9) and that his position, as a humble chainbearer in the surveying team employed by Mordaunt Littlepage, is near the base. His opposition to the squatters on the Littlepage estate brings about his own death, but it affirms the interesting principle that "all the knowledge, and all the arts of life that the white man enjoys and turns to his profit, come from the rights of property" (*C*, 123). The Chainbearer's antagonists are the Yankee squatter, Aaron Thousandacres, who has no respect for law and property, and Jason Newcome, the pedagogue–land agent of the Littlepages, "a law honest" conniver. Coejemans is thus the lower-class exemplar of respect for law and property and for the deference due to men of high degree.

It is principally in the contrast between New England Yankees and Dutch-English New Yorkers, however, that Cooper makes the most searching examination of manners in the Littlepage Manuscripts—that is, in the contrast between Jason Newcome and his descendants and the Littlepage family. In *Satanstoe*, the Littlepages' social status lies somewhere between "the higher class of the yeomanry and those who, by their estates, education, connections, official rank, and hereditary consideration, formed what might justly be called the aristocracy of the colony" (*S*, 14). Because Newcome is only a Yankee schoolteacher, he has no position in genteel society. Cooper makes him out to be the personification of barbarism. His taste is crude, his manners are unformed, and he has no respect for social station. A democratic leveler, his constant aim is to prove himself the social equal of the Littlepages. Through Corny, Cooper undertakes to explain the origin of the difference between New Englanders like Newcome and respectable folk of the middle colonies:

There was and is little sympathy, in the way of national feeling, between the colonies of New England and those which lie farther south. We are all loyal, those of the east as well as those of the south-west and south; but there is, and ever has been, so wide a difference in our customs, origins, religious opinions, and histories, as to cause a broad moral line, in the way of feeling, to be drawn between the colony of New York and those that lie east of the Byram River. I have heard it said, that most of the emigrants to the New England states came from the west of England, where many of their social peculiarities and much of their language are still to be traced, while the colonies farther south have received their population from the more central counties, and those sections of the island that are supposed to be less provincial and peculiar. [S, 17]

Cooper points up distinctions between Corny and Jason in their attitudes toward the government authority, professions, trades, callings, dress, pronunciation, learning, taste, and manners. That Jason is a Yale A.B. while Corny is a graduate of Nassau Hall (as Princeton was first called) is as important an index of social status in this novel as the social differences between the Gibbsville boys who attend Yale and Harvard and those who attend Lafayette and Muhlenberg in O'Hara's *Ten North Frederick*. Jason is a puritan of the standing order, Corny a kneeling Episcopalian; Jason is nosy, inquisitive, Corny discreet, well-bred; Jason fawns before wealth and aristocratic titles, Corny accepts them as necessary concomitants to civilization. "In this respect," Corny writes, "Jason was always a moral enigma to me; there being an absolute absence in his mind, of everything like a perception of the fitness of things, so far as the claims and rights of persons were connected with rank, education, birth and experience" (S, 326).

By the 1780s, when the events of *The Chainbearer* occur, the effects of Jason's false principles in political and social relationships are beginning to appear. Newcome, the new man or invader, has wormed his way into the position of land agent of the Littlepage family, but, as a renter at Ravensnest, he is one of the principal malcontents at lease-time, as well as a co-conspirator with the squatter Thousandacres to subvert the law and defraud Mordaunt, Corny's son. While the plot business goes on, Cooper reconstructs the social history of New York as a new state. All ranks have been abolished in the new republic, of course, but some class distinctions still persist. Moreover, the Yankees have introduced a number of unhappy innovations into the usages of the state, but "among the upper real New York families," Cooper assures us, "women do not even now attend funerals," a fact which Mordaunt mentions "lest some antiquarian, a thousand years hence, might light on this manuscript, and mistake our customs" (*C*, 461–62). Other customs Cooper notes are these: only intimate friends shake hands, the custom of shaking at introductions being "imported from some of our sister states" (*C*, 58); grown sons may presume "to take a plate at the table of the father without observing the ceremony of asking, or of being asked," because "Heaven be praised! We have not yet reached this pass in America" (*C*, 42); social classes are still "broadly distinguished by dress, no man even affecting to assume the wardrobe of a gentleman, without having certain pretensions to the character" (*C*, 255–56); propriety forbids Kate Littlepage from accepting Tom Bayard's proposal at once because her brother Mordaunt is away and does not know the gentleman—even though every other member of the family including her father does know Tom and approves of the match; travelers departing on the Hudson are waved at with hats and handkerchiefs, though Cooper editorializes, "It would be a bold woman who would think now of waving a handkerchief to a Hudson river steamboat!" (*C*, 95n). These customs, principally those of the better class of New Yorkers, are held to, Cooper argues, because "most of the usages of those highly improved conditions of society are founded in reason, and have their justification in a cultivated common sense . . ." (*C*, 42). Few assumptions about social usage are less open to challenge than this of Mordaunt's. For most historians of manners, the changing patterns of social usage reflect an arbitrary exercise of social power by an elite class. Reason or common sense has little to do with the perpetuation of customs and manners.

In *The Redskins*, Cooper brings his notation of New York manners down into the present, the 1840s. Matters which concern him here are the invasion of the Irish as a servant class, the decline of the "two-man" and "three-man" beds in the best New York inns ("at no respectable New York inn is a gentleman now asked to share even his room, without an apology and a special necessity, with another, much less his bed; but the rule does not hold good as respects pedlars and music-grinders" (*R*, 218), the practice of men's sitting at table after the women have left it ("among other customs to be condemned that we have derived from England"), and so on. One usage is central to the conflict between the renters and the landlord—the Littlepage canopied pew at St. Andrew's Episcopal Church. "A relic of . . . colonial opinions and usages" (*R*, 56), this wooden canopy is denounced by the tenants as a symbol of Littlepage aristocratic pretension—a thing especially obnoxious to them in that it is flaunted in a House of God, where earthly distinctions are vain. "Lest this manuscript should get into the hands of some of those who do not understand the real condition of New York society," Hugh Littlepage sarcastically observes, "it may be well to explain that 'aristocrat' means, in the parlance of the country, no other than a man of gentleman-like tastes, habits, opinions, and associations" (*R*, 224). These qualities suggest the class which Cooper most wished to see dominant in America, a class of gentlemen possessed by "the great indispensables of tastes, manners, and opinions, based on intelligence and cultivation . . ." (*R*, 172). But thanks to the forces of mediocrity and democratic leveling, not only is the social power of this class threatened—its very foundation, property, is being undermined by the renters.

To establish the really complex causes of the antirent agitation required more political objectivity than Cooper could muster in the trying decade of the 1840s. Agitated as he was, he could only reduce the complex phenomena of New York politics to a theory, based on his personal bias, of New England subversion, and dramatize the theory in a parable of social disorder. Cooper argued passionately against the breakup of the baronial estates because it threatened what to him was the ideal social order. New Englanders were a danger to the status quo because they came from a state of society where every husbandman could farm his own land and thus could be the social equal of his neighbors. And this menace threatened the survival of the landed gentry in New York. Cooper believed that in a country like the United States not small freeholders but "a landed gentry is precisely what is most needed for the higher order of civilization" (R, 462). Composed of Christian ladies and gentlemen, this class, as the repository of genteel manners and enlightened opinion, would elevate the general tone of society and provide models of imitation for the lower orders, who would still be properly subservient to the claims of wealth, property, and merit in a republican society. As Uncle Ro points out, a landed gentry "is the very class which, if reasonably maintained and properly regarded, would do the most good at the least risk of any social caste known" (R, 462).

But the idea of a landed gentry, even if it constituted no political risk, was alien to the social ideal of many "Middle States" men, as well as to those Yankees and Europeans who migrated westward looking for an equal share in the evolving Jacksonian social order. Like Edith Wharton, who attacked the midwestern businessmen and post–Civil War "lords of Pittsburgh" for destroying the urbane social aristocracy of Old New York, and like Marquand, who resented the increasing power of the Boston Irish, Cooper sought through his novels of manners to prevent the antirent faction from destroying his social dream. But, ironically, even as Cooper was attacking the Yankee antirenters as influences foreign to the spirit of New York social and political institutions, the State Assembly of New York was debating legislation that would effectively break up the huge manorial estates, legislation that made it possible for small farmers, of whatever regional origin and social class, to own their own farms and shape for themselves a destiny consonant with the American dream of true democratic equality. Nevertheless, in the Littlepage Manuscripts, as in the other novels I have discussed, Cooper has given us fascinating instances of the novel as social history, as a record of the changing times and manners, brought to life by the vitality of his characters and their dramas.

3

❧ HENRY JAMES

The Superstitious Valuation
of Europe

James's ambivalent feelings about America led him to crisscross the Atlantic in the early 1870s, testing his impressions of the viability of the Old World and the New as subject and setting of his art. Yielding to "the importunate presence of tradition of *every* kind—the influence of an atmosphere electrically charged with historic intimations and whisperings,"[1] young James suffered from "the great American disease"—"the appetite, morbid and monstrous, for colour and form, for the picturesque and romantic at any price."[2] In Europe, where life seemed "raised to a higher power, because more richly charged, more significantly composed, and more completely informed,"[3] James, like Cooper before him, embarked on a passionate pilgrimage to escape the bland homogeneity of life in America; the passion for money-making and the indifference to culture, social grace, and intellectual refinement here; the absence of a genuine variety of social types, and, as a consequence, the superficial American literary culture crippling to the aspiring artist. Summing up, he observed of Howells's *A Foregone Conclusion* that "our native-grown imaginative effort" had to make "small things do great service. Civilization with us is monotonous, and in the way of contrasts, of salient points, of chiaroscuro, we have to take what we can get."[4]

Troubled, at the same time, by the feeling that America ought to be a rich enough ground for the writer, he debated with himself the value of complete expatriation. His inner dialogue on this vexing point lasted more than forty years; it constitutes, in its way, an extensive catalogue of counterstatements, a rich commentary on the relation of the artist to his regional and moral environs. At times he felt that the American writer "*must* be tethered in native pastures."[5] Even Hawthorne, he occasionally felt, "forfeited a precious advantage in ceasing to tread his native soil"; and he envied Turgenev that "like those of all great novelists" his works "savour strongly of his native soil."[6] His intermittent doubt of the value of expatriation even led him to urge his brother William to insure that his sons contracted "local saturations and attachments in respect to their *own* great and glorious country, to learn, and strike roots into, its infinite beauty . . . and variety." He felt that if his nephews did sink themselves in America, "they won't, as I do now, have to assimilate, but half-heartedly, the alien splendours." He urged William to make the boys "stick fast and sink up to their necks in everything their *own* countries and climates can give," since "its being that 'own' will double their *use* of it."[7] James is said to have complained to Hamlin Garland that "the mixture" of the Old World and the New in him "proved disastrous" because it "made of me a man who is neither American nor European."[8]

But these counterstatements, usually provoked by homesickness, were at best generally valid for the would-be expatriate, not ultimately true for James himself. Brooks and Parrington felt that James's expatriation ruined his writing because it deprived him of the subjects and situations, the social order and the moral orientation, that might have generated great art.[9] But for James, as William Troy has argued, "residence in England, rather than being a source of sterility and corruption, was an indispensable condition of fulfillment."[10] As James ultimately decided: "My choice is the Old World—my choice, my need, my life."[11]

At the time of his departure in 1875, James was known chiefly as a reviewer, essayist, and short story writer. His first novel, *Watch and Ward* (1871), had not brought him recognition. "Conceived as a study of Boston manners," the novel dealt, as Leon Edel has rightly observed, "rather with the moeurs of Quincy Street."[12] James consistently disclaimed it in later years and spoke of *Roderick Hudson* as his first novel, and critics have generally been pleased to do the same. But the early stories, reviews, and travel essays constituted a gathering in of the preparations for what was to be his great theme as a novelist of manners —"The Americano-European legend." In "A Bundle of Letters" (1879) Louis Leverett spoke his author's mind in saying, "I am much interested in the study of national types; in comparing, contrasting, seizing the strong points, the weak points, the point of view of each."[13] The decade from 1872 until 1882 most interests the student of James's international novels—and I limit myself, arbitrarily, to this period—for it is the chief period "of his studies in comparative national psychology and manners," the period when "he spent part of his time on one side of the water and part on the other, and the people in his stories followed in his footsteps."[14]

I

Emerson had observed in his essay "Manners" that society would "pardon much to genius and special gifts, but, being in its nature a convention, it loves what is conventional, or what belongs to coming together. That makes the good and bad of manners, namely, what helps or hinders fellowship."[15] How much society would pardon to genius James tested in his first major novel of manners, *Roderick Hudson* (1875). Simple in the configuration of its plot, *Roderick Hudson* develops a surprisingly complex drama of social and moral ambiguities. Wealthy Rowland Mallet, visiting his cousin in Northampton, Massachusetts, makes the acquaintance of Roderick Hudson, a young sculptor of such promise that Mallet offers to take him to Italy to study art. They leave behind Roderick's mother and Mary Garland, his fiancée (with whom Rowland has fallen in love). In Italy, Roderick's talent has barely begun to flourish when he falls in love with beautiful Christina Light. Christina's mother wants to marry her off to wealth and a title, certainly not to a penniless American artist.[16] Roderick's thwarted passion for Christina eventually destroys him as an artist. Responsible for having brought him to Europe, Rowland tries to revive Roderick's inspiration and to retrieve him from the moral debauchery into which he sinks. But when Roderick asks Rowland for money in order to effect an assignation with Christina, Rowland, confessing that he loves Mary Garland, denounces Roderick's heartlessness. Roderick disappears into a storm and is later found dead at the base of a cliff. Totally absorbed by the energy of his art and willing to sacrifice everyone, including himself, and every social and moral convention to achieve its realization, Roderick embodies the destructive egotism of the Romantic temperament. The novel tests the tolerability of Romantic genius, as exemplified in Roderick, against the mature consciousness that the complex business of life often requires subordination of the self and deference to the sensibilities of others. The spectacle of his youth and genius involves the question of manners or the relation of individualism to the conventions of society.

New England society, represented by Northampton, is repressive and inhibiting. To the townspeople and his family, Roderick is strange and different—given to thoughtlessness, insults, and "ill-mannered speech." His behavior may thus in some ways be justified by the repressive condition of his environment. But the "heterogeneous society" of the foreign colony in Rome is not repressive, and there is no apparent cause for Roderick to behave, in his social engagements, as if society were an inhibition to be resisted, its conventions so many constraints upon his perfect freedom. Still, misbehave he does. "Roderick's manners on the precincts of the Pincian were quite the same as his manners on Cecilia's verandah; they were no manners, in strict parlance, at all. . . . He interrupted, he contradicted, he spoke to people he had never seen and left his social creditors without the smallest conversational interest on their loans; he lounged and yawned, he talked loud when he should have talked low and low when he should have talked loud. Many people in consequence thought him insufferably conceited and declared that he ought to wait till he had something to show for his powers before assuming the airs of a spoiled celebrity." Roderick received "from various sources, chiefly feminine," enough "finely adjusted advice" to make him "an embodiment of the proprieties," but on the whole he ignores society, social conventions, customs, and manners.[17]

What saves Roderick from his own boorishness is that sexual

charisma which makes him somehow "perfectly inoffensive" to many people, particularly to women. He belonged to that race of mortals, Rowland reflects, "to be pitied or envied according as we view the matter, who are not held to a strict account for their aggressions" (*RH*, 31). But this charisma is more reported than shown, more ascribed than dramatized, so that while Rowland, Mary, Christina Light, and others are fascinated by Roderick, the reader is at a loss to account for it. Christina tries to explain the paradox to Rowland Mallet: "There's something strange about him. To begin with he has no manners. You may say that it's not for me to blame him, since I have none myself. That's very true, but the difference is that I can have them when I wish to (and very charming ones too; I'll show you some day); where-as Mr. Hudson will never, never, never arrive—and thank God after all—at the least little *tenue*. For somehow one sees he's a gentleman. He seems to have something urging, driving, pushing him, making him restless and defiant. You see it in his eyes. They're the finest, by the way, I ever saw. When a person has such eyes you forgive him his bad manners. I suppose they rep-resent what's called the sacred fire" (*RH*, 212–13).

As this passage suggests, it is difficult to exaggerate James's preoccupation with polite manners in dramatizing and testing values in conflict. Christina, fully as egotistical as Roderick, who is no gentleman, knows that her manners can be instruments of self-assertion: she can have them when she wishes to, and when she does not she can make life miserable for those about her. She is, in fact, the temperamental counterpart of Roderick. One eve-ning at a large musical party, Roderick conspicuously sits next to Christina, although all of the other men are standing. In the long pause before the music begins, Christina crosses the whole length of the immense room, with everyone staring at her, to approach Rowland: "Please remind Mr. Hudson," she tells him, "that he's not in a New England village, that it's not the custom in Rome to address one's conversation exclusively, night after night, to the same poor girl." The next day, when Rowland reports this request to Roderick, he replies:

"Oh, the charming 'cheek' of her! She does everything that comes into her head."

"Had she never asked you before not to talk to her so much?" Rowland inquired.

"On the contrary, she has often said to me, 'Mind you now, I forbid you to leave me. Here comes that beast of a So-and-so.' She cares as little about the custom of the country as I do. What could be a better proof than her walking up to you with five hundred people looking at her? Is that, for beautiful watched girls, the custom of the country?" [*RH*, 199–200]

Though we do not see many of the private sessions between Christina and Roderick, he appears to have accurately identified Christina's way of expressing herself—by violating the custom of the country, even while invoking its protection.

These violations of the accepted social order—as tolerant as it is in the foreign colony at Rome—bring Roderick under criticism from his patron Rowland Mallet. Roderick's defense is the principle artists have so often invoked to sacrifice the conventions of society in pursuit of self-realization:

"I think that when you expect a man to produce beautiful and wonderful works of art you ought to allow him a certain freedom of action, you ought to give him a long rope, you ought to let him follow his fancy and look for his material wherever he thinks he may find it. . . . You demand of us to be imaginative, and you deny us the things that feed the imagination. In labour we must be as passionate as the inspired sibyl; in life we must be as regular as the postman and as satisfactory as the cook. It won't do, you know, my dear chap. . . . Shoot them, the poor devils, drown them, exterminate them, if you will, in the interest of public morality: it may be morality would gain—I daresay it would. But if you suffer them to live, let them live on their own terms and according to their own inexorable needs!" [*RH*, 224]

Roderick's arguments, however, are doubly suspect. First, although James certainly sympathizes with this position, Roderick's rhetoric exaggerates the extent to which Roman society imposes social and moral restraints on the artist. As we have already seen, Roderick's acquaintances—particularly the women, who control the machinery of society—are disposed to grant him unheard-of freedom from the accepted norms of conventional Roman behavior. Second, Roderick's claim to freedom clashes with his own belief that men are driven, fated, conditioned to behave as they do; it conflicts with his belief that "there's a certain group of circumstances possible for every man, in which his power to choose is destined to snap like a dry twig." For Rowland, however, "The power to choose *is* destiny. That's the way to look at it" (*RH*, 141).

In fact, Roderick's New England conscience and his artistic imagination lie very near, and it is the paralyzing effects of guilt that keep him from producing sculptures. His disintegration—gambling, drinking, and unspecified attentions to women memorable only for certain graceful lines—is far from determined. It is rather the effect of self-indulgence, Hawthorne's sin of egotism, masquerading as artistic freedom. For Rowland Mallet—and for James, if the example of his biography is any clue—"a man of genius owes as much deference to his passions as any other man, but not a particle more, and I confess I have a strong conviction that the artist is better for leading a quiet life" (*RH*, 49). But Roderick, an uneasy member of the cult of experience, is incapable of the quiet life, and his "inexorable needs" lead him to betray Mary Garland, to pursue Christina Light after her marriage to the Prince, even to try to borrow money from Mary and from Rowland, who loves Mary, to effect his assignation with Christina. In these perfidies, it is clear, Roderick is "without that indispensable aid to completeness, a feeling heart" (*RH*, 220).

The crisis of the novel is brought on by Rowland's refusal to give Roderick enough money to follow the Princess. The final interview between them is a passage of great emotional intensity, one of the best in the book. The discovery by Roderick that he has been blind to Rowland's love for Mary glitters with savage grace. But Roderick's "illumination" is only intellectual; it is accompanied by no sense of the feelings of the others involved—Mary, Rowland, or even the Prince, whom he aspires to cuckold. As Roderick wanders away from Rowland into the mountains, he accuses himself of only stupidity. Rowland, meanwhile, reflects, "It was egotism always—the shock of taste, the humiliation of a proved blunder, the sense, above all, of a flagrant want of grace; but never a hint of simple sorrow for pain inflicted" (*RH*, 513). We are left to wonder, therefore, whether Roderick's death expresses the selfless motive Oscar Cargill has supplied for him: ". . . an effort to square himself with his patron, or to free him

in relation to Mary Garland."[18] For Roderick has been presented
to us as "never thinking of others save as they figured in his own
drama," of possessing an "extraordinary insensibility to the inju-
rious effects of his own eloquence," of being "perfectly indifferent" to "sympathy or compassion": "The great and characteristic
point with him was the perfect separateness of his sensibility. He
never saw himself as part of a whole; only as the clear-cut, sharp-
edged isolated individual, rejoicing or raging, as the case might
be, but needing in any case absolutely to affirm himself" (*RH*,
429). When he no longer finds it possible to affirm himself, he
dies as probably a suicide—although the motives, as well as the
actual circumstances, of his death, are, as Professor Cargill points
out, wonderfully ambiguous.

Roderick Hudson is thus the imperial self through whom the
early James criticized that autonomous individualism of nineteenth-century transcendentalism. Roderick's view of the self
and others is held up as destructive both to the individual who
so indulges himself and to the society that tries to accommodate
him in spite of his rebellion against its formal conventions. The
moral norm of the novel—indeed, it is quite possible to speak of
it as the social norm as well, since the question of the artist's morality is a social question—is not embodied in the attitudes of
Northampton society or even the society of the foreign colony
in Rome. Rather, it is Rowland Mallet whose personal standards
constitute a paradigm of the correct relation of the individual to
society. Rowland balances an appreciation of aesthetic values
with a fine moral sensibility. He calls himself "the most rational
of men," but he has a generous heart, instanced by his offering
on three days' acquaintance to take Roderick with him to Europe, and by a deep love for Mary Garland. He is a man of leisure, but he believes in the *application* of genius. Above all, he
embodies a commitment to civilized manners that stands in admirable contrast to Roderick's anarchic individualism; it is a code
of manners, moreover, squarely based on a sensitivity to moral
claims: "False positions were not to his taste; he shrank from
imperious passions, and the idea of finding himself jealous of an
unsuspecting friend could only disgust him. More than ever then
the path of good manners was to forget Mary Garland . . ."

(*RH*, 111–12). Though he has a moral conscience, he is not a prude. One of the Children of Light, he has the saving sense of beauty. It is his disinterestedness which first attracts him to the romantic American youth and then permits him to tolerate ill-mannered behavior which another might have immediately rebuked. Rowland, like James himself, above all, realizes the differences between ideal and actual social existence, as he meditatively conforms to the conventions of the foreign colony: "He enjoyed the quiet corner of a drawing-room beside an agreeable woman," James writes, "and, though the machinery of what calls itself society seemed to him to have many superfluous wheels, he accepted invitations and made visits punctiliously, from the conviction that the only way not to be overcome by the ridiculous side of most of such observances is to take them with ordered gravity" (*RH*, 99–100). This statement expresses what James felt to be a satisfactory view of the nature of social experience: that groups of people call themselves "society"; that the ordered social observance of the drawing room can be extremely agreeable; that insistence on polite manners is, *sub specie aeternitatis*, absurd; but that their agreeableness makes them worth observing punctiliously, with "ordered gravity." The quality of Rowland's social and moral perceptions makes him by far the most interesting character in the book, certainly of far more interest to Christina Light than Roderick Hudson cares to admit. Rowland is, in fact, the real center of the novel, and it is thanks to James's unerring instinct for the right angle from which to tell the story that we are able to see the drama in its fullness. "My subject, all blissfully, in the face of difficulties, had defined itself—and this in spite of the title of the book—as not directly, in the least, my young sculptor's adventure. This it had been but indirectly, being all the while in essence and in final effect another man's, his friend's and patron's, view and experience of him."

The real "center of interest" in the novel is thus "Rowland Mallet's consciousness, and the drama is the very drama of that consciousness," the whole of the novel being "the sum of what 'happened' to him,"—which, as James defined it, was above all his feeling "certain things happening to others, to Roderick, to Christina, to Mary Garland, to the Cavaliere, to the Prince, so

the beauty of the constructional game was to preserve in everything its especial value for *him*."[19] While Rowland is the center,
and while the plot is focused on the love relationships among
Rowland, Mary, Roderick, and Christina, the novel in fact deals
with "certain things happening" in the domain of manners.

The clash of manners largely arises from "the keynote of the
contrasted European order." The novel opens with four chapters
set in Northampton, a backwater New England village. Full of
high moral seriousness, the town is an inadequate environment
for the aspiring artist because it has no tradition of the arts and,
indeed, suspects that art is morally insidious. As Cecilia observes
of Roderick: "The flame smoulders, but it's never fanned by the
breath of criticism. He sees nothing, hears nothing, to help him
to self-knowledge. He's hopelessly discontented, but he doesn't
know where to look for help. Then his mother, as she one day
confessed to me, has a holy horror of a profession which consists
exclusively, as she supposes, in making figures of people divested
of all clothing. Sculpture, to her mind, is an insidious form of
immorality, and for a young man of possible loose leanings she
considers the law a much safer training" (*RH*, 29). In such a
community, it is clear, Roderick's talent will wither if not trans-
planted to a more congenial artistic climate. James went to great
pains, in the preface of the novel composed many years later, to
criticize the absence of "intensity" in his portrait of Northampton. He had wished to create, he wrote "some more or less vivid
antithesis to a state of civilization providing for 'art,' " a "humane
community," but one which was still incapable of nourishing
artistic genius. He erred in thinking, on the basis of Balzac's example, that to name a place is to represent it and that to address
himself to the surfaces of the life of a *ville de province* was somehow to penetrate its mass. Balzac, he observed, "tackled no group
of appearances, no presented face of the social organism (con-
spicuity thus attending it), *but* to make something of it. To name
it simply and not in some degree tackle it would have seemed
to him an act reflecting on his general course the deepest dis-
honour."[20] Still, Northampton's artistic thinness is sufficiently
suggested to the alert reader who cannot miss its intended
significance.

Rome, on the other hand, offers Roderick the opportunity for a "high aesthetic revel" (*RH*, 92). "He declared," James wrote with delicious irony, "that Rome made him feel and understand more things than he could express; he was sure that life must have there for all one's senses an incomparable fineness; that more interesting things must happen to one there than anywhere else" (*RH*, 92). Rome impresses him by "the element of accumulation in the human picture," for the "infinite superpositions of history," for the density of a high old tradition in arts and society. The "dusky swarming purlieus of the Ghetto" strike him as "weighted with a ponderous past," "blighted with the melancholy of things that had had their day" (*RH*, 275). The Vatican fascinates Roderick as "what he had been looking for from the first, the sufficient negation of his native scene." Like Hawthorne in *The Marble Faun*, James presents Rome as "the immemorial city of convention," and he calls the pope, in fact, "the most impressive convention in all history . . . visible to men's eyes in the reverberating streets, erect in a gilded coach drawn by four black horses" (*RH*, 92).

To James, the spectacle of the American's "assimilation" of Europe was rich ground for reflection, for he had seen hundreds of American travelers managing to miss, for all practical purposes, the real meaning of the experience. To his mother he complained in 1869 of "the absolute and incredible lack of *culture* that strikes you in common travelling Americans. The pleasantness of the English," he went on, "comes in a great measure from the fact of their each having been dipped into the crucible, which gives them a sort of coating of comely varnish and colour. They have been smoothed and polished by mutual social attrition. They have manners and a language. We lack both. . . ."[21]

The reactions of three such traveling Americans—Mr. Leavenworth, the American millionaire and "patron" of the arts, Mrs. Hudson, and Mary Garland—illustrate how much high comedy James could create in handling the American philistine in Europe confronting the "undraped paganism" everywhere. Certain of the New England "self-regarding virtues" are tested in the persons of these three, particularly in Mary Garland, who has come of a race of ministers. Rowland Mallet wishes to initiate her into full consciousness of Europe, to soften her Puritan angles, to cultivate in her "a motive for curves" (*RH*, 344). But for all the potential Rowland sees in her, Mary, like the awesomely "pure" Madame de Mauves, is not much changed by the experience of Europe. The transformation of the provincial American requires a greater openness to experience and willingness to change than she can command. Consequently, when Rowland escorts the ladies back to America after Roderick's death, Mary Garland is about as self-righteous as she was at the beginning, when Rowland took Roderick away. Mary's egotism, so fatally characteristic of Roderick, is indicated in James's final observation on Rowland's fate: "During the awful journey back to America, made of course with his assistance, she had used him, with the last rigour of consistency, as a character definitely appointed to her use" (*RH*, 526–27).

In the spectrum of moral and social values suggested in the novel, only Rowland triumphs over that crass egotism James associates with the American character and reconciles himself to an actual social order—whatever its defects and however absurd in certain lights the performance of its rituals may seem. He does this out of his commitment to the civilized beauty of the selfless life. In this, Rowland is a reflection of James himself. The criterion of civilized life he projected as "Europe" is, in fact, an ideal of society, one which he defined for Grace Norton in 1879 as a standard "of wit, of grace, of good manners, of vivacity, of urbanity, of intelligence, of what makes an easy and natural style of intercourse!"[22]

II

James's decision to settle in Paris was an unwise one. Although he was boasting to Howells in May of 1876 that he was "turning into an old, and very contented, Parisian" who felt as if he had "struck roots into the Parisian soil, and were likely to let them grow tangled and tenacious there,"[23] before long he was complaining that he really saw nothing of Parisian society. No one introduced him; he had no entrée into the exclusive drawing rooms of the Faubourg St. Germain. He felt cut off from the aristocracy which gave *ton* to the civilization he wished to portray. His situation was not much better than it had been earlier when he complained that "the waiters at the *restaurants* are as yet my chief society." By July he was confiding to William "a long-encroaching weariness and satiety with the French mind and its utterance," a desire "only to feed on English life and the contact of English minds." All he could claim for the experience of Paris was having learned the Théâtre Français by heart, "a good deal of Boulevard and third rate Americanism."[24] "The longer I live in France, the better I like the French personality," he observed to William, "but the more convinced I am of their bottomless superficiality."[25] These feelings underlay his move to London in December of 1876.

It is not surprising that James's response to Paris colored the novel he was then writing and that the exclusiveness of French society and the "bottomless superficiality" of the French mind found satiric expression in his new novel, *The American*. For one thing, his choice of a French setting discharged one obligation James felt to be incumbent on the American novelist of manners, the "terrible burden" of having to deal with Europe: "The burden is necessarily greater for an American—for he *must* deal, more or less, even if only by implication, with Europe; whereas no European is obliged to deal in the least with America. No one dreams of calling him less complete for not doing so. . . . The painter of manners who neglects America is not thereby incomplete as yet; but a hundred years hence—fifty years hence perhaps—he will doubtless be accounted so."[26]

The most direct stimulus to his new novel seems to have been the insult to the American character in the *L'Étrangère* (1876) of Alexandre Dumas *fils*, then playing at the Théâtre Français. Both James's letters of the period and his review of the play in the *New York Tribune* suggest that "surge of patriotic indignation" which aroused his "desire to refute the play."[27] In defending the American character, James took hints from Turgenev's *A Nest of Gentlefolk* (1858) and employed a dramatic device, borrowed from Augier, called the "intrusion plot." In its simplest form, this term describes the arrangement of dramatic actions which constitutes for James the structure of his formal themes: "Into a group there comes an intruder whose presence is resisted by one or more persons and accepted by one or more, with resulting conflict, until someone's eyes are opened to the true situation, to the danger, or to a possible solution. Different outcomes are possible, but the most frequent is the elimination of the intruder."[28]

The intruder, in this case, is a young American millionaire who goes to Paris to cultivate himself and falls in love with the daughter of an aristocratic family who first permit Newman's attentions, then reject him as a possible son-in-law because he is a "commercial person." In the quality of his response to the de Bellegardes and of theirs to him, James reveals the character of Newman and his antagonists and tests the values expressed in the manners of the two cultures they represent.

Christopher Newman, as his name suggests, is meant to represent the new man of the New World—a kind of Christopher Columbus in reverse—confronting the complexity and mystery of the Old World, where the qualities that have elevated him in America are of little social significance. A casual optimist with few principles but an extraordinary "unconscious *sang-froid*," a San Franciscan who is "horribly Western" and who knows nothing about culture, a democrat innocent of the knowledge of hierarchical class arrangements and ignorant of social forms, Newman is a young self-made man of action and enterprise, a pragmatist who has made his way up from a battlefield commission in the Civil War to the zenith of American commercial success: he is a millionaire manufacturer of leather goods and washtubs. The novel opens in the Salon Carré of the Louvre, where, with an "aesthetic headache," Newman sits on an ottoman, his long legs casually extended, lounging "in profound enjoyment of his posture." To the interested observer, Newman is a comic example of the American "national mould." His expression has that typically American "vagueness which is not vacuity, that blankness which is not simplicity, that look of being committed to nothing in particular, of standing in an attitude of general hospitality to the chances of life, of being very much at one's own disposal, so characteristic of many American faces. It was our friend's eye that chiefly told his story; an eye in which innocence and experience were singularly blended."[29]

The experience which his appearance suggests is that of a man who has "sat with Western humorists in knots, round cast-iron stoves, and seen 'tall' tales grow taller without toppling over," whose "sole aim in life had been to make money" (*A*, 36), but who has rejected the Darwinian business ethic of the Gilded Age, renounced revenge on his competitors, and given up business itself. The innocence which his glance suggests is that of a man who has only recently discovered in Europe "a very rich and beautiful world" which had "not all been made by sharp railroad men and stock-brokers" (*A*, 89). If Culture had once seemed to him "a proceeding properly confined to women, foreigners, and other unpractical persons" (*A*, 78), Raphael and Titian and Rubens had "inspired our friend, for the first time in his life, with a vague self-mistrust" (*A*, 18). In order to improve his mind, he takes in Europe, for his world is "a great bazaar, where one might stroll about and purchase handsome things" (*A*, 78). Europe he regards as made for him. He wishes to cultivate art and sees 470 churches; he wishes to cultivate society and becomes the familiar of M. Nioche and his daughter, a coquette. Above all, he wishes to marry "a magnificent woman," a "great woman," a beautiful woman—"I mean beautiful in mind and in manners, as well as in person. It is a thing every man has an equal right to . . ."(*A*, 52). In wanting to possess "the best article in the market," Newman is, as Mrs. Tristram puts it so precisely, "the great Western Barbarian, stepping forth in his innocence and might, gazing a while at this poor effete Old World, and then swooping down on it" (*A*, 48).

In Claire de Cintré he almost manages to make off with its best prize. But not quite. If she suggested to Newman "the sense of an elaborate education," she had passed "through mysterious ceremonies and processes of culture in her youth"; she had been "fashioned and made flexible to certain exalted social needs." A woman of "goodness, beauty, intelligence, a fine education, personal elegance," and noble birth, she is, in fine, exactly what Newman has been looking for. As he says to her younger brother Valentin, adumbrating Gatsby's conception of Daisy, "She is my dream realized" (*A*, 128).

The family, however, is another affair, and it is in Christopher

Newman's confrontation with the de Bellegardes that some of James's finest comedy emerges. They are a family with an eight-hundred-year-old name; their secluded hotel is in the exclusive Faubourg St. Germain; they constitute "the skim of the milk of the old noblesse" (*A*, 54). They are exclusive, associating only with their peers, among whom are some of "the best-preserved specimens" of "the Legitimists and the Ultramontanes" (*A*, 54). They admit of no changes, no intrusions of the modern. The Marquis has but a "single political conviction": "He believed in the divine right of Henry of Bourbon, Fifth of his name, to the throne of France" (*A*, 186). The gentlemen in their drawing rooms perpetuate the wig and carry on the "profuse white neck cloth of the fashion of 1820" (*A*, 174). They do not go out; they do not know Paris. Few of them have ever seen an American, although the city is crawling with them; and only a few remember having seen the great Dr. Franklin. To the American Mrs. Tristram, they are "mounted upon stilts a mile high, and with pedigrees long in proportion" (*A*, 54).

The dowager Marquise de Bellegarde is described as a "feudal countess of a mother" who "rules the family with an iron hand" and who allows Claire to "have no friends but of her own choosing, and to visit only in a certain sacred circle" (*A*, 55). She is preeminently "a woman of conventions and proprieties" whose "word is the world of things immutably decreed" (*A*, 145). If Newman is rich, she is proud, and in her world her power over her children counts for more than his money. Her son, the Marquis, is, as his name indicates, urbane. Valentin remarks, "He is a very remarkable man; he has the best manners in France. He is extremely clever; indeed he is very learned. He is writing a history of The Princesses of France Who Never Married" (*A*, 123). Opposed to Newman's suit, Urbaine is capable of a fine "transcendent patronage" in dealing with an American who in all tranquillity does not suspect "the relativity of his own place in the social scale" (*A*, 185). It is principally through Urbaine de Bellegarde and Newman that James dramatizes the conflict between the manners of the American democrat and the French aristocrat. The Marquis's deportment is always mechanically polite, correct, polished, aristocratic, and impersonal: "His manners seemed to indicate a fine, nervous dread that something disagreeable might happen if the atmosphere were not purified by allusions of a thoroughly superior cast" (*A*, 168). To Newman he is "a man of forms and phrases and postures; a man full of possible impertinences and treacheries" (*A*, 169). "What under the sun is the man afraid of?" Newman asks himself. "Does he think I am going to offer to swap jack knives with him?" (*A*, 168) In a Paris filled with American tourists demanding fried ham and cornbread for breakfast, who could be sure?

What the Marquis fears is, simply, Newman as a brother-in-law. Newman is unprepared to feel the social delicacy of his candidacy for marriage to Claire. After all, the de Bellegarde women had always married well; none had ever married into even the *petite noblesse*; there has never been a case, as Valentin tells Newman, of "a misalliance among the women." But it is characteristic of Newman that he believes that anything is possible—with a strong will, good intentions, and enough cash. That there should be anything more powerful than his will seemed to him impossible, and it is a mark of his comic optimism that he is never in doubt about his final goal (to win Claire) but only about the precise means of achieving it (the "everlasting proprieties" that have a hand in everything that she does).

The title of the novel suggests that Newman is intended to be representative of the American character. And in one sense he is. For Newman synthesizes some of the most salient characteristics of the American people. Although James thoroughly deplored some of these characteristics, it is those personal, individualizing traits of his large, generous, easy nature which distinguish him from the other Americans in the novel—particularly Tom Tristram and Mr. Babcock—and which justify James's sympathy with him. Tristram is an idle expatriate who judges a country by the quality of its cigars, who has lived amidst the beauty of Paris for years but who has never been inside the Louvre, and who cannot allude to America without superciliousness: "He irritated our friend by the tone of his allusions to their native country, and Newman was at a loss to understand why the United States were not good enough for Mr. Tristram. He had never been a very conscious patriot, but it vexed him to see them treated as little better than a vulgar smell in his friend's nostrils, and he finally broke out and swore that they were the greatest country in the world, that they could put all Europe into their breeches' pockets, and that an American who spoke ill of them ought to be carried home in irons and compelled to live in Boston." Tristram's attitudes illustrate what James called "the baleful spirit of the cosmopolite," the "uncomfortable consequence of seeing many lands and feeling at home in none." If the passionate pilgrimage produced only Tom Tristrams, it were better not taken. As James was later to observe, no doubt apropos of the many Tristrams in Europe, "To be a cosmopolite is not, I think, an ideal; the ideal should be to be a concentrated patriot."[30]

Mr. Babcock illustrates the opposite danger. If Newman is the Westerner, Babcock is the New Englander, a minister from Dorchester travelling in Europe on funds supplied by his congregation in order to improve his mind and culture. But for all his reverence before the treasures of Europe, "European life seemed to him unscrupulous and impure." He wished to give himself up to its beauty, but like Mary Garland he had a too highly developed set of moral prejudices. Art and Life are Extremely Serious Things to Babcock, but, deprived of spontaneity, he responds to Europe in terms of how he thinks he ought to feel about what he sees.

Newman falls between these two types. He is neither the deracinated expatriate, at home nowhere, nor the American ascetic moralist-patriot, at home only in "safe" Dorchester. James's inclusion of these other Americans indicates his perception, as Irving Howe has suggested, that "the notion that there is a 'national character' is impossible to defend as an abstract proposition."[31] Yet few writers, in fact, were more "obsessed, and to some extent enthralled, by the manifold paradox of our American self-consciousness"[32] than James, and few writers have understood more perceptively how the institutionalization of our social experience gives shape and form to the American "identity." Writing to Thomas Sergeant Perry, James defined his sense of the relationship between the developing American identity, coming to consciousness in the New World, and the fixed condition of national types in the Old: "We are Americans born—*il faut en prendre son parti.* I look upon it as a great blessing; and I think that to be an American is an excellent preparation for culture. We have exquisite qualities as a race, and it seems to me that we are ahead of European races in the fact that more than either of them we can deal freely with forms of civilization not our own, can pick and choose and assimilate and in short (aesthetically &c) claim our property wherever we find it. To have no national stamp has hitherto been a regret and a drawback, but I think it not unlikely that American writers may yet indicate a vast intellectual fusion and synthesis of the various National tendencies of the world is the condition of more important achievements than any we have seen."[33] James's objection to the provincialism of America lay precisely in our failure to realize the possibility of choice in creating a new, unique, national body of manners. As Frederick Hoffman has observed, this relationship between freedom and consciously chosen forms links James to the central American situation: "The American self is free to choose; no premium is put upon his adherence to traditional form or manners."[34] Isabelle Archer in *The Portrait of a Lady* appeals to us because, having come to Europe to observe the formal order of social experience, she uses her knowledge—as she tells Mrs. Touchett—to *choose* whether or not she will assimilate any of its conventions. Newman, though far richer, has paradoxically less freedom than she. Although Osmond respects "a magnificent form" as much as the Bellegardes, she can disobey him without serious consequences for their already estranged relationship. Newman, however, must accommodate himself to arbitrary European customs—vexing and irrational as they seem to the pragmatic American mind—in order to win Claire and to show the European aristocracy that "we aren't barbarians."

Though Newman cares little for the proprieties of the Faubourg St. Germain, he loves Claire deeply enough to want to learn "to do what is required over here" (*A*, 125), to comply with all the proper usages, to establish his claim to equality with the de Bellegardes—on their terms. He therefore pleads for instruction, begs to be tutored in the forms. This tourist attitude led James to observe in a review of Albert Rhodes's *The French at Home* that "the American demand for information about Parisian manners and customs seems to amount to what is commercially called a 'steady run.' . . ."[35] Thus Newman demands of Valentin: "If there is any thing particular to be done, let me know and I will do it. I wouldn't for the world approach Madame de Cintré without all the proper forms. If I ought to go and tell your mother, why I will go and tell her. I will go and tell your brother, even. I will go and tell any one you please. As I don't know any one else, I begin by telling you" (*A*, 125–26).

Newman's ignorance of polite manners, however, his ignorance of even what constitutes a social obligation, in view of his ambition, cannot help producing a broad comedy of manners. He at first mistakes Urbaine for the butler; he is on terms of easy familiarity with cicerones, guides, couriers, and the coquette Noémi Nioche. He telegraphs his engagement to America before it is formally announced and then brandishes the congratulatory replies in the face of Mme de Bellegarde. He threatens to stage an engagement party at his hotel, unaware that the "everlasting proprieties" require that Mme de Bellegarde give it. He parades the old marquise around the room on the evening of the party, mortally embarrassing her in the presence of her guests. And the result of these violations of decorum is a comedy which—from the viewpoint of the complicated artifice of European social forms—shows that Newman is indeed the barbarian. As one critic in the *Nation* observed in 1878: "America is not a good training-school of manners for the multitude. Not that Americans wish to be offensive—on the contrary, they are very good-natured; but they seem not to know the kind of treatment or attention (*égard* is the French word) a civilized being has the right to expect from a stranger."[36]

Despite his vulgarity, the real source of Newman's appeal is that he can perceive the distinction between "natural" and "artificial" behavior, between "the special intention" and "the habit of good manners," between urbanity and sincerity. Newman insists, on the ground of nature and sincerity, that he is both civilized and noble. His is precisely the claim Cooper's Eve makes in *Home As Found*, that the American gentleman enjoys the highest social station among civilized nations. To be sure, Mr. Effingham would very probably never have admitted Newman to the character of a gentleman, but the democrat Newman cannot understand why he is not as good as anybody. As Laboulaye observed, "*Tout Américaine à Paris se croît gentilhomme.*" When Valentin is horrified at Newman's ambition to marry Claire because he is not noble, Newman exclaims: "The devil I am not!"

> "Oh," said Bellegarde a little more seriously, "I did not know you had a title."
> "A title? What do you mean by a title?" asked Newman. "A count, a duke, a marquis? I don't know anything about that. I don't know who is and who is not. But I say I am noble. I don't exactly know what you mean by it, but it's a fine word and a fine idea: I put in a claim to it."
> "But what have you to show, my dear fellow, what proofs?"
> "Anything you please! But you don't suppose I am going to undertake to prove that I am noble. It is for you to prove the contrary."
> "That's easily done. You have manufactured wash-tubs."
> Newman stared a moment. "Therefore I am not noble? I don't see it. Tell me something I have *not* done—something I cannot do."
> "You cannot marry a woman like Madame de Cintré for the asking."
> "I believe you mean," said Newman slowly, "that I am not good enough."
> "Brutally speaking—yes!" [*A*, 126-27]

Newman is defeated because he wages his campaign in the arena of European manners and customs. He seeks to appropriate for himself proprieties and amenities which are totally foreign and too complex for him to grasp. As an American he has not developed a social style that is both expressive of the national character and distinguished and beautiful enough to oppose to the European. Instead he has sought to ape the European, and, repeatedly caught in the postures of imitation, Newman appears all the more grotesque. "Am I stepping about like a terrier on his hind legs?" (*A*, 233) Much of the time, unfortunately, he is. As one observer of Americans in Paris argued in 1878, "it is much better form to be American and to have a national individuality of one's own than to offer to foreign eyes a pale imitation of European models."[37]

Newman is, from the democratic viewpoint, admirable enough

—although we cannot help seeing the ridiculous in his playing the wrong kind of game with the wrong kind of people. What one of Howells's characters says in *Through the Eye of the Needle* is perfectly apropos, that "we haven't socially evolved from ourselves; we've evolved from the Europeans, from the English. I don't think you'll find a single society rite with us now that had its origin in our peculiar national life, if we have a peculiar national life."[38] Instead of exploiting the freedom of a unique social experience to create beautiful, new, and distinctive social forms, Americans sought both to impose on the democratic New World an aristocratic social pattern developed in the Old World and, returning to the Old, to beat the Europeans on their own ground. Much later, when James toured the United States after the turn of the century, he took little comfort in the uses to which Americans had put their freedom in the intervening quarter century. Virtually, he discovered, Americans had no manners or forms: "The ugliness—one pounced, indeed, on this as on a talisman for the future—was the so complete abolition of *forms*; if, with so little reference to their past, present or future possibility, they could be said to have been even so much honoured as to be abolished."[39]

This passage of time also put in clearer perspective the social character of the exclusive houses of the Faubourg St. Germain. And in the preface to *The American* he later argued that if he had properly gauged the depths of their cynicism, the de Bellegardes "would positively have jumped . . . at my rich and easy American, and not have 'minded' in the least any drawback. . . ."[40] Virtually isolated from the society he had tried to examine, his portrait failed of verisimilitude. Leon Edel has observed that "the Faubourg which Henry creates is in part the Faubourg of literature, rather than that of life. . . ."[41] But to have permitted the marriage of Claire and Newman would have been to pander to the sentimentality of an audience brought up on Maria Cummins, Mrs. Southworth, and Augusta Jane Evans Wilson, to throw, as James put it, "a rather vulgar sop to readers who don't really know the world and who don't measure the merit of a novel by its correspondence to the same." In defense of his conclusion, James observed to Howells that the marriage of

Claire and Newman "would have been impossible: they would have been an impossible couple, with an impossible problem before them. For instance—to speak very materially—where would they have lived? It was all very well for Newman to talk of giving her the whole world to choose from: but Asia and Africa being counted out, what would Europe and America have offered? Mme. de C. couldn't have lived in New York; depend upon it; and Newman, after his marriage (or rather *she*, after it) couldn't have dwelt in France. There would have been nothing left," he added facetiously, "but a farm out West."[42] It would be a mistake to underrate James's objection here, for the question of where such an exotic couple might have lived was a real one, as Howells had discovered in *A Chance Acquaintance* and *The Rise of Silas Lapham*, where the socially mismatched couples must settle in California and Mexico. James tackled the paradox of the aristocratic woman married to an American living in New York in "Lady Barberina." In this tale the social impasse comes right down to the practical question of "Who in New York society is possibly distinguished enough to lead Lady Barberina into dinner?"

III

The problem, for the American writer, of such social dilemmas is amplified in James's biography *Hawthorne*, published in 1879 for the English Men of Letters series. As he wrote the book— largely out of Lathrop's biographical notice and Hawthorne's notebooks—James discovered that the materials available to him needed interpretation for the foreign reader. James's problem was the difficult one of getting at Hawthorne through a set of notebooks which revealed well enough the details of Hawthorne's daily life in Concord and Salem and his appetite for actuality. But Hawthorne's random notations did not constitute the sort of dialogue with the self that helps to explain the creative imagination. Forced to abandon them as a way of getting at Hawthorne's mind and intellect, James exploited them for the inferences they offered about "his social circumstances."[43] In other words, Hawthorne's notebooks were important as a means of "documenting"

James's thesis about the thinness of the social environment in which Hawthorne lived.

The text for his disquisition on Hawthorne's environment James took from a passage in the preface to *The Marble Faun*. It is so crucial to the history of the novel of manners in America and to the criticism that surrounds the genre, as well as to James's particular practice as a novelist of this type, that although I have briefly touched upon it in chapter 1, we would do well to explore it more fully here. In the preface to that novel, Hawthorne observed that "Italy, as the site of his Romance, was chiefly valuable to him as affording a sort of poetic or fairy precinct, where actualities would not be so terribly insisted upon as they are, and must needs be, in America. No author, without a trial, can conceive of the difficulty of writing a romance about a country where there is no shadow, no antiquity, no mystery, no picturesque and gloomy wrong, nor anything but a commonplace prosperity, in broad and simple daylight, as is happily the case with my dear native land. It will be very long, I trust, before romance writers may find congenial and easily handled themes, either in the annals of our stalwart republic, or in any characteristic and probable events of our individual lives. Romance and poetry, ivy, lichens, and wall-flowers, need ruin to make them grow."[44]

For James, Hawthorne's notebooks constituted "a practical commentary" on the dilemma expressed in this passage. The notebooks suggested, above all, "the lightness of the diet to which his observation was condemned" (*H*, 47). The absence of antiquity, of mystery, and of the picturesque evils associated with Europe operated to deprive Hawthorne, James felt, of appropriate subjects for his romances. And to press home to his English audience "the negative side of the spectacle on which Hawthorne looked out," James launched into a well-nigh ludicrous enumeration of "the items of high civilization, as it exists in other countries, which are absent from the texture of American life" (*H*, 47–48): "No State, in the European sense of the word, and indeed barely a specific national name. No sovereign, no court, no personal loyalty, no aristocracy, no church, no clergy, no army, no diplomatic service, no country gentlemen, no palaces, no castles, nor manors, nor old country houses, nor parsonages, nor thatched cottages, nor ivied ruins; no cathedrals, nor abbeys, nor little Norman churches; no great Universities nor public schools —no Oxford, nor Eton, nor Harrow; no literature, no novels, no museums, no pictures, no political society, no sporting class—no Epsom nor Ascot! Some such list as that might be drawn up of the absent things in American life—especially in the American life of forty years ago, the effect of which, upon an English or a French imagination, would probably be appalling" (*H*, 48).

This indictment, so reminiscent of Cooper's *Notions of the Americans*, also recalls Hawthorne's complaint that Americans were too pragmatic to appreciate fantasies set in "a neutral territory, somewhere between the real world and fairy-land, where the Actual and the Imaginary may meet, and each imbue itself with the nature of the other."[45] As a romancer, Hawthorne wished "to claim a certain latitude, both as to its fashion and material, which he would not have felt himself entitled to assume had he professed to be writing a Novel." As he observed in the preface to *The House of the Seven Gables*, though the novel is "presumed to aim at a very minute fidelity, not merely to the possible, but to the probable and ordinary course of man's experience," the romance "has fairly a right to present that truth [of the human heart] under circumstances . . . of the writer's own choosing or creation."[46] Again and again, Hawthorne came back in his prefaces to the plight of the romancer in a country where sober common sense seemed to devalue the soaring rhapsodies of the imagination. For Hawthorne, the success of the gothic writers and the historical romances of Scott and his imitators attested to the more encouraging environment of Europe for the romancer. As he complained in the preface to *The Blithedale Romance*, "in the old countries, with which fiction has long been conversant, a certain conventional privilege seems to be awarded to the romancer; his work is not put exactly side by side with nature; and he is allowed a license with regard to everyday probability, in view of the improved effects which he is bound to produce thereby." But in America, "there is as yet no such Faery Land, so like the real world, that, in a suitable remoteness, one cannot well tell the difference, but with an atmosphere of strange enchantment, beheld through which the inhabitants have a propriety of their own. This atmosphere is what the American romancer needs." Without it, "the beings of the imagination" are held up beside "actually living mortals," and the artifice of the writer, "but too painfully discernible," is virtually discredited.[47]

I go into these perhaps already familiar matters in order to make a distinction not always noted by critics of nineteenth-century American literature. Cooper condemned American society as a field for the novelist; Hawthorne indicts it as a field for the romancer. In their purest forms, these genres are in nowise identical, and the basis of the two criticisms of Cooper and Hawthorne is totally antithetical. Cooper's judgment was based on the absence of social levels and the rituals of class; Hawthorne was not concerned with the anatomy of American social life. "He was not at any time what would be called a sociable man," James observed, and "thoroughly American in all ways, he was in none more so than in the vagueness of his sense of social distinctions, and his readiness to forget them if a moral or intellectual sensation were to be gained by it" (H, 27, 50). Such comments are hardly applicable to Cooper, and they indicate the extent to which the needs of the romancer differ from those of the novelist.

In fact, there are three separable issues involved in the allegation that America was inhospitable to the writer. The first has to do with the nature of American society itself. Certainly America never had a rigidly class-structured society in the European sense. But that is not to say that America did not, and does not, have distinctive social "classes" available to the novelist. As Cooper conceded, however reluctantly, New York had its social hierarchy. And so did Salem. James speaks disparagingly of the "small and homogeneous society" in which Hawthorne lived (H, 15). But as Lathrop's biography reveals, "there existed at Salem, during the early part of Hawthorne's life, 'a strong circle of wealthy families,' which 'maintained rigorously the distinctions of class,' and whose 'entertainments were splendid, their manners magnificent' " (H, 49). From Lathrop's description as well as from a study of nineteenth-century social history, the modern critic may rightly conclude that the materials for the social novel, or the novel of manners, were as available in Salem as in Coopers-town, but that Hawthorne was simply not interested in exploiting them. James tells his English readers that Lathrop's description of Salem "is a rather pictorial way of saying that there were a number of people in the place—the commercial and professional aristocracy, as it were—who lived in high comfort and respectability, and who, in their small provincial way, doubtless had pretensions to be exclusive" (*H*, 49–50). This observation, in tone and attitude, seems to dismiss the very reality of "class" distinctions to which Lathrop attested. In resumé, one basis of the argument that the novel of manners cannot exist in America is that American society is classless; so it is in the European sense. But social distinctions are available to the novelist of manners; we see them in Cooper's work, even in that of James.

The second issue derives from the alleged superiority of the romance to the novel—an allegation that explains why Simms, Hawthorne, and Cooper wrote romances. Although towns like Salem offered distinctions in class, manners, and customs (how Marquand makes use of them in his Newburyport novels!), Hawthorne preferred fantasy to actuality, the fairy land, the moonlit room, where the beings of the imagination could be arranged and rearranged according to improbabilities allowable only in the romance, which makes no claim to verisimilitude. Because it offered them more scope to be "imaginative," "fanciful," and rhapsodic, writers like Hawthorne naturally praised the romance over the novel, which was dismissed as a mere reportorial description of the everyday events of the commonplace world. But very few nineteenth-century romancers (or twentieth-century critics) have been willing to allow that the realistic novel, or novel of manners, may also make great demands on the imagination.

This leads us into the third issue—the limitation of a writer's sensibility. Hawthorne knew that novels of manners could be written about the social life of Salem and Concord. But he simply could not write them. Though his notebooks reveal an appetite for concrete social detail, he had a confessed "weakness" for the romantic allegory. In the preface to *Twice-Told Tales* he conceded that his stories had "the pale tint of flowers that blossomed in too retired a shade. . . . Instead of passion there is sentiment; and, even in what purport to be pictures of actual life, we have allegory, not always so warmly dressed in its habiliments of flesh and blood as to be taken into the reader's mind without a shiver." Melville himself felt that Hawthorne needed a greater sense of material actualities, that his fiction needed a little more "roast-beef." And in candid moments Hawthorne himself conceded that "my own individual taste is for quite another class of works than those which I myself am able to write. If I were to meet with such books as mine, by another writer, I don't believe I should be able to get through them." And he confessed to Fields, his publisher, that Anthony Trollope, one of England's great historians of manners, was his favorite novelist.

What I am trying to suggest is that Hawthorne rationalized a personal limitation in exploiting the romance because his sensibilities were unequal to the task of writing the novel of social life in America. In the Custom House chapter of *The Scarlet Letter* he made what to my mind is one of the most painful admissions ever made by an American writer. Speaking of his romance of history, he wrote: "It is my belief . . . that had I attempted a different order of composition, my faculties would not have been found so pointless and inefficacious. I might, for instance," he went on, "have contented myself with writing out the narratives of a veteran shipmaster, one of the Inspectors, whom I should be most ungrateful not to mention, since scarcely a day passed that he did not stir me to laughter and admiration by his marvellous gifts as a story-teller. Could I have preserved the picturesque force of his style, and the humorous coloring which nature taught him how to throw over his descriptions. . . ." But Hawthorne could not—the mimetic impulse was not in him. "It was a folly," he went on, "with the materiality of this daily life pressing so intrusively upon me, to attempt to fling myself back into another age; or to insist on creating the semblance of a world out of airy matter, when, at every moment, the impalpable beauty of my soap-bubble was broken by the rude contact of some actual circumstance. The wiser effort," he believed, would have been "to diffuse thought and imagination through the opaque substance of to-day, and thus to make it a bright transparency; to spiritualize the burden that began to weigh so heavily; to seek, resolutely, the true and indestructible value that lay hidden in the petty and wearisome incidents, and ordinary characters, with which I was now conversant. The fault was mine." Some humor, but more than modesty, underlies this mea culpa. But it does not weaken the seriousness of his conclusion: "The page of life that was spread out before me seemed dull and commonplace, only because I had not fathomed its deeper import. A better book than I shall ever write was there; leaf after leaf presenting itself to me, just as it was written out by the reality of the flitting hour, and vanishing as fast as written, only because my brain wanted the insight and my hand the cunning to transcribe it. At some future day, it may be, I shall remember a few scattered fragments and broken paragraphs and write them down, and find the letters turn to gold upon the page."[48]

Committed to the world of fancy and imagination, rather than to the actualities of his daily life, Hawthorne, in other words, even if he had lived in Europe, would doubtless have written Spenserian, Bunyanesque allegories. This is surprising, in its way, for Hawthorne gives intimations from time to time of a penetrating realistic vision based on his own experience. It might even be possible to say that the real strength of *The Blithedale Romance* lies not in its mystical veils but in those scenes of vivid realism that mark the kind of fiction Hawthorne personally preferred to read but felt that he could not successfully write—Coverdale's journey to Brook Farm in the snowstorm, his illness, his farewell to the pigs, Priscilla riding the ox, the moving episode of dragging the pond for Zenobia's body.

In any event, the historically informed literary critic cannot be too credulous when writers like Cooper and Hawthorne complain about "the conditions of American life." What we should endeavor to realize is that their views conceal debatable artistic assumptions (e.g., the romance as "superior" to the novel) and the perfectly understandable tendency of the writer to rationalize the limitation (which may be also the strength) of his own sensibility. In the long run, no one can really be sorry that Hawthorne, in writing *The Scarlet Letter*, employed his particular talents as he did. It is, after all, one of the great imaginative works of nineteenth-century fiction. But if I emphasize Hawthorne's "denigration" of the book, I do so only to point out that, although Melville ranked him with Shakespeare, Hawthorne's talent was a limited one—as he himself recognized.

Looking at the notebooks, James accepted the description of America, as Hawthorne implied it, at face value. Salem seemed so isolated, New England culture so impoverished, that the most distinctive adjective he could ascribe to Hawthorne was "provincial." He observed that "it takes so many things, as Hawthorne must have felt later in life, when he made the acquaintance of the denser, richer, warmer European spectacle—it takes such an accumulation of history and custom, such a complexity of manners and types, to form a fund of suggestion for the novelist" (H, 47). The moral of Hawthorne's story, he concluded, was that "the flower of art blooms only where the soil is deep, that it takes a great deal of history to produce a little literature, that it needs a complex social machinery to set a writer in motion" (H, 16). And, of course, America could not provide those necessities. The positive side of the social spectacle on which Hawthorne looked out was that the thin, democratic society in which he grew up had the beneficial effect of emphasizing the importance of the individual. "The individual counts for more, as it were," James argued, "and, thanks to the absence of a variety of social types and of settled heads under which he may be easily and conveniently pigeon-holed, he is to a certain extent a wonder and a mystery" (H, 53). If it had no other effect, James felt, the mystery of the American individual caused Hawthorne to care for "the deeper psychology" (H, 64) and to focus on the complexity of his moral, not social, relations.

The attack on James's *Hawthorne* by American critics was prompt and shrill. Howells went directly to the point in asserting that the substance of fiction is not the institutions of European society but human life: "After leaving out all those novelistic 'properties' as sovereigns, courts, aristocracy, gentry, castles, cottages, cathedrals, abbeys, universities, museums, political class, Epsoms, and Ascots, by the absence of which Mr. James suggests our poverty to the English conception, we have the whole of human life remaining, and a social structure presenting the only

fresh and novel opportunities left to fiction, opportunities manifold and inexhaustible. No man would have known less what to
do with that dreary and worn-out paraphernalia than Hawthorne...."[49]

But having abandoned provincialism in favor of an ideal of civilization at its highest, most international character, James was in
no mind to agree with Howells. He thanked Howells for his review, but observed that *Hawthorne* was "a tolerably deliberate
and meditated performance" and that he was "prepared to do
battle for most of the convictions expressed" in it. He apologized
for the number of times he had used the word "provincial" in
connection with Hawthorne, but he argued that "certain national
types are essentially and intrinsically provincial. I sympathize
even less," he went on, "with your protest against the idea that it
takes an old civilization to set a novelist in motion—a proposition
that seems to me so true as to be a truism. It is on manners, customs, usages, habits, forms, upon all these things matured and established, that a novelist lives—they are the very stuff his work is
made of; and in saying that in the absence of those 'dreary and
worn-out paraphernalia' which I enumerate as being wanting in
American society, 'we have simply the whole of human life left,'
you beg (to my sense) the question. I should say we had just so
much less of it as these same 'paraphernalia' represent, and I think
they represent an enormous quantity of it." James argued that the
proof of Howells's position would be the emergence of a real
novelist—"(setting the present high company—yourself and me—
for obvious reasons apart)"—an American Balzac or Thackeray.
And since he felt that he was arguing so theoretical a possibility,
James went on to admit to Howells that "such a genius will get
on *only* by agreeing with your view of the case—to do something
great he must feel as you feel about it." But he doubted whether a
"man of the faculty of Balzac and Thackeray" could agree with
Howells. "When he does," James went on, "I will lie flat on my
stomach and do him homage—in the very centre of the contrib-
utor's club, or on the threshold of the magazine, or in any public
place you may appoint!" He concluded by praising Howells for
not feeling the want of a complex paraphernalia in the European
sense: "You are certainly right—magnificently and heroically

right—to do so, and on the day you make your readers—I mean the readers who know and appreciate the paraphernalia—do the same, you will be the American Balzac. That's a great mission— go in for it!"[50]

James himself was clearly disqualified from becoming the American Balzac—he hadn't Balzac's passion for business—but it is possible to see in *The Princess Casamassima* James's attempt to encompass, after the manner of Balzac and Thackeray, the whole range of English social experience and a good many of those novelistic properties and paraphernalia absent in America. T. W. Higginson criticized James for insufficiently appreciating "the strong point of republicanism, in that it develops real individuality in proportion as it diminishes conventional distinctions."[51] But *The Princess Casamassima* does address itself precisely to the political question underlying James's criticism of America in *Hawthorne*. For in Hyacinth Robinson's dilemma over the forms of civilization is posed the question of culture or anarchy. James's novel defines the cost to society of a class like the aristocracy and the quality, beauty, and style of life associated with it. Hyacinth is torn between the alternatives: from his mother's side comes his passionate awareness of the miserable plight of the poor, his ardent socialism, and even his solemn anarchist vow to assassinate "an enemy of the people." But from his father's side he derives his feeling for the style of aristocratic life, his sense of taste, and his passionate desire to surround himself with beauty and distinction. He does not kill himself because his politics have changed and he no longer believes in the bald logic of the anarchist argument. He takes his life because he is paralyzed by the counterbalancing claims of politics and art, of morality and beauty—by the insistent needs of the deprived workingmen and the need for beauty and grace which would be starved if the aristocracy and its modes of expression were liquidated. As he writes to the princess after having seen the glories of European civilization on the Continent:

The monuments and treasures of art, the great palaces and properties, the conquests of learning and taste, the general fabric of civilization as we know it, based if you will upon all the despotisms, the cruelties, the exclusions, the monopolies, and the rapacities of the past, but thanks to which, all the same, the world is less of a 'bloody sell' and life more of a lark—our friend Hoffendahl [the leader of the conspirators] seems to me to hold them too cheap and to wish to substitute for them something in which I can't somehow believe as I do in things with which the yearnings and the tears of generations have been mixed.... He would cut up the ceilings of the Veronese into strips, so that everyone might have a little piece. I don't want everyone to have a little piece of anything and I've a great horror of that kind of invidious jealousy which is at the bottom of the idea of redistribution.[52]

Is the beauty, grace, and charm of the princess's world worth the labor, poverty, and anguish of the workers who support the social mass? This is a nice question—one which Mrs. Wharton and Fitzgerald ask about the sacrifices which produced Lily Bart and Nicole Diver in *The House of Mirth* and *Tender Is the Night*. Hyacinth's suicide at the end of the novel is an index of how impossible it is to answer whether an exquisite civilization created by a leisure class is worth the cost in human life of the laborers who make it possible. Howells was to argue that the poverty of the workingman justified immense sacrifices of privilege to the claims of democracy and socialism, but James was ambivalent. As he observed in *Transatlantic Sketches*, the "constant sense of the beautiful scenic properties of English life" suggests that Conservatism in England "has all the charm, and leaves dissent and democracy nothing but their bald logic. Conservatism has the cathedrals, the colleges, the castles, the gardens, the traditions, the associations, the fine names, the better manners, the poetry; dissent has the dusky brick chapels in provincial by-streets, the names out of Dickens, the uncertain tenure of the *h*, and the poor *mens sibi conscia recti*."[53] James's leaning here toward the forms, institutions, and manners of a civilization that had been produced by English Conservatism should be seen in the light of his severe criticism of the cultural nudity of America, where, in the absence of "continuity, responsibility, transmission," there "couldn't *be* any manners to speak of" because "the basis ... was somehow wanting for them; and ... nothing, accordingly, no image, no presumption of constituted relations, possibilities, amenities, in the social, in the domestic order, was inwardly projected."[54] Democracy, James observed in *The American Scene*, "represents an immense boon," but at the same time, he wanted to know, "what does the enjoyment of the boon represent?" (*AS*, 53). The "huge democratic broom" had swept the social field clean, and James was appalled at how "the working of democratic institutions" had managed to vulgarly "determine and qualify manners, feelings, communications, modes of contact and conceptions of life" (*AS*, 53). The only consolation he could derive was in "the possible evolution of manners, the latent drama to come" (*AS*, 25), the development of paraphernalia, what he called "the great adventure of a society reaching into the apparent void for the amenities, the consummations, after having earnestly gathered in so many of the preparations and necessities" (*AS*, 12).

Yet at the same time that James admired a class system that had produced the cathedrals and colleges and castles, he knew that the British aristocracy was corrupt. "The upper classes are too refined," he noted, "and the lower classes are too miserable."[55] To Charles Eliot Norton he remarked "the already very damaged prestige of the English upper class" and noted that "the condition of that body seems to me to be in many ways very much the same rotten and collapsible one as that of the French aristocracy before the revolution...."[56] His disillusionment at the failure of the English aristocracy to approximate his ideal society led him to express, through the princess, the imagination of disaster, the fear that English society is "the old regime again, the rottenness and extravagance, bristling with every iniquity and every abuse, over which the French Revolution passed like a whirlwind; or perhaps even more a reproduction of the Roman world in its decadence, gouty, apoplectic, depraved, gorged and clogged with wealth and spoils, selfishness and scepticism, and waiting for the onset of the barbarians."[57] America might lack those social institutions and forms which are useful to the novelist; but at least in terms of the common life James would have agreed with Colonel Higginson that republicanism permits the greater development of the average man. Still, he found little cheer in what seemed to him a choice between decadence and barbarism.

While Howells was "going in for" the American Balzac—he nearly made it in *A Hazard of New Fortunes*—James was meanwhile complaining that the novel he was at work on, *Washington*

Square, made him "feel acutely the want of the 'paraphernalia.' "[58]
One doubts that the paraphernalia were as objectively necessary
as James argued, but it is clear that they were important to him,
and the felt lack of them handicapped his work, leading him to
compose (for English readers?) long paragraphs of social history
which establish Washington Square's claim to having had something of a social character. This discursive reportage is a mark of
the novel of manners. Rare enough in James, the tendency to indulge in extended passages of social history helps the novelist to
make clear the where and why of the societies dealt with. Marquand's long discussions of Clyde, Massachusetts; Mrs. Wharton's
essays on the transitions in Old New York social history; O'Hara's
long and highly repetitive set pieces distinguishing Lantenengo
Street and Christiana Street in Gibbsville—all of these point up the
need of the novelist of manners to establish his social world, to
appropriate its social reality, and to recreate it through the medium
of language. This kind of expository description in his "tale
purely American" annoyed James, however, for, as he observed
to Norton, "to write well and worthily of American things, one
need even more than elsewhere to be a *master*. But unfortunately
one is less!"[59]

Partly to avoid the problem of recreating social history, James
gradually turned from the novel of manners to what might broadly be called "the psychological novel." He shifted the field, that
is, from the external world of manners and customs to the impact
of manners on the consciousness of his personae. *The Portrait of
a Lady*, which the *Nation* called a work of "romantic sociology,"[60] illustrates the turning point in James's method. It is clearly
a novel of manners in its attention to social rituals; in Isabel's
resistance to the conventions of Gardencourt and her wish for
knowledge so as to choose whether or not she will observe them;
in Henrietta Stackpole's "boarding-house manners"; in the deferential manners of the Molineux ladies; in the perfect obedience
to her father's wishes of Pansy, the convent-educated *jeune fille*,
who possesses "the *achieved* manners of an old civilization"; and
in Osmond's reverence before that "something sacred and precious—the observance of a magnificent form."[61] The novel, rich
in its attention to manners, has been so superbly analyzed by

Edel and others, that perhaps it will seem sufficient if I select only an instance or two of James's changing relation to these materials.

It is, in fact, Osmond's failure to observe a form, a point of manners, that provides James with his first major occasion to explore the psychology of Isabel, to begin working his way toward the novels of "the major phase." On the evening when, returning unexpectedly to the Palazzo Roccanera, Isabel glimpses Madame Merle and Osmond together in the large drawing room, she has her first intimation of the true nature of her marriage: "Madame Merle was there in her bonnet, and Gilbert Osmond was talking to her; for a minute they were unaware she had come in. Isabel had often seen that before, certainly; but what she had not seen, or at least had not noticed, was that their colloquy had for the moment converted itself into a sort of familiar silence, from which she instantly perceived that her entrance would startle them. Madame Merle was standing on the rug, a little way from the fire; Osmond was in a deep chair, leaning back and looking at her. Her head was erect, as usual, but her eyes were bent on his. What struck Isabel first was that he was sitting while Madame Merle stood; there was an anomaly in this that arrested her."[62]

That Osmond does not ask her to sit down, does not himself stand, is a minor point of good form. But it has the deepest implications for Isabel as that night she sits up until four in the morning meditating on her marriage to Osmond. It would be too much to expect Isabel to infer from this scene that Madame Merle has been Osmond's mistress and is, in fact, the mother of Pansy. Isabel's powers at this point are not that perceptive. Still, the "remembered vision—that of her husband and Madame Merle unconsciously and familiarly associated" (*PL*, II:205)—activates those frightening reflections which lead Isabel deeply into the failure of her own marriage and ultimately to the knowledge that this incident "expresses."

As he looked back in writing the preface, James took a singular satisfaction in this long meditation in chapter 42 of the novel, for it signaled the shift away from the documentary representation of manners as "actions" in the external world toward dramatic scenes existent in the consciousness of his central characters. Manners still continue to be highly important in the later James (it tells much that Chad has removed his coat in the canoe with Mme de Vionnet), but James's interest is henceforth the impact of manners on those who are imaginative enough to guess what deeper significance they express. As Christof Wegelin has observed of this shift: "The comedy based on the conflict between American and European manners has now given way to the serious, sometimes tragic, problem piece, in which manners function as conventions determining morals."[63]

To extrapolate somewhat further, the fiction of Howells and James illustrates the two directions it is possible for the novelist of manners in America to take. Howells, in the late eighties, turned more and more from the comedy of manners based on the foibles of social mobility toward the novel of social protest, a shift from the manners of the American social classes toward the economic inequities upon which status and manners rest. James shifted in the other direction, leaving the comedy of international contrasts in manners for the deeper psychology of his characters, for what Frederick Crews has called "the tragedy of manners."

But James's later interest in the aesthetic arrangement of the content of human awareness—in a style complex, involuted, and appropriately expressive of the data of consciousness—should not obscure for us the fact that he never lost his interest in manners. For James, style and language were an indispensable index of manners. This much is clear from *The Question of Our Speech* (1905). Ostensibly a plea for discrimination in our use of the *vox Americana*, it claims language to be the very groundwork of civilization. For James, one's native tongue is a "touchstone of manners," the representative note of its having achieved civilization.

With the question of our speech, he argued, "verily we raise and set up the question of our manners as well, for that is indissolubly involved. To discriminate, to learn to find our way among noted sounds, find it as through the acquisition of a new ear; to begin to prefer form to the absence of form, to distinguish color from the absence of color—all this amounts to substituting manner for the absence of manner: whereby it is *manners themselves*, or something like a sketchy approach to a dim gregarious conception of them, that we shall (delicious thought!) begin to work round to the notion of." The idea of the civilized use of one's language and the idea of good manners—both are inextricably involved in James's definition of good breeding: "The idea of good breeding—without which intercourse fails to flower into fineness, without which human relations bear but crude and tasteless fruit —is one of the most precious conquests of civilization, the very core of our social heritage," he argued. To preserve and enlarge the value of good breeding, or "*secure* good manner," James felt a conscious mission for himself. For "no danger would be more lamentable," he observed, "than that of the real extinction, in our hands, of so sacred a flame."[64]

His discussion of the civilized use of language, "this highest of the civilities," in its way bears upon the style of the late James. Indeed, *The Question of Our Speech* is a beautiful illustration of that sophisticated and infinitely interesting medium. I mention the later style only because it brings us back around to the earlier, and because it establishes the connection between complexity of manners (so abundantly illustrated in the earlier novels) and complexity of style (so clearly the mark of the later). Henry James claims the distinction of being America's greatest novelist of manners not because his notation of the customs of the social worlds he knew was extensive or "true." He is our best novelist of manners because he is our best novelist. And his sense of character in relation to society, his commitment to civilization, his artistic intelligence, his command of language, the particular felicity of his style, the characteristic comedy of his phrasing and diction—it is these that make him not only America's best novelist of manners but our best novelist. One can appreciate the early novels of manners which made James's reputation and set him on the high road, without, I am happy to say, disparaging the novels of the later period, the "major phase."

4

❦ WILLIAM DEAN HOWELLS

Equality as the Basis of Good Society

Howells has suffered a decline in popularity for reasons not too difficult to understand. Many readers, particularly the young, are not really interested in the way Howells approached the issues that generated his art. The romance of money is dead; men who pursue wealth for its own sake are not our avowed culture heroes now; and our millionaires have abandoned conspicuous consumption for anonymity. Portraits of the domestic circle no longer entertain; families are hardly families any longer, in the old sense; and novels of family life, unless they are ethnic portraits of castrated sons, are no longer felt to reveal viable truths in the modern world. The dynamics of social ambition are apparently no longer taken very seriously, and at a time when we are all being adjured to "tune in, turn on, and drop out," the drama of social climbing is an anachronism to many young people. Upward social mobility and the old antagonisms of class are as real as ever. But since the thirties other social issues have concerned us. Accidents of the Zeitgeist thus have a way of seeming to render obsolete the social center of a writer's work.

Howells still deserves to be read, though, and read with affection. For few writers of his time brought to life so vividly the social experience of nineteenth-century America or dramatized so convincingly the problems of middle-class existence in fiction. Howells knew the East and the West, the city and country, the rich and the poor. He knew the range of their manners, their ambitions and values, their style and idiom. And his social awareness, matched by a notable psychological acumen, served him well in that most challenging of all the novelist's tasks—the creation of convincing characters, like Bartley Hubbard, Silas and Persis Lapham, Basil and Isabel March, Squire and Marcia Gaylord. These two preoccupations, character and manners, place his novels at the midpoint between sensibility and social history; they unify in themselves the extremes of self and society.

What makes Howells of particular interest to the student of the novel of manners in America is the considerable art with which he embodied the democratic social assumptions of the developing West in which he grew up. The son of an Ohio newspaperman, Howells spent his youth in small-town newspaper offices unconsciously assimilating the Western egalitarianism that marked the politics of Jackson and Lincoln. Later, when he came to have a wider knowledge of the world, "the vision of the West as the ideal land of freedom, equality and purity was constantly present in his mind and could only occasionally be blurred by dark events. It became a constant source of inspiration to him," as Olov Fryckstedt has observed, and "it is only from this experience that we can fully understand the enthusiasm and the loving care with which he depicted the commonplace realities of American life in novel after novel."[1] Even after Howells had become the editor of the *Atlantic Monthly* and the intimate friend of the New England Brahmins, who constituted the arbiters of taste in America, he did not repudiate his Western egalitarian values. As Henry Steele Commager has rightly suggested of the mature Howells, "the dictator of literary Boston and, eventually, of literary America, Howells never forgot his frontier origins or abandoned his democratic simplicity."[2] This point deserves to be made, and to be made emphatically, because Howells has been too readily accused of toadying to the genteel aristocracy of the East.

The fact is that few men of his time were more capable than Howells of representing accurately in fiction the social contradictions that characterized American life in the last quarter of the nineteenth century. He saw the spectacle of simple Westerners like himself thrown up against hypercivilized Boston snobs, of provincial country folk deracinated and struggling to find themselves in the developing cities, of the underworld of the laboring poor, and of newly rich millionaires trying to crash polite society. He saw, in other words, a broad spectrum of social experience which could be brought into dramatic relief through the medium of the travel narrative and the social novel.

I

Howells's first novel, *Their Wedding Journey* (1872) is composed of that sharp observation and notation of social differences that bring to life the novel of manners. Hardly fiction, it is more nearly a travelogue. As Howells himself once observed, "I was a traveller long before I was a noveler, and I . . . mounted somewhat timidly to the threshold of fiction from the high-roads and by-roads where I had studied manners and men."[3] The experience that provided him with the narrative organization of *Their Wedding Journey* was a trip he and his wife had taken into the northeastern United States and Canada. For the westerner Howells, Rochester, Niagara Falls, the St. Lawrence River, and Montreal were rich in dramatic contradictions. Studying the people he met on trains and ships, in the cathedrals and on the streets, Howells saw a way of turning his journey to good account by rendering a new and distinctive portrait of American manners. To his father he observed: "At last I am fairly launched upon the story of our last summer's travels, which I am giving the form of fiction so far as the characters are concerned. If I succeed in this—and I believe I shall—I see clear before me a path in literature which no one else has tried, and which I believe I can make most distinctly my own."[4]

Perhaps more by accident than design, Howells was working his way, through the travel narrative, toward one of the most effective devices in the novel of manners: the neutral setting which brings together characters from a variety of social backgrounds and generates its action out of the conflict of opposing manners. His aim in *Their Wedding Journey* was quasi-fictional social history. He wanted to capture some of the commonplace realities of American life—not the exciting and picturesque episodes of exotic travel narratives, but the simplicity of American manners in the northeast United States in the early 1870s; to seize the significant detail which could be rendered dramatically and pose it as the representative expression of American manners. He wished simply "to talk of some ordinary traits of American life," "to speak a little of well-known and easily accessible places, to present now a bit of landscape and now a sketch of character."[5] His aim, as he told J. M. Comly, was to try to make *Their Wedding Journey* "a faithful study of our American life."[6]

The traveling couple of whom Howells undertook to give character sketches are Basil and Isabel March, a pair of almost middle-aged newlyweds whose wedding journey transacts the plot. It had every right to be a sentimental journey, but Howells continually undercut their romantic illusions. Basil is an insurance salesman with unfulfilled literary yearnings, and Isabel is a conventional woman who interprets everything she sees—couples necking in public, Niagara Falls, discourteous hotel clerks and ticket-sellers, disappointingly civilized Indians, picturesque and wild landscapes, and the old-world curiosities of Montreal and Quebec—in the light of her Boston prejudices. Basil, whose charming irony continually qualifies her impetuous judgments, offers a whimsical commentary on American manners which endeared Howells to the American reading public. It is clear from this tale and from the other "March family narratives" that Howells intended them to represent an ordinary middle-class couple whose manners are somehow typical of the average American. Howells's characteristic themes and interests are here explored: love and matchmaking, the oddities of the womanly temperament, the ironic humor of the American male, the variety of manners that distinguish American social classes, and the national pride of the American who compares his country with a foreign culture.

Nothing in particular happens during the journey: Howells cautions us not to expect of Basil and Isabel any "romantic adventures" of the kind that interested Cooper, Simms, and Hawthorne. But the exciting things that do not happen are trivial compared to the charming things that do. Garrulous and talky, Howells had yet to learn the lesson of dramatic objectivity from Turgenev, and as Basil and Isabel drift from place to place, he turns to the reader and asks: "Do I pitch the pipe too low? We poor honest men are at a sad disadvantage; and now and then I am minded to give a loose to fancy, and attribute something really grand and fine to my people, in order to make them worthier of the reader's respected acquaintance. But again, I forbid myself in a higher interest . . ." (*TWJ*, 239). The higher interest which governed Howells's treatment of his characters and plot was a growing sense of the value of verisimilitude in fiction.

This verisimilitude is evident in both his description of national manners and in the psychology of his characters. No details were apparently too trivial to engage Howells's interest—from the grandeur of Niagara Falls to the commonplaceness of the pedlar boy on the train with his prize candies, gum-drops, popcorn, papers, books, magazines, and police gazettes. Emerson had sung the transcendental value of the smallest facts of the material world—"the meal in the firkin; the milk in the pan"—but Howells was feeling his way, through these details, toward the realist's perception of the intrinsic value of the actual. His love for the ordinariness of American experience—for example, the manners of a young American boy flirting with a pair of girls—moved him to observe: "Ah, poor Real life, which I love, can I make others share the delight I find in thy foolish and insipid face?" (*TWJ*, 67).

The book is divided into two parts, the first dealing with the sights and scenes of America as the Marches go by night boat and train to Niagara and beyond, the second with Canadian scenes in Montreal and Quebec. The balanced structure permits Howells to offer a series of observations contrasting the commonplace features of American life with the exotic and picturesque purlieus of a Canadian scene more European than American. Montreal suggested the antique feudalism of the Old World with its churches and convents, old buildings and bridges, narrow streets and dark mysterious shops, the color and pageantry of European influences absent from Boston and New York. Montreal gave the Marches a profounder sense of the past, of "the ties which exist for us only in history." It cast over the present "a glamour of olden time to the new land; it touched," Howells observed, "the prosaic democratic present with the waning poetic light of the aristocratic and monarchical tradition." It makes comprehensible to them, but not totally admirable, the Canadians' "veneration for things we have tumbled into the dust" (*TWJ*, 201). Absurdly sentimental, Basil and Isabel look in Montreal and Quebec for romantic associations with the literature they have read. They poeticize the landscape, the streets, and churches. They yearn for the sensations such associations are supposed to create. But for Howells the ideal had to embrace the real; men had to get over their absurd reluctance of facts; they needed to find the poetic in the here and now. Howells does not condemn the Marches for romanticizing what they see and for feeling disappointed occasionally with the ordinariness of America. But he was constrained to ask: "Why, in fact, should we wish to find America like Europe? Are the ruins and impostures and miseries and superstitions which beset the traveller abroad so precious, that he should desire to imagine them at every step in his own hemisphere? Or have we then of our own no effective shapes of ignorance and want and incredibility, that we must forever seek an alien contrast to our native intelligence and comfort?" (*TWJ*, 202–3).

Their Wedding Journey is a light performance, but it turned out to be surprisingly popular. Howells's sharp eye for the significant detail, the appeal of a winsome personality that showed through the narrative, the delicacy of his humor and irony, the believability of his newlyweds, a style marked by what one critic has called his "phrasal excellencies"[7]—all of these qualities won for him an appreciative audience. "Where did you find that impossibly happy way of saying everything?" John Hay asked him, and Henry Adams praised Howells's gift for delineating our manners, his "photographic truth to nature, and remarkable delicacy and lightness of touch."[8] Even Dreiser, who thought Howells wrote a lot of "pewky and damn-fool" books, praised *Their Wedding Journey* because there was "not a sentimental passage in it, quarrels from beginning to end, just the way it would be, don't you know, really beautiful and true."[9] But for all its light comedy and phrasal excellencies, the aim of *Their Wedding Journey* was more than descriptive. In its conclusion, through the conversations of Basil and Isabel, Howells rises to an affirmation of the character and manners of American life— picturing the New World as a place of fresh opportunity and new possibilities, a kind of Eden, in its way, "a new chance afforded the race for goodness and happiness, for health and life" (*TWJ*, 206).

II

In *A Chance Acquaintance*, Howells dealt again with social tensions in American society and once more affirmed the social value of the democratic political ideal. Traveling up the Saguenay to Quebec and down to Boston, Colonel Ellison and his wife Fanny, from Milwaukee, who make a brief appearance in *Their Wedding Journey*, encounter the Marches at Niagara Falls. With them is their niece Kitty Ellison, of Eriecreek, New York, who has come along for a one-day excursion. All three are plain people of the provincial republic who have no pretensions to social class or position, though Isabel is surprised, as she remarks in *Their Wedding Journey*, at the existence of civilization in a westerner like Kitty. On the way up the Saguenay, the Ellisons accidentally make the acquaintance of Miles Arbuton, a Bostonian whom they mistake for an Englishman. In the course of the novel, despite the "incompatibility of Boston and Eriecreek traditions,"[10] Miles and Kitty fall in love. Although they have practically nothing in common except their youth and good looks, they head back to Boston betrothed.

The crisis in their relationship occurs at an inn where Miles unexpectedly meets two Boston ladies whom he knows. Surprised at seeing them so far from home, Miles neglects to introduce them to Kitty, and as they draw him further down the piazza, Miles is "obliged" to leave Kitty sitting on the porch and to accompany them all the way to their boat. Being abandoned mortifies Kitty, but it turns, she believes, on a point of manners: "Why, how stupid I am!" she thinks. "Of course a gentleman can't introduce ladies; and the only thing for him to do is to excuse himself to them as soon as he can without rudeness, and come back to me" (*CA*, 260). But the real problem is that Miles is too ashamed to introduce Kitty to the fashionable Boston ladies because she is too countrified, in her homemade dress, to make their acquaintance. And Kitty knows it. When he finally returns, and her shame convicts him of his rudeness, he has the honesty to recognize that his manners have been outrageous. "He saw it with paralyzing clearness; and, as an inexorable fact that confounded quite as much as it dismayed him, he perceived that throughout that ignoble scene she had been the gentle person and he the vulgar one" (*CA*, 267). The story thus weighs the Boston gentleman in the balance and finds him wanting. Arbuton—with his exquisite and aristocratic bearing, his sophisticated and civilized style, his "fastidious good looks and his blameless manners"—is shown to be proud of place, arrogant of social distinctions, and deficient in human feeling—the feeling of common human brotherhood. By his rudeness to Kitty, in fact, he proves himself to be "all gloves and slim umbrella,—the mere husk of well-dressed culture and good manners" (*CA*, 152).

To put *A Chance Acquaintance* into political terms, in terms of the distinction between the Jeffersonian *aristoi* and the Jacksonian common man, is not at all to distort the social significance of the novel. Howells was distressed at the incapacity of the classes to interact amicably. Shortly after seeing him in 1871, E. L. Godkin told Charles Eliot Norton that Howells talked "despondently like everybody else about the condition of morals and manners."[11] But the arrogance of the *aristoi* in Boston bothered him more than the innocent vulgarity of the immigrants, the Boston working class, and the country folk who had wandered into the city. In Kitty Ellison, Howells created a truly democratic heroine, the lovely average of American girlhood capable of putting to shame the so-called civilized Boston snob. As Kitty writes of Miles to her girl friends in Eriecreek: "He has been a good deal abroad, and he is Europeanized enough not to think much of America, though I can't find that he quite approves of Europe, and his experience seems not to have left him any particular country in either hemisphere." In addition, he "believes in 'vulgar and meretricious distinctions' of all sorts, and . . . hasn't an atom of 'magnanimous democracy' in him. In fact," she goes on, "I find, to my great astonishment, that some ideas which I thought were held only in England, and which I had never seriously thought of, seem actually a part of Mr. Arbuton's nature or education. He talks about the lower classes, and tradesmen, and the best people, and good families, as I supposed no-

body in *this* country *ever* did,—in earnest" (*CA*, 134–35). Kitty
has no experience with aristocratic attitudes of this type; they
strike her as the stuff of sentimental romances, not facts of life,
and she can hardly believe that Arbuton seriously means what he
says.

Kitty's inability to understand Arbuton's snobbishness is to
be accounted for by the republican conditions of American life
and history that have shaped her sense of values. Kitty is the
daughter of a small country editor, a Free Soil man in Kansas before the Civil War who was murdered in one of the border feuds.
Taken in by an uncle in Eriecreek, she grew up among a family
of ardent abolitionists whose house was a stopover for slaves on
the underground railroad to Canada. She had sat in the lap of
Osawatomie John Brown and heard him sing "Blow ye the trum-
pet, blow!" For Kitty and her family, Boston represented a place
of "humanitarian pre-eminence," the home of the great New
England abolitionists, "of the author of the 'Biglow Papers,' of
Senator Sumner, of Mr. Whittier, of Dr. Howe, of Colonel Higginson, and of Mr. Garrison" (*CA*, 9). For the Ellisons, Boston
was "not only the birthplace of American liberty, but the yet
holier scene of its resurrection." When he learns that Kitty is
going to Boston, her uncle reminds her that "there everything
that is noble and grand and liberal and enlightened in the national
life has originated, and I cannot doubt that you will find the
character of its people marked by every attribute of a magnanimous democracy. If I could envy you anything, my dear girl,"
he concludes, "I should envy you this privilege of seeing a city
where man is valued simply and solely for what he is in himself,
and where color, wealth, family, occupation, and other vulgar
and meretricious distinctions are wholly lost sight of in the consideration of individual excellence" (*CA*, 10).

Kitty's feelings about the glory of New England receive a rude
shock in the person of Miles Arbuton, the Boston snob. He wakes
her to reality. And it is a mark of her intelligence that she understands the character of this quasi aristocracy and recognizes that
she and Miles could never be happy together as man and wife.
Her rejection of Miles, then, is an affirmation of democratic
American manners. Arbuton is not a peer, but Kitty's refusal of

his marriage proposal tells as convincingly for American social values as Bessie Alden's rejection of Lord Lambeth in James's "An International Episode" (1878) or Isabel's refusal of Lord Warburton in *The Portrait of a Lady* (1881). In fact, it is possible to say that James saw in *A Chance Acquaintance* how the comedy of manners could be used to assert distinctively American social values.

In *William Dean Howells: The Development of a Novelist*, George N. Bennett has claimed that "*A Chance Acquaintance* need not be narrowly interpreted as a novel of manners."[12] This may be true. Still, I see no other way to penetrate to the social significance that lies at the heart of the novel—the moral superiority of "natural nobility" to artificial forms of gentility—than to recognize at the outset that the crux of the novel is a point of manners. Arbuton's bad manners occur in a context where we cannot possibly mistake Howells's overriding intention—to affirm egalitarian political and social values. To recognize this is not to narrow its significance but rather to get to the heart of Howells's conception of manners. He cherished the novel of manners. He loved its potential for the realistic notation of our commonplace, democratic, middle-class American life. His greatest achievements—*A Modern Instance* and *The Rise of Silas Lapham*—distinguish the form. Until he turned to the economic romance in the 1890s, Howells's work suggests how skillfully he charged the novel of manners with those implied political and social considerations which brought it to a high level of achievement.

The indictment of aristocratic manners in *A Chance Acquaintance* was certainly not lost on his Boston readers. Quite a few Bostonians thought Howells a western upstart who had never known a gentleman or who knew only one kind of Bostonian. But his most sensitive critics recognized it as "the first of a long series of attacks on Proper Boston."[13] Thomas Sergeant Perry commended Howells's "national spirit" in the *Century Magazine*. He praised "the way Mr. Howells shows the ... emptiness of convention and the dignity of native worth." It is "one of the main conditions of American, if not of modern, society," Perry observed, "that inborn merit has a chance to assert itself." And this possibility was nowhere more tellingly asserted than in the comparison of Kitty and Arbuton. If the old lines were being destroyed, Perry observed, it was because "the democratic hero" had done much in literature to speed up the process. "After all, what can realism produce but the downfall of conventionality? Just as the scientific spirit digs the ground from beneath superstition, so does its fellow-worker, realism, tend to prick the bubble of abstract types. Realism is the tool of the democratic spirit," Perry concluded, "and Mr. Howells's realism is untiring."[14]

Henry James was less complimentary, but he did think Kitty a real creation—"in bringing her through with such unerring felicity, your imagination has *fait ses preuves*."[15] Howells agreed that the relationship of the couple was contrived and that Miles was something of a straw man, but "well- or ill-advisedly," he replied, "I conceived the notion of confronting two extreme American types: the conventional and the unconventional. These always disgust each other, but I amused myself with the notion of their falling in love, which would not be impossible, if they were both young and good-looking. Now conventionality is, in our condition of things, in itself a caricature; and I did my best for the young man, but his nature was against him, and he is the stick you see." Howells always felt that the rituals of polite society were artificial, and he could not help representing them as play-acting, a kind of drawing-room theatrical, an elaborate charade of the European conventionalities, or, better yet, a stage farce which could not be taken very seriously by anyone. He concluded by saying that he felt that he had "learnt a great deal in writing the story," and that if it did not destroy his public he would be "weaponed better than ever" for a career in fiction.[16]

In view of Howells's assault on genteel Boston, his manifest preference for the simplicities of small-town life, it is surprising that so many critics have misunderstood him. One can do nothing with Bernard Smith's claim that when Howells found in Boston "the culture, the temper, the manners he admired, he gave himself to it unreservedly and was stamped genteel for life," or with C. Hartley Grattan's claim that Howells "accepted the New England environment at Boston's evaluation and took Boston's judgments as his own."[17] For these comments grossly oversimplify a complex attitude to New England. They ignore the fact that there were many Bostons and that Howells principally admired the Boston which stood for plain living and high thinking, the "cleanly decencies" of American life, the excellence of New England writing, and the pure simplicity of an unassuming social organization. Family counted for something in Boston, for example, he later wrote, "but family alone did not mean position, and the want of family did not mean the want of it." Money was less important than family: "One could be openly poor in Cambridge without open shame, or shame at all, for no one was very rich there, and no one was proud of his riches." Howells's real Boston interests "were the intellectual interests, and all other interests were lost in these to such as did not seek them too insistently."[18] The Boston Howells did not like, as *A Chance Acquaintance* makes clear, was "a Boston of mysterious prejudices and lofty reservations; a Boston of high and difficult tastes, that found its social ideal in the Old World, and that shrank from the reality of this; a Boston as alien as Europe"; a city "that seemed to be proud only of the things that were unlike other American things; a Boston that would rather perish by fire and sword than be suspected of vulgarity; a critical, fastidious, and reluctant Boston, dissatisfied with the rest of the hemisphere, and gelidly self-satisfied in so far as it was not in the least the Boston of her [Kitty's] fond preconceptions" (*CA*, 151–52). But Howells's egalitarian attack on the social snobbery of genteel New England is lost on some of his modern critics, who cannot discriminate the many Bostons as well as could the westerner Howells.

III

Their Wedding Journey and *A Chance Acquaintance* employed the travel structure to bring into dramatic relief the variety and multiplicity of American manners in Boston and the provinces and the differences between the commonplace world of America and the picturesque antiquities of the Canadian scene. In both books Howells had made extensive use of his own experiences, working his way toward the novel of manners through the recreation of autobiographical materials. *A Foregone Conclusion* (1875), *The Lady of the Aroostook* (1879), and *A Fearful Responsibility* (1881) continue this pattern. But in these novels

Howells Europeanized the setting to take full advantage, with Henry James, of the international theme. Each documents the minutiae of international manners—the quaint Italian custom of cutting up all of one's meat beforehand; the American breakfast of hot beefsteak and fried potatoes; the scandal of European fingernails; the custom of tucking one's napkin into his collar. And the plot of each novel turns on some major expression of national manners.

The success of these minor novels led friends like Charles Dudley Warner to clamor for a big book that would justify their faith in his power as a novelist of manners, "a large canvas with many people in it." Howells believed that the "paraphernalia" of social life were present in America, but a large novel was beyond his power in the 1870s. He wanted to know whether "the real dramatic encounter" was not "always between two persons only? Or three or four at most?"[19] He did not believe that a novel had to be long in order to be great, and in the early novels he had not wanted "much world, or effect of it, in my fictions." On taking stock at the age of forty, he declared, "I find that . . . I don't care for society, and that I do care intensely for people. I suppose, therefore," he went on, "that my tendency would always be to get my characters away from their belongings, and let four or five people act upon each other."[20] This preference clarifies Howells's method through the 1870s in the novels I have mentioned. His method was to lift people out of the social milieux which separate them, free them of their belongings, confine them aboard a ship or in a train or boarding house, put them into some sort of dramatic juxtaposition, and study their manners and values under the pressure of the experience. He was increasingly aware, moreover, that "the real test of the manners and morals of a nation is not by comparison with other nations, but with itself." He was coming to judge society by the form of its intrinsic development. Colonel Higginson had argued that "manners, like morals, are an affair of evolution, and must often be a native product,—a wholly indigenous thing."[21] Howells wanted to come to terms with the indigenous article, to trace the historical development of some of our social institutions and their effect on individual life. In *A Modern Instance* (1882), Howells confronted the problem more boldly than he had ever done before. Abandoning the international comedy of manners, Howells gave expression to what he called the feeling "for the human relation, as the social climate of our country qualifies, intensifies, generally conditions and colours it."[22] The result was by all counts one of his best novels of manners.

As he planned the book, he meant *A Modern Instance* to treat "an enormous fact" of American life which had "never been treated seriously"—the question of divorce. He intended to take "a couple who are up to a certain point about equally to blame for their misery" and show their love marriage falling into ruin "through the undisciplined character of both."[23] Not a tract against divorce, it was rather to be a serious exploration of marital incompatibility—free from the cant of religious moralizing, an explanation of its causes and its consequences for American society. Character would be the focus of the novel, as usual, but for the first time Howells would be looking at character as inseparable from the manners and values of the society in which it had developed. He would not separate his characters from their belongings and juxtapose them aboard a ship in this novel. Instead, he would show them as reflections of the social milieu which had shaped and conditioned them.

Bartley Hubbard, the husband in this marital drama, is a self-made man. An orphan who through native talent and minimal application eked out a college education, Hubbard has managed to get the editorship of a country newspaper and has moved to Equity, Maine, to set up shop. He values appearances highly, is quick-tempered, and has a tendency to evade his responsibilities. As one character puts it, he has no more moral nature than a baseball. An impulsive boy, Bartley elopes and marries Marcia Hubbard, a beautiful, passionate, and wildly jealous young girl, the daughter of a lawyer in Equity whose ruling passion is a studied village atheism. Neither of them has any grounding in the social or religious values which organize and unify society; neither has a grip on what Howells defined as "all that really holds human society together for good,—marriage, the family, religion, subordination."[24]

The novel opens in Equity, a little backwater village in a state of cultural dry rot. There were doubtless complex causes for the condition of small-town life in the eighties as Howells looked at it—economic fluctuations as the older agrarianism gave way to the new industrial order, the influx of thousands of immigrants, the migration of the best young people from the country to the cities. But what principally interested Howells was the religious condition of the American small town. Equity is a Calvinist village in which religion "had largely ceased to be a fact of spiritual experience, and the visible church flourished on condition of providing for the social needs of the community."[25] Orthodoxy has proved unequal to the new Darwinian science, and the churches have begun to attend to social needs rather than to the necessities of the soul. Pleasant Sunday schools, oyster suppers, popular lectures, secular music, and social dancing in the church basements— these signal the moral flabbiness and the uncertain doctrinal aims of the churches in New England.

In this milieu Bartley Hubbard achieves popularity by giving a series of readings from the poets for the benefit of each congregation. He shops around from church to church, with the approval of the various memberships, because "the editor of a paper devoted to the interests of the whole town ought not to be of fixed theological opinions" (*MI*, 18). Squire Gaylord, Marcia's father, is an avowed infidel, but in the "rather chaotic liberality into which religious sentiment had fallen in Equity" (*MI*, 18), there is something refreshing almost in his "puritan" contempt for "the idea that souls were to be saved by church sociables" (*MI*, 25). Marcia's mother still wears her black silk on Sunday, but "her social life had ceased, like her religious life." In this household, alienated from the religious and social life of the village, Marcia Gaylord is brought up. She is unchristened and unschooled in the doctrines of the Christian religion, which had been the foundation and main support of the social and moral values of communities like Equity. When she later tells Mrs. Halleck that she wants her daughter brought up in the Congregationalist church because "that's where the good people are," Mrs. Halleck is scandalized by her discovery that "there was any person in a Christian land, except among the very lowest, that seemed to understand so little about the Christian religion, or any scheme of salvation" (*MI*, 203).

The problem of the collapse of religious doctrine is not limited to villages like Equity. Howells wanted to show the effect of skepticism in cities like Boston as well. In the religious uncertainty of the age, the elder Hallecks hang on grimly to the old orthodox ways, however antiquated, while the children, profoundly dislocated, become alienated from the older generation. Olive Halleck goes into the Unitarian church, where a tolerant rationalism prevails, and Ben Halleck renounces religion entirely, cynically doubting whether or not he believes in anything. Howells's concern for the spiritual condition of America in *A Modern Instance* does not turn on the question of whether or not people ought to believe the doctrines of the Christian religion but rather on the question of what happens to individuals when the religious and marital institutions, the manners, the morals, and the social values of communities begin to collapse under a disintegrating pressure like skeptical science.

The clear assumption of the novel is that up to the Civil War or thereabouts the Christian churches provided the institutional structure embodying and expressing a standard of personal and social morality. With the collapse of the doctrines on which public and private morality was based, people like the Hubbards and the younger Hallecks, thrown upon their own inadequate emotional and intellectual resources, are doomed to that moral anarchy which attends the disintegration of society. In this confusion, the old restraints that separate people from each other and help them to sublimate and harmonize their destructive impulses pass away. Marcia perceives something of this problem when she tells Mrs. Halleck: "I've thought a great deal about it, and I think my worst trouble is that I've been left too free in everything. One mustn't be left too free. I've never had any one to control me, and now I can't control myself at the very times when I need to do it the most . . ." (*MI*, 202).

It would be easy to ascribe Marcia's wild jealousy and Bartley's gradual deterioration, their mindless elopement and their subsequent estrangement, to the cultural conditions in which they have grown up. I do not wish to do that. Howells shows them to have many personal defects that partly account for the collapse of their marriage. But there can be no doubt that Howells saw the collapse of fundamentalist orthodoxy in the post-Darwinian period as a social phenomenon radically disorienting to *all* the characters of the novel: the squire's agnosticism now rendered pointless, he can only ridicule the latitudinarianism of the sects; Mrs. Gaylord, cut off from church and society, becomes hopelessly narrow; Bartley never develops a sense of personal responsibility because religion has lost its moral authority; and the Halleck children fall into skeptical rationalism or private cynicism.

Against this background of the larger decay of American society and the new moral anarchy, Howells tells the story of Bartley and Marcia and the impact of changing social conditions on their lives and upon those of their family and friends. Howells realizes the experience through a close notation of those commonplace details that create a comprehensive social milieu and make for a national identity. To emphasize its representative character, Howells thought about calling the book "An American Marriage," "A Native American Romance," or "Here and Now." With almost a sociological approach of the kind Taine had recommended in his history of English literature, Howells specified the distinctively American character of our manners. Of the custom of young people of the opposite sex writing letters to each other, he says "Every one who has lived the American life must have produced them in great number" (*MI*, 19); in describing Mrs. Gaylord's habits he speaks of "the pathetic idiosyncrasies of a certain class of American mothers" (*MI*, 29); of Bartley he remarks that "his friend of the Chronicle-Abstract introduced him lavishly, as our American custom is" (*MI*, 137). These references to the customs of "Americans" suggest how the sociological perspective of Taine and Spencer had led Howells to contemplate America with "scientific" detachment. They also show how conscious of our native customs the experience of Europe had made him. "The American who has known Europe much can never again see his country with the single eye of his old ante-European days," Howells confessed after his return from Venice. "This is inevitable; there may be an advantage in it, but if there is none, it is still inevitable. It may make a man think better or worse of America; it may be refinement or it may be anxiety; there may be no compensation in it for the loss of that tranquil indifference to Europe which untraveled Americans feel, or it may be the very mood in which an American can best understand his fellow-Americans. More and more, in any case, it pervades our literature. . . ."[26] For Howells, the experience of Europe revealed with startling clarity American customs and manners of which, earlier, he had been unconscious. And what he saw led him to believe that if European readers were to understand us and if we were to understand ourselves he would have to specify "our American customs," to hold them out for inspection and thought, to show what was happening to them and to us in the current radical transitions in religion, morals, business, and politics. "It was a significant turning point in Howells's career as an artist," as Olov Fryckstedt has observed, "when he realized that the American values in which he never ceased to believe—egalitarianism, freedom, and purity of manners—had to be defended and guarded in order to be maintained."[27]

Howells enriches *A Modern Instance* with those sharply observed details, minor in themselves but marvelously representative, which signify social differentiae: the customs of courtship in rural New England, where a young couple are alone after everyone else in the house has gone to sleep—a situation "scarcely conceivable to another civilization" but "characteristic of the New England civilization wherever it keeps its simplicity" (*MI*, 4); styles of dress like Squire Gaylord's black tie (no collar), cassimere pantaloons, satin vest, and the dress-coat which old-fashioned country lawyers were still wearing in the seventies, or Bartley Hubbard's "two-button cutaway, his well-fitting trousers, his scarf with a pin in it" (*MI*, 88)—an ensemble so elegant that despite "the assumption of equality between all classes in Equity," the common townsfolk "stood in secret awe of his personal splendor" (*MI*, 49); the oddities of the social hierarchy in a little town where the local printer ranked "a little above the foreman of the saw-mill in the social scale, and decidedly below the master of the Academy" (*MI*, 23); the tendency of mothers in rural America to let their daughters' "fancied knowledge of the world . . . outweigh their own experience of life" and to let their children "order the social affairs of the family" (*MI*, 29); the fact that Ben and Olive are not "the first chop" in Boston because Ben did not go to Harvard and Olive did not go to Papanti's—even though they were rich enough to do both; the unfashionableness of the elder Hallecks, who built on Rumford Street only to see society drift toward the Back Bay; and so on.

In *The American Novel and Its Tradition* Richard Chase observes that the European novel of manners "always achieved its effect by bringing people of different social class into conflict" but that this juxtaposition of classes is impossible in the American novel because "nearly everyone a novelist of manners might be interested in has been middle-class, and has very likely prided himself on manners indistinguishable from the lower class which is always incipiently middle-class itself."[28] But American social experience has always been markedly diversified. In *A Modern Instance*, Howells offers a careful comparison of the manners of the simple folk of Equity and the more sophisticated people of Boston. In Boston itself, the unfashionable Hallecks are offset by the prominent Athertons. Uncultivated people like Kinney, the travelers aboard the train, and the Indiana folk in Tecumseh serve to create a larger national perspective in the story which is absent from Howells's earlier novels, where he limited the dramatic encounter to three or four persons. Howells provides extensive notes about the social differentiae between the bare Portland hotels where Squire Gaylord "puts up" and the Boston hotels with their three-burner chandeliers and marble mantels. The elegance of the luxury hotels is contrasted with Mrs. Nash's rooming house; and the Revere House dining room is juxtaposed against the cheap little "eating-house" where country girls and Irish immigrants consume hulled corn and milk, baked beans and squash pie. Howells plays off the expensive but ugly fashions of the Halleck House on Rumford Street (overstuffed sofas and black walnut furniture) against the Hubbards's first little house on Clover Street and against the luxury of the Atherton's house on the New Land. And he rounds out his portrait of these Bostonians and Down East New Englanders by balancing it against the portrait of the West, the gradual relaxation of polite manners as the train moves across the Appalachians toward Indiana—the mixing of the passengers, the pipe-smoking women, the tobacco-chewing men, the openness and friendliness of the people in the middle border states.

The journey of the Hubbards from Equity to Boston expresses the rhythm of modern American life inasmuch as "the steady stream of young people from the farms and small rural communities to the manufacturing and commercial centers was one of the important events of postwar America."[29] Uppermost in How-ells's mind as he traced the story of the Hubbards was the un-certainty that afflicts the outlander, the provincial, the new man, when he tries to ascend to the next level of social existence. In Boston, Marcia is terrified at doing anything countrified; even Bartley does not know whether ladies wear their bonnets in the Revere House dining room. Marcia is dazzled by the gaslights at Bowdoin Square, and Bartley crows because the theater "is packed with Beacon Street swells" (*MI*, 115). But months after they have been in Boston, they are still countrified, still isolated from the class who frequent the theaters and expensive restau-rants. "In the meantime," Howells wrote, "their life went on ignorantly in the obscure channels where their isolation from society kept it longer than was natural." They had "scarcely any knowledge of the distinctions and differences so important to the various worlds of any city. So far from knowing that they must not walk in the Common, they used to sit down on a bench there, in the pleasant weather, and watch the opening of the spring, among the lovers whose passion had a publicity that neither surprised nor shocked them." Later, when they learn that the "best people" never go there, "they resorted to the Public Garden, where they admired the bridge, and the rock-work, and the statues. Bartley, who was already beginning to get up a taste for art, boldly stopped and praised the Venus, in the presence of the gardeners planting tulip bulbs" (*MI*, 143).

Howells's insight into the process by which country folk ad-just to the city was never sharper. It is matched only by his sense of what happens to people too rigid to adapt. Boston cramps Squire Gaylord; it's too tight a fit; he can't find himself in it: "He suffered from the loss of identity which is a common affliction with country people coming to town. The feeling that they are of no special interest to any of the thousands they meet bewilders and harasses them." After the narrowness and gossip of towns like Equity, "the fact that nobody would meddle in their most intimate affairs if they could, is a vague distress. The Squire not only experienced this, but after reigning so long as the censor of morals and religion in Equity, it was a deprivation for him to pass a whole week without saying a bitter thing to any one. He was tired of the civilities that smoothed him down on every side" (*MI*, 193).

Gradually, the Hubbards touch the periphery of Boston's social life, thanks to one of those chance acquaintances which Howells loved to indulge. Through his college acquaintance Ben Halleck, Bartley and Marcia are led into the social life of the Hallecks, Clara Kingsbury, and Atherton. But the rustic Hubbards are anomalies in the social life of Boston. Clara believes that she ought to pay Marcia some attention and decides "to bring them out in Boston society" (*MI*, 176). But the Hubbards are so bereft of the social amenities that Clara's party "remained a humbug. It had seemed absurd to invite anybody to meet two such little, unknown people as the Hubbards; and then, to avoid marking them as the subjects of the festivity by the precedence to be observed in going out to supper, she resolved to have tea served in the drawing-room, and to make it literally tea, with bread and butter, and some thin ascetic cakes" (*MI*, 179–80).

The failure of the Hubbards to make a place for themselves in Boston society is not the result of their poverty or even their rusticity. For they live respectably enough through Bartley's newspaper work and gradually catch on to the manners of society. The problem is that neither of them has had the kind of social education that makes for self-discipline and the control of the feelings. The larger social evils in America which Howells had touched on are reflected in Bartley's moral flabbiness—his deviousness, his theft of Kinney's article, his gambling and growing dependence on tivoli and Norwegian beer, his blackmail of Witherby, and his growing disrespect for the sacredness of marriage—and in Marcia's wild jealousy of other women, her nagging, her stinginess, and her violent temper. They mean well but they just cannot control themselves.

The novel thus raises the question of the natural goodness of the individual. Although Howells's views are difficult to infer from *A Modern Instance*, owing to his self-effacement, Atherton seems to express the meaning of the Hubbards's experience for American social life in general. Clara argues that "natural goodness" counts for something, but Atherton points out that "natural goodness doesn't count. The natural man is a wild beast, and his natural goodness is the amiability of a beast basking in the sun when his stomach is full. The Hubbards," he argues, "were full of natural goodness . . . when they didn't happen to cross each other's wishes." What really makes for harmony in society is "the implanted goodness," "the seed of righteousness treasured from generation to generation, and carefully watched and tended by disciplined fathers and mothers in the hearts where they have dropped it. The flower of this implanted goodness," Atherton concludes, "is what we call civilization" (*MI*, 332–33). The idea of disciplining natural impulses through cultivating the conventions of the civilized life is reminiscent of Howells's later claim that "the great fault of our manners, when we have them . . . is that they are personal and occasional manners. These, when they are good, are very good, but when they are bad they make you wish that the person's behavior was governed by a convention or a tradition of breeding which prescribed a certain type of conduct, not to be varied at will." This diagnoses the problem of Bartley and Marcia. Having no social tradition, no external rule of conduct, they surrender to their passions, act out, in fact, that beastliness which marks the natural man. Howells went on to say that he thought the condition of our deplorable manners was transitional: "We have no manners because we are waiting to get the best. . . . But we must not wait too long! Manners are one of the most precious heritages from the past," he argued. "We may disuse forms, but we must not disuse forms a great while. Goodness of heart, purity of morals, show themselves in forms, and practically do not exist without them." He went on to say that "forms in conduct are like forms in art. They alone can express manners; and they are built slowly, painfully, from the thought, the experience of the whole race."[30] Since Marcia and Bartley are uneducated, they have no usable past, no tradition handing down to them the forms whereby goodness of heart, purity of morals, and graciousness of manners can be expressed.

But for Atherton and Clara, the problem is not so much what people like the Hubbards do—for they are hopelessly beyond the possibilities of civilization. The problem is what the Ben Hallecks do. When the divorce notice strays into his hand, must Ben pass it on to Marcia? When he discovers that Bartley is trying to get rid of her, should Ben tell her that she no longer has any responsibility to her husband or to their marriage vows? After Bartley is killed in a gunfight, can Ben *then* propose to a woman whom he had loved while she was another man's wife? The effect on Ben Halleck of the Hubbards's estrangement is what most draws Atherton and Clara into the Hubbards's affairs. They do not like being drawn in, but it is the question of what Ben will do that most interests them and Howells. "I thought it was bad enough having a man, even on the outskirts of my acquaintance, abandon his wife," Clara observes, "but now Ben Halleck, who has been like a brother to me, to have him mixed up in such an affair in the way he is, it's intolerable!" (*MI*, 334)

Atherton agrees that it is. His view of the world and of civilization is like Howells's: "This whole thing is disorderly." But Atherton argues that he and Clara have a share in it, that they cannot renounce responsibility for it. "It's intolerable, as you say. But we must bear our share of it. We're bound together. No one sins or suffers to himself in a civilized state,—or religious state; it's the same thing. Every link in the chain feels the effect of the violence, more or less intimately. We rise or fall together in Christian society. It's strange that it should be so hard to realize a thing that every experience of life teaches" (*MI*, 334). Though the question is perhaps too delicate for the modern sensibility, if Ben appealed to Marcia while she was married, "through teaching her to think of escape from her marriage by a divorce," he would be committing "a crime against her and against society" (*MI*, 332), a violation of that constituted order which Atherton calls civilization. What makes civilization viable, Atherton argues, is precisely the existence of men like Ben Halleck, whose moral perceptions are so sensitive that they refuse to let Nature overcome Culture, to let appetite destroy the seed of implanted goodness. Even after Bartley's death, Ben still cannot bring himself to approach Marcia because even if he were to appeal to her now "there could only be loss—deterioration,—lapse from the ideal" (*MI*, 362).

The issue of divorce, a burning question in the 1880s, is no longer pressing. But the question which Howells raises in the novel is still relevant—whether civilization can survive if the morally educated do not nurture the flower of implanted goodness from generation to generation. Whether or not the Hallecks and Athertons themselves could survive the disintegrating forces of modern American society was a question Howells was not yet willing to explore. In the end, he did not want to commit himself too fully. However persuasive Atherton's social and cultural perceptions are, the reader cannot help seeing that Ben is a crippled, maladjusted man whose example offers little to emulate. Even so, *A Modern Instance* suggests that Howells was beginning to value more highly those conservative social forces supporting culture. He was rethinking the problem of personal responsibility for the condition of civilization. He was gradually working toward the doctrine of "complicity," developed in *Annie Kilburn*—the view that we are interdependently responsible for the evils that infect a culture. Disorder, violence, disintegrative force affect all classes of society equally and have to be dealt with. How he did not know yet. But, as Atherton put it, "we rise or fall together in Christian society."

IV

A Modern Instance marked a major achievement in Howells's art. All of the elements of his wide and various experience had begun to coalesce. His knowledge of the West, of the intellectual and social life of Boston and Europe, his increasing knowledge of history, psychology, literature, and life—all these were combining to provide a rich fund of material from which the novelist began to draw. In addition, he was maturing. And age he counted one of his major assets: "A young writer may produce a brilliant and very perfect romance, just as he may produce a brilliant and very perfect poem," Howells once observed, "but in the field of realistic fiction, or in what we used to call the novel of manners, a writer can only produce an inferior book at the outset. For his work he needs experience and observation. . . . Until he is well on towards of forty, he will hardly have assimilated the materials of a great novel, although he may have amassed them."[31] *A Modern Instance* was published when Howells was forty-five. He was at the height of his powers, at his best as a social witness.

But by nearly every estimate, *The Rise of Silas Lapham* (1885) is Howells's greatest achievement. As a novel of manners, it has few equals in the nineteenth century for accuracy of social observation and comprehensiveness of sociological detail.[32] A masterpiece of sustained social analysis, it probes the values of American business life against a background of class antagonisms. Its links with *A Modern Instance*—the Boston setting, recurrent characters, concern for the condition of American civilization— suggest that Howells was beginning to see Boston steadily and to see it whole—to see it, that is, as a world where the drama of social life was acted out in an interdependent way. Set in the age of self-made millionaires, *Silas Lapham* projects the romance of money and social ambition against the background of great business enterprise and industrial expansion. It poses the question of personal morality in a business world most aptly described by the term "social Darwinism." The focus of the novel is the character of the representative American businessman under pressure to use jungle methods to maintain his fortune. The novel reveals him to be basically honest but tempted to do wrong, occasionally succumbing perhaps, but capable of triumphing over human weakness by deliberately chosen, ethically motivated conduct based on a sense of fair play and Christian charity. *Silas Lapham* rejects the notion of social Darwinism both as a modus operandi and as an adequate description of the American world of business.

Silas is a great creation, and Howells's characterization was nearly perfect, for he realized how fully manners could be expressive of Lapham's values. One of the brilliant techniques by which Howells sustains our affection for Silas and Persis is to give their comic social climbing a winsome unselfishness. They want to get into society not so much to ratify their own ambition as to provide for their daughters. Both are country folk who have kept their provincial ways and who, too old to change, are satisfied enough with the life of business and home. But like most parents they want the best for their children. As Persis observes: "I presume we ought to try to get them into society, some way; or ought to do something." Why not? Silas replies: "There's money enough."[33] Their social ambitions for Pen and Irene are intensified by the Corey ladies and the incomprehensible attentiveness of Tom to Persis and her daughters. And because Tom is a suitable match for Irene, Silas and Persis decide to move from their unfashionable house on Nankeen Square to the Back Bay area, where the Coreys and their friends live.

The scenes between Silas and Persis over whether they should build on the New Land contain some of the most charming banter in all of Howells's novels. He was in his element in their bluff raillery about whether Silas could take care of his own furnace on the Back Bay and whether it would be proper to shovel his own sidewalks. The "history of a man's rise from poverty and obscurity to distinction and to a place of greatest influence," Howells wrote of Horace Greeley, "is a perpetual romance; it delights and touches all, for in this nation it is in some degree the story of every man's life or the vision of his desires."[34] Howells might have been talking of himself—or of Silas Lapham. They're not all "big-bugs" on Beacon Street. "You can have just as much style there as you want, or just as little" (*RSL*, 27). And Silas concludes, "A man can be a man on Beacon Street as well as anywhere, I guess" (*RSL*, 31). So he and Persis decide to crack the inner citadel of Boston society and build on the New Land.

The inner citadel, as represented by the Coreys, is concealed by an imposing edifice. Though Bromfield Corey's irony always undercuts Anna's view of their exalted social status, Corey likes to remember that "we are Essex County people, and that in savour we are just a little beyond the salt of the earth" (*RSL*, 54). Exclusive, cultivated, possessed of the finest manners, Corey embodies the aristocrat's disbelief in the value of work. The son of an old India merchant, he took the fortune his father had made, "travelled about over Europe, and travelled handsomely, frequenting good society everywhere, and getting himself presented at several courts, at a period when it was a distinction to do so."

Later he set up a studio in Rome, dabbled at painting, and rounded out "the being inherited from his Yankee progenitors, till there was very little left of the ancestral angularities" (*RSL*, 57). When he returned to America, he "continued a dilettante, never quite abandoning his art, but working at it fitfully, and talking more about it than working at it" (*RSL*, 57). Devoted to idleness, on aesthetic principles, Corey is the perfect antithesis to the self-made paint manufacturer Silas Lapham.

It is a mark of Howells's social insight that he saw the old aristocracy beginning to disintegrate under the economic stresses of modern American life. The family reserves have drastically declined in the postwar depression. There is still enough for Tom to live the gentleman's life, with certain sacrifices—moved by "the example of persons of quality in Europe," as Bromfield says, "which I alleged in support of the life of idleness" (*RSL*, 78). But Tom is too restless. He is unwilling to be idle and is ashamed to live on his father. With the industry and energy of the new generation, he wants work. And the work he wants is with Silas Lapham's paint concern. When Tom tells his father this, Bromfield replies: "Ah, we shall never have a real aristocracy while this plebeian reluctance to live upon a parent or a wife continues the animating spirit of our youth. It strikes at the root of the whole feudal system. I really think you owe me an apology, Tom. I supposed you wished to marry the girl's money, and here you are, basely seeking to go into business with her father" (*RSL*, 55). In this speech, Howells's skill in characterization is brilliantly apparent. For we see him delicately balancing the seriousness of Corey's views, as an expression of his class, against his mocking exaggeration of them.

Howells also knew that, despite their dwindling reserves, the aristocratic class would try to preserve its exclusiveness and avoid the social entanglements business life sometimes creates, and Tom's mother warns him against "the kind of people you would be mixed up with" (*RSL*, 59). But Tom is indifferent to his mother's passion for exclusiveness. Tom's largeness of perspective, his easy tolerance of the Laphams, is accounted for by his having spent some time in the West. As Tom confesses to his father, "I suppose that in a new country one gets to looking at people a little out of our tradition; and I dare say that if I hadn't passed a winter in Texas I might have found Colonel Lapham rather too much" (*RSL*, 53). It is not that people or conditions are worse in Texas. It is that the manners and customs of the West have given him a new perspective on the manners and customs of the East, and he sees that it is not quite fair to judge Lapham by the standards that prevail in Boston.

The new perspective created by exposure to the larger world—which leads young people to abandon the social values of their own tightly ordered little world—is one of the major themes of the Boston novel of manners, as the fiction of John P. Marquand suggests. Tom's tolerance of Lapham comes of what Bromfield Corey calls "the error which I have often deprecated": "In fact I am always saying that the Bostonian ought never to leave Boston. Then he knows—and then only—that there can *be* no standard but ours. But we are constantly going away, and coming back with our convictions shaken to the foundations. One man goes to England, and returns with the conception of a grander social life; another comes home from Germany with the notion of a more searching intellectual activity; a fellow just back from Paris has the absurdest ideas of art and literature; and you revert to us from the cowboys of Texas, and tell us to our faces that we ought to try Papa Lapham by a jury of his peers. It ought to be stopped—it ought, really. The Bostonian who leaves Boston ought to be condemned to perpetual exile" (*RSL*, 53). Corey's snobbishness, in a less whimsical man, would be vicious. We cannot help liking him, however, for the self-mockery underlying his most serious but extravagant opinions.

Tom's relationship with Lapham succeeds—so long as it is a business relationship and the two families are kept apart. Complications arise when Bromfield wonders whether Lapham wants to give their relation "any sort of social character" (*RSL*, 97) and whether it would be decent of him to make Lapham's acquaintance. Silas is innocent of Persis's charge of being "crazy to get in with those people," but he does not see why he cannot invite Bromfield down to a "fish dinner at Taft's" if he takes a notion. But it cannot be their part to make the first social overtures. As Persis tells Silas, Bromfield Corey has been "all his life in society, and he knows just what to say and what to do, and he can talk about the things that society people like to talk about, and you— can't" (*RSL*, 98). Bromfield is no better than Silas, she says, but it does put him "where he can make the advances without demeaning himself, and it puts you where you can't." They're simply not on the same social level, she tells Silas. "He's got a better education than you, and if he hasn't got more brains than you he's got different. And he and his wife and their fathers and grandfathers before 'em, have always had a high position, and you can't help it. If you want to know them, you've got to let them make the advances. If you don't, all well and good" (*RSL*, 98).

But the business relationship of Silas and Tom carries a built-in dilemma. If the Laphams cannot make any kind of social overture, the Coreys—for Tom's sake—cannot afford to imply any "social distrust of them" (*RSL*, 143). The Coreys consider introducing the Laphams into society, but they have, socially speaking, nothing to offer. Would they be an "addition" to society? On this question Tom hedges, praising the Laphams' good sense and right ideas. But as Bromfield points out, "If society took in all the people of right ideas and good sense, it would expand beyond the calling capacity of its most active members. Even your mother's social conscientiousness could not compass it. Society is a very different sort of thing from good sense and right ideas. It is based upon them, of course, but the airy, graceful, winning superstructure which we all know demands different qualities. Have your friends got these qualities—which may be felt, but not defined?" (*RSL*, 113) Regretfully, Tom concedes that they do not, that they do not even understand society in Corey's sense, that they have probably never even given a dinner party. "Horrible!" says Bromfield in mock dismay, "how is society to assimilate them?" (*RSL*, 113)

At the same time, Lapham has fixed ideas about the Coreys. He knows something about old Phillips Corey, the India merchant, and he knows some of the anecdotes about Bromfield, who had done nothing but spend his father's money, live idly, and say smart things—most of which are lost on Lapham. "He knew who the Coreys were very well, and, in his simple, brutal way, he had long hated their name as a symbol of splendour which, unless he should live to see at least three generations of his descendants gilded with mineral paint, he could not hope to realise in his own." To Lapham, Bromfield Corey, "the tall, slim, white-moustached man, with the slight stoop, was everything that was offensively aristocratic" (*RSL*, 74–75). The possible conflict is thus sharply drawn. The seeds of an ugly contest in social rivalry are clearly implied in the relationship as posed. But with Howells class relationships are never abstract or ideological. The "personal equation" always modifies and qualifies class attitudes. When Silas meets Tom he cannot help liking the boy, and when the Corey's invitation to dinner arrives, the Laphams cannot refuse.

The Laphams' preparations for the dinner party are fully as comic as the dinner party itself, which is one of the great scenes in American fiction. Never having given a dinner, the Laphams are oblivious of "the awful and binding nature of a dinner engagement" (*RSL*, 147). Pen ignores the invitation and stays at home without forewarning Mrs. Corey. Never having gone to a dinner, none of them knows what to wear. The ladies spend days with the dressmaker, and the industry of Persis and her minions even begins to frighten Silas with "vague apprehensions in regard to his own dress." He refuses to wear a dress coat because, "for one thing, he considered that a man looked like a fool in a dress-coat, and, for another thing, he had none—had none on principle." He decides to go in a frock coat and black pantaloons, "and perhaps a white waistcoat, but a black cravat anyway" (*RSL*, 149).

None of the family can agree to this costume, and in the usual American way, they solve their argument by consulting a book of etiquette. But manuals of etiquette have never been equal to the task of socially instructing the American middle class. For although their book of etiquette "settled the question adversely to a white waistcoat," the author, "after being very explicit in telling them not to eat with their knives, and above all not to pick their teeth with their forks—a thing which he said no lady or gentleman ever did—was still far from decided as to the kind of cravat Colonel Lapham ought to wear: shaken on other points, Lapham had begun to waver also concerning the black cravat. As to the question of gloves for the Colonel, which suddenly flashed upon him one evening, it appeared never to have entered the thoughts of the etiquette man, as Lapham called him. Other authors on the same subject were equally silent, and Irene could only remember having heard, in some vague sort of way, that gentlemen did not wear gloves so much any more" (*RSL*, 150).

The dinner party itself, the center of the novel, is the ground where the two alien social groups engage. An unequal contest, it ends in hilarious disaster. Silas goes in saffron-tinted gloves, his large fists dangling down "like canvased hams" (*RSL*, 154). He cannot get the right one buttoned, and when he sees with horror that Tom Corey is not wearing gloves, he begins, "with as much indifference as he could assume," to pull them both off and stuff them into his pocket. After a false start going in to dinner, the hostess incomprehensibly latched on to his arm, Silas settles down in his chair feeling "safe from error if he kept a sharp lookout and did only what the others did." Whether or not to stick his napkin into his collar presents a delicate problem, and what to do with his wineglasses another, for Silas is a prohibitionist on principle at home. "He had a notion to turn them all down, as he had read of a well-known politician's doing at a public dinner, to show that he did not take wine; but, after twiddling with one of them a moment, he let them be, for it seemed to him that it would be a little too conspicuous, and he felt that everyone was looking. He let the servant fill them all, and he drank out of each, not to appear odd" (*RSL*, 156). Before long he is thirsty and talkative, drinking glasses of Madeira and Apollinaris at a single swallow. Howells counterpoints the inner anxieties of Silas with other people's conversation and behavior, and the result is a brilliant social comedy which illustrates how hilarious the comedy of manners can be. When the ladies leave the men to their cigars, Tom runs and opens the dining room door for his mother and the ladies: "Lapham thought with shame that it was he who ought to have done that; but no one seemed to notice, and he sat down again gladly, after kicking out one of his legs which had gone to sleep" (*RSL*, 163).

With a good cigar and a roomful of men, Lapham is more

nearly in his own element. Before long he is bragging about his money, Tom's application for a job, his new house, and his war experiences. His brain foggy, vaguely aware of the odd way the guests are looking at him, Silas is finally pried loose and taken home. The reiterative style here suggests how much Howells owed to Twain's farces: "He made cordial invitations to each of the gentlemen to drop in and see him at his office, and would not be satisfied till he had exacted a promise from each. He told Charles Bellingham that he liked him, and assured James Bellingham that it had always been his ambition to know him, and that if anyone had said when he first came to Boston that in less than ten years he should be hobnobbing with Jim Bellingham, he should have told that person he lied. He would have told anybody he lied that had told him ten years ago that a son of Bromfield Corey would have come and asked him to take him into the business" (*RSL*, 169). In the "clarity with which he exposes all this," as Alexander Harvey has accurately observed, "Howells is the supreme historian of manners, one of the great psychologists."[35]

Throughout the early period of his employment with Lapham Tom knows exactly how to treat his employer because theirs is a purely business association. Tom feels "the social difference between Lapham and himself," but "in his presence he silenced his traditions, and showed him all the respect that he could have exacted from any of his clerks" (*RSL*, 89). But Howells does not discount the effect on young Corey of Silas's drunkenness and his maudlin self-abasement the next day. As he looks at the shirt-sleeved porter cleaning up the office, "he said to himself that Dennis was not more plebeian than his master; that the gross appetites, the blunt sense, the purblind ambition, the stupid arrogance were the same in both, and the difference was in a brute will that probably left the porter the gentler man of the two." Lapham's ignorance of society and his falling afoul of its manners seem to Tom "the insult of clownish inexperience." And "amidst the stings and flashes of his wounded pride, all the social traditions, all the habits of feeling, which he had silenced more and more by force of will during the past months, asserted their natural sway, and he rioted in his contempt of the offensive boor, who was even more offensive in his shame than in his trespass" (*RSL*, 173).

Tom's resentment seems justified in the light of Lapham's outrageous behavior at the party. Yet even as he revels in righteous indignation, he sees how totally his is a class point of view. He has the honesty to admit that Lapham's inexperience really told in his favor, "that he was so guiltless in the past." He asks himself whether he has shown Lapham the sympathy due his remorse or whether "he had met him on the gentlemanly ground, sparing himself and asserting the superiority of his sort, and not recognising that Lapham's humiliation came from the sense of wrong, which he had helped to accumulate upon him by superfinely standing aloof and refusing to touch him" (*RSL*, 174). And he has to own that while his own behavior has been exactingly polite, he has failed to show human sympathy. It would be misleading not to say that Tom's love for Pen plays a part in his sympathy for her father. But Tom is no Miles Arbuton. He is civilized and sensitive; he has to struggle to prevent the prejudices of his class from blinding him, but he succeeds.

It is in fact the power of love that triumphs over the conventions of society, as is so often the case in the comedy of manners. The symbolism of the wedding of Tom and Pen is inescapable. Howells meant their marriage to unite the best of the urban, aristocratic manners of Boston and the best of the humbler, more natural, spontaneous, up-country democratic manners of the Laphams. The hope of the future, Howells felt, lies with couples like Pen and Tom, who rise above the arbitrary social conventions that separate their parents. Even Bromfield recognizes that a new day is dawning: "We represent a faded tradition," he tells his wife. "We don't really care what business a man is in, so it is large enough, and he doesn't advertise offensively; but we think it fine to affect reluctance" (*RSL*, 82–83). If Silas's money is "fairly and honestly earned, why should we pretend to care what it comes out of, when we don't really care? That superstition is exploded everywhere" (*RSL*, 76).

With the fading of the Corey tradition, "Gentlemaning as a profession," in the words of Silas, "has got to play out in a generation or two." But what would take the place of the civilization created and sustained by the upper class? Howells was optimistic. He believed that civilization was less and less a class phenomenon. "We think it is an affair of epochs and of nations. It's really an affair of individuals." "I've occasionally met young girls," Bromfield observes, "who were so brutally, insolently, wilfully indifferent to the arts which make civilisation that they ought to have been clothed in the skins of wild beasts and gone about barefoot with clubs over their shoulders. Yet they were of polite origin, and their parents were at least respectful of the things that these young animals despised" (*RSL*, 95). As Bromfield points out, it is not enough to be quick, shrewd, and sensible. "I have no doubt that some of the Sioux are so. But that is not saying that they are civilised. All civilisation comes through literature now, especially in our country. A Greek got his civilisation by talking and looking, and in some measure a Parisian may still do it. But we, who live remote from history and monuments, we must read or we must barbarise" (*RSL*, 96).

But as long as civilization is defined in terms of polite manners, those outside the aristocracy do not stand much of a chance of social acceptance. When Pen and Tom married, "there was a brief season of civility and forbearance on both sides," but the tension of their family situation is intolerable. Bromfield Corey "made a sympathetic feint of liking Penelope's way of talking," but he really did not warm to her. Anna put up a brave front, but she too was unhappy. Even the Corey girls are hopelessly incapable of appreciating the personal qualities in Pen that Tom admires. Nanny tries to encourage her parents with the notion that "as she's unformed, socially," there is "a chance that she will form herself on the Spanish manner" (*RSL*, 295). But with a feeling of relief on everybody's part, Tom and Pen go off to Mexico at the end of the novel. Pen will not feel any stranger among the Mexicans than she has among the Boston aristocrats, and the Coreys are happy that, at that distance, they can correspond.

Constance Rourke has criticized *The Rise of Silas Lapham* and *The Lady of the Aroostook* for failing to come to terms with the tragic implications inherent in the differences between the Laphams and the Coreys and the families of Staniford and Lydia

Blood. Packing Pen and Tom off to Mexico and the Stanifords off to California she called an evasion of the real problem.[36] But the conclusion of these novels clearly indicates how profoundly irremediable Howells felt the problems created by the love of social unequals to be: such love could produce no satisfactory social life for them in Boston. The Bloods and the Laphams are too provincial. "Are we not provincial?" Colonel Higginson asked in "Acts of Homage." No doubt. But for Higginson "all the manners of the great world are but little affairs of spoons and napkins and visiting-cards compared with those essential ingredients of manners which lie in 'self-reverence, self-knowledge, self-control'; and which may be acquired in a log cabin or a sod shanty or an Indian tepee from parents who know their business. Given this foundation, the great world can add much in respect to minor details; but without this foundation the teachings of the great world can do little."[37]

Howells believed in the rightness of Higginson's observation. Yet the ending of *A Chance Acquaintance*, *The Lady of the Aroostook*, and *The Rise of Silas Lapham* implies that such egalitarian optimism is socially irrelevant. Kitty could never marry Miles unless he gave up life in Boston for life in Eriecreek; Staniford had to choose either South Bradfield or California; and Pen found Mexico less alien to her than Tom's Boston. It was sad but true, Howells concluded, that until the aristocracy faded away, personal qualities would have little relevance in the way common people were judged. As Howells ruefully observed at the end of *Silas Lapham*, "our manners and customs go for more in life than our qualities. The price that we pay for civilisation is the fine yet impassable differentiation of these. Perhaps we pay too much; but it will not be possible to persuade those who have the difference in their favour that this is so. They may be right; and at any rate, the blank misgiving, the recurring sense of disappointment to which the young people's departure left the Coreys is to be considered. That was the end of their son and brother for them; they felt that; and they were not mean or unamiable people" (*RSL*, 296).

In the course of a long and distinguished career, for which Taine praised him as "a precious painter and a sovereign witness,"[38] Howells created a substantial body of fiction, much of it of high quality, portraying the range and variety of manners in America and Europe, the East and the West, the country and the town. As I have sought to suggest in this discussion of his early novels, Howells documented his time, first, as a travel writer who turned to the novel in order to dramatize the comedy of manners, then as a satirist of the spectacle of social climbing and aristocratic snobbishness. Later, as the conditions of American life in the postwar period rapidly altered the character of American social experience, Howells came increasingly to see the spectacle as less a comedy than a tragedy of manners in which unchecked economic forces made society itself the arena of competitive struggle. But although he turned to the utopian romance, he never surrendered his belief in the ultimate triumph of political, economic, and social equality. "Equality," he once wrote, "is such a beautiful thing that I wonder people can ever have any other ideal. It is the only social joy, the only comfort." He was optimistic enough to believe that the class structure which produced the exclusiveness of the Coreys would eventually disappear from America. Far from producing vulgar conformity, equality, "when we have it, will be the highest yet attained by the exceptional few. The purest ideals of the philosophers and the saints are not too fine to be realized," he concluded, "in the civility which shall be the life of the whole people."[39]

5

✖ EDITH WHARTON

Social Historian of Old New York

Edith Wharton undertook her first novel of manners at the age of eleven with the opening lines: " 'Oh, how do you do, Mrs. Brown?' said Mrs. Tompkins. 'If only I had known you were going to call I should have tidied up the drawing-room.' Timorously I submitted this to my mother," Mrs. Wharton later observed, "and never shall I forget the sudden drop of my creative frenzy when she returned it with the icy comment: 'Drawing-rooms are always tidy.' " Her mother's response to this trial flight was "so crushing to a would-be novelist of manners," Edith later wrote, "that it shook me rudely out of my dream of writing fiction."[1] Still, Edith Wharton broke with the proprieties of her own social class, the commercial aristocracy of post-Civil War America in New York City, and became a writer. She wrote from the premise that "manners are your true material, after all"[2]—as George Frenside tells the aspiring novelist Vance Weston in *Hudson River Bracketed* (1929). She recognized that the surfaces of Old New York social life were rich enough to feed her imagination and that to capture the sense of reality she needed only to study the conscious and purposive behavior of the men and women of that society. The excellence of her fiction has led Blake Nevius to observe that Mrs. Wharton is, next to James, "our most successful novelist of manners—not an extravagant claim in view of the limited competition in what to Americans seems to be an alien and difficult genre."[3] Edith Wharton's difficulty, however, was less with the genre than with her family and class. In satirizing the manners of the narrow, exclusive social group—who principally stood for good grammar, a well-stocked wine cellar, and freedom from novelty and unpleasantness—she proclaimed not merely her intellectual independence but also her rebellion against them. In her seventies, looking back at her career, Mrs. Wharton observed that "none of my relations ever spoke to me of my books, either to praise or blame—they simply ignored them; and among the immense tribe of my New York cousins, though it included many with whom I was on terms of affectionate intimacy, the subject was avoided as though it were a kind of family disgrace, which might be condoned but could not be forgotten."[4]

To escape the intellectual and artistic limitations of New York society, Edith Wharton moved to Paris in 1907. Henry James felt that Edith *"must* be tethered in native pastures, even if it reduces her to a backyard in New York."[5] But from her European vantage point Edith Wharton used what she knew of New York society to compose a brilliant but uneven series of satirical studies of the social history of New York beginning with *The House of Mirth* (1905) and including *The Custom of the Country* (1913), *The Age of Innocence* (1920), *The Glimpses of the Moon* (1922), *Old New York* (1924), *The Mother's Recompense* (1925), *Twilight Sleep* (1927), *The Children* (1928), *Hudson River Bracketed* (1929), *The Gods Arrive* (1932), and *The Buccaneers* (1938). Taken together, they establish Mrs. Wharton as the major link between the generation of Howells and James and that of Fitzgerald and Lewis, between the nineteenth- and twentieth-century American novel of manners.

I

In analyzing the point of view from which these novels were written it is instructive to remember her attitude toward American society as a field for fiction. Siding with James, she denied Howells's claim that if we dispose of all the paraphernalia of societal institutions the novelist still has the whole of human nature as his subject. In "The Great American Novel," Mrs. Wharton asked whether *human* nature could exist if denuded of "the web

of custom, manners, culture it has elaborately spun about itself?"
Her point was that human nature can exist only in relation to
social forms. If you strip away the web of custom and manners,
she argued, the only thing left is "that hollow unreality, 'Man,'
an evocation of the eighteenth-century demagogues who were
the first inventors of 'standardization.' " She went on to assert
that "human nature" and "man" are mere intellectual abstractions, whereas real men are bound up with the effects of climate,
soil, laws, religion, wealth, and leisure.[6]

In her most representative novels, Mrs. Wharton returned
again and again to the idea of tradition and continuity as important factors affecting the quality of individual life. She continually argued the necessity of commitment to the cultural
tradition; the danger of alienation from it; the catastrophe that
ensues when social upheavals like revolution and war destroy the
slowly and delicately spun web of that tradition; and the necessity of imaginatively preserving—if necessary even reconstructing
—the precious values of the past. Her dramatization of the theme
of tradition involved two methods. The first was to illustrate
through plot and character the importance of the web of culture
and manners which enclose men and to warn of the disaster in
store for those who become culturally deracinated or alienated
and for those who destroy the delicate web in a radical obsession
to change it. And the other method, most evident in the final
years of her life, was an impulse to reconstruct—archaeologically,
as it were—the social world of her youth: the traditions which
vitalized the culture of Old New York in the period from about
1840 to 1880. Her aim was to memorialize a set of slowly evolved
cultural values destroyed by a succession of disastrous changes in
American life beginning in the 1880s—including the rise of the
industrial plutocracy ("the lords of Pittsburgh," as she sarcastically called them); the massive immigration, which totally altered
the ethnic character of New York City; World War I, the Depression and the New Deal; and the nationalistic hatreds, at the
close of her life in 1937, building toward World War II.

The House of Mirth (1905), set in contemporary New York
high society, was her first major novel of manners. It is fundamentally the story of a failure of connections, of Lily Bart's fail-

ure to get into relation with an order of cultural values superior to the goal of worldly pleasure pursued by the fashionable haut monde. Lily rejects Lawrence Selden, the cultivated but poor young man who loves her, angles for a rich husband, fails because of her fastidious tastes, wastes her meager inheritance, and dies in a cheap boardinghouse of an overdose of chloral. Failing to find a wealthy husband, she falls in the social hierarchy—from the Trenor set and the Dorsets down to the level of the Welly Brys, Sam and Mattie Gormer, down to the Hotel Emporium level of Norma Hatch. In this descent, carefully discriminated in levels by Mrs. Wharton's precise notation of varying nuances of custom and manners, wealth is absolute power. In antagonizing Bertha Dorset, Lily exposes herself to the most powerful influence in New York society. "That influence, in its last analysis," Mrs. Wharton wrote, "was simply the power of money: Bertha Dorset's social credit was based on an impregnable bank-account."[7]

Lily's expulsion from society because she borrows money from Gus Trenor turns upon a careful point of manners in the relationship between the sexes and the handling of this power of money—"the tiresome distinction between what a married woman might, and a girl might not, do. Of course it was shocking for a married woman to borrow money—and Lily was expertly aware of the implication involved—but still, it was the mere *malum prohibitum* which the world decries but condones, and which, though it may be punished by private vengeance, does not provoke the collective disapprobation of society" (*HM*, 92). Unmarried, of course, lacking the protection of a husband, she stands falsely accused by society of being Trenor's mistress. Disillusioned by the realization that "the maintenance of a moral attribute should be dependent on dollars and cents" (*HM*, 197), she learns, as the sociologist William Graham Sumner observed in *Folkways* (1906), that "from shells to gold the ethics of social relations has clung to money."[8]

Mrs. Wharton concludes *The House of Mirth* with the implication that the absence of wealth may be just as great an attribute of freedom as its possession. Susy Lansing in *The Glimpses of the Moon* celebrates "the blessed moral freedom that wealth confers." But Lily must learn that the condition of moral freedom—the "republic of the spirit"—may be attained only by indifference to wealth. But taught by her mother to believe that "to be poor . . . seemed such a confession of failure that it amounted to disgrace" and that "acquiescence in dinginess was evidence of stupidity," she produced her expensive triumphs of beauty so effortlessly that "she almost felt that other girls were plain and inferior from choice" (*HM*, 103, 39). In a review of Howard Sturgis's *Belchamber*, written shortly after she had finished *The House of Mirth*, Edith Wharton defined the effect of such materialism upon sensitive natures: "A handful of vulgar people, bent only on spending and enjoying, may seem a negligible factor in the social development of the race; but they become an engine of destruction through the illusions they kill and the generous ardor they turn to despair."[9] Lily Bart must certainly have been in her mind when Mrs. Wharton made this observation. For *The House of Mirth* condemns the materialism of wealthy New York as destructive of illusions and generous ardors and productive of only despair. It is not from these socialites that Lily learns the meaning of life. It is from a poor working girl, Nettie Struther, who risks an uncertain future for the continuity of a family. Nettie seems to Lily "to have reached the central truth of existence"—a major claim for the interconnective value of love, children, and the family. It is melodramatic in context, but nonetheless it was true for Mrs. Wharton because she felt personally deprived of them.

Lily Bart is not a tragic heroine, but her fate is full of pathos because it is as much caused by the crassness of her social world as by her own whims. Balancing the social determinisms against Lily's personal vacillations, Mrs. Wharton showed that Lily fell from her high station, after her money was gone, because "there was no center of early pieties, of grave endearing traditions, to which her heart could revert and from which it could draw strength for herself and tenderness for others" (*HM*, 371). The biblical title implies the significance of the action: "The heart of the wise is in the house of mourning; but the heart of fools is in the house of mirth" (Ecclesiastes 7:4). As Mrs. Wharton told Erskine Steele, the meaning of the book is expressed in the idea that "in whatever form a slowly-accumulated past lives in the blood—whether in the concrete image of the old house stored with visual memories, or in the conception of the house not built with hands, but made up of inherited passions and loyalties—it has the same power of broadening and deepening the individual existence, of attaching it by mysterious links of kinship to all the mighty sum of human striving" (*HM*, 371).[10]

In her memoirs Edith Wharton defined her artistic problem in *The House of Mirth* as the effort to show how a group of irresponsible pleasure seekers added to the "old woe of the world," to show how their superficial values had a deeper significance than they themselves could guess. How could their trivial actions assume tragic significance, she asked herself, or be worth telling about in a novel? The answer was that "a frivolous society can acquire dramatic significance only through what its frivolity destroys. Its tragic implication lies in its power of debasing people and ideals."[11] The meaning of Mrs. Wharton's chronicle of the very rich lies in the ruin of exquisite creatures like Lily Bart by a society which has failed to provide her, thanks to the surrender of its traditions, with that supporting "web of custom, manners, culture" human nature elaborately spins about itself in traditional societies.

It may be observed here, in conclusion, that although it is often concerned with an aristocracy, the novel of manners is rarely the stuff of tragedy. Its mode is more often than not irony or pathos, if not satire. Northrop Frye has observed that "the best word for low mimetic or domestic tragedy is, perhaps, pathos, and pathos has a close relation to the sensational reflex of tears. Pathos presents its hero as isolated by a weakness which appeals to our sympathy because it is on our own level of experience. I speak of a hero, but the central figure of pathos is often a woman or a child (or both, as in the death-scenes of Little Eva and Little Nell), and we have a whole procession of pathetic female sacrifices in English low mimetic fiction from Clarissa Harlowe to Hardy's Tess and James's Daisy Miller. We notice that while tragedy may massacre a whole cast, pathos is usually concentrated on a single character, partly because low mimetic society is more strongly individualized."[12]

One prominent motive in the genesis of the nineteenth-century novel of manners, it is worth pointing out, was the disgust of the post–Civil War realists with the excess of pathos infecting the low mimetic "tragedy." The so-called Domestic Sentimentalists— Susan Warner, Mrs. E.D.E.N. Southworth, Maria Cummins, and Augusta Jane Evans Wilson, for example—exploited the mode of pathos in scores of books that shamelessly appealed to the melodramatic sensibility of the mid-century. Later realists deflated the prevailing emotionalism through ridicule and irony. In its satire on the sentimentality of the Pen-Tom-Irene triangle, *The Rise of Silas Lapham* illustrates how ironic variations could be played on this popular pathetic mode. In *The House of Mirth* Lily only approaches the tragic condition; only the implications of her story are tragic. As Louis Auchincloss has observed, "pathos has a bigger place than tragedy in the study of manners."[13]

II

America's failure to preserve any kind of traditional system of values led Mrs. Wharton to complain that, in her youth, "the Americans of the original States, who in moments of crisis still shaped the national view, were the heirs of an old tradition of European culture which the country has now totally rejected."[14] *The Glimpses of the Moon* (1922), *The Mother's Recompense* (1925), *Twilight Sleep* (1927), and *The Children* (1928), though seriously defective works of art, deal with the plight of rootless and ephemeral people like Lily in the postwar world, morally adrift, ignorant of the social connections that enrich life, falling back finally on the meaningless pleasures of the moment.

As she witnessed the Jazz Age spectacle after the war, Edith Wharton tried to recover and imaginatively project some of the values expressed in the social and moral traditions of her youth. *The Age of Innocence* (1920) and *Old New York* (1924) memorialize a social world swept away by the acceleration of historical forces which only Henry Adams, of her generation, had adequately described. In these works she claimed for Old New York in the age of innocence a certain kind of social norm. Nostalgic the novel certainly is; but Mrs. Wharton's characteristic irony continually undercuts her temptation to sentimentalize the age. For there is no question that Old New York was an imperfectly developed culture—marked by sexual hypocrisy, intellectual narrowness, civic irresponsibility, and class snobbery. But at its best it preserved dignity and decorum; a sensitivity to feeling and emotion, however inhibited by convention; an appreciation for pictorial beauty and a feeling for the grandeur of the English language; an unshakable belief in the civilizing power of education; a high (but conservative) social style; and a commitment to personal rectitude in public life—all of these qualities seemingly obsolete in the age of flappers, jazz babies, flagpole sitters, and bathtub gin.

As a period piece *The Age of Innocence* lovingly records the manners of the world of Edith Wharton's youth—the opera evenings in the old Academy of Music in the seventies when Christine Nilsson sang *Faust,* the theater evenings at Lester Wallack's where the latest Dion Boucicault play was appearing, the formal dinners, the rounds of visits and card-leavings, the rituals of betrothal, the Grace Church weddings, the summers in Newport and on the Hudson alternating with winters in Washington Square and the Fifth Avenue brownstones, and the effect on the lives of her urbane Old New Yorkers of inventions like electricity, the telephone, the fountain pen, the Hudson Tunnel, and other "Arabian Nights marvels." When she showed the manuscript to her cousin Walter Van Rensselaer Berry, he observed: "Yes; it's good. But of course you and I are the only people who will ever read it. We are the last people left who can remember New York and Newport as they were then, and nobody else will be interested."[15]

These details of New York's social life are interesting, but the novel deserves rather to be read for the portrait of the age it provides. Others had analyzed it before Mrs. Wharton. Twain and Charles Dudley Warner had condemned its materialism in *The Gilded Age,* and Henry Adams had exposed the corruption of our politics in *Democracy* (1880). But for Edith Wharton the 1870s was uniquely the age of "innocence." She meant by this term a combination of manners and unspoken assumptions about values endemic in the very social life of this small pyramid of families constituting the "society" of Old New York. In one sense, their innocence was preserved through their exclusiveness. In the language of the social anthropologist, Mrs. Wharton calls them a "tribe" of "Aborigines" living on the "reservation" of Washington Square. Their manners are "rituals" and "taboos." They communicate by an in-group code: "In reality they all lived in a kind of hieroglyphic world, where the real thing was never said or done or even thought, but only represented by a set of arbitrary signs. . . ."[16] Ruled by a matriarch who could command the obedience of all the members of the family, this tribe could close ranks and repel outsiders or discipline would-be rebels like Ellen Olenska and Newland Archer.

Reminiscent of Arnold's "barbarians," these aristocrats are typified in May Welland, who is striking for her "radiant good looks" and for "her health, her horsemanship, her grace and quickness at games"; but she has only a "shy interest in books and ideas." Afraid of French Sundays, European morals, and "foreignness" in general, they avoid Europeans when abroad "in conformity with the old New York tradition that it was not 'dignified' to force one's self on the notice of one's acquaintance in foreign countries" (*AI*, 192). They have little interest in art or the life of the mind. They have no "intellectual liberty," "critical independence," or capacity for breathing the "air of ideas." New Yorkers of the age of innocence, in short, did not "look life in the face." But if they had "a blind dread of innovation, an instinctive shrinking from responsibility," Mrs. Wharton still found admirable their good taste, their polished style, and their "scrupulous probity in business and private affairs."[17]

One of Mrs. Wharton's aims in *The Age of Innocence* was to explore Old New York attitudes toward the relation of men and women, particularly the double standard in sexual education and behavior. For her, the education of the young in this aristocratic society did not adequately fit them for life and the realities of human nature. In the opening chapter of the novel, as they witness the seduction scene in *Faust*, Archer reflects that May does not even know what is going on on stage. She is expected to know nothing before marriage, but he is expected to know, theoretically, everything. If a decent fellow had had any experience of sex before marriage, it would doubtless have been with a class of outlawed women or with a foolish conniver from whom the females of the tribe would have to protect him. "What could he and she really know of each other, since it was his duty, as a 'decent' fellow, to conceal his past from her, and hers, as a marriageable girl, to have no past to conceal" (*AI*, 41). And yet on the night of her marriage, May Welland, "the centre of this elaborate system of mystification," would be plunged "into what people evasively called 'the facts of life'" (*AI*, 42–43). May's innocence is actually ignorance, an "artificial product," a "factitious purity" which has been "cunningly manufactured by a conspiracy of mothers and aunts and grandmothers and long-dead ancestresses, because it was supposed to be what he wanted, what he had a right to, in order that he might exercise his lordly pleasure in smashing it like an image made of snow" (*AI*, 43).

If May is "innocent," Archer is "experienced," as his affair with Mrs. Thorley Rushworth, one of the "connivers," attests. Archer has in fact claimed a sexual freedom which he believes women should enjoy as freely as men. But May is so thoroughly the product of a factitious purity that she can never fully satisfy a husband. Before he can extricate himself, the families announce their betrothal and Archer finds himself a married man.

Archer's marriage is nearly destroyed by the Countess Ellen Olenska. She is far more realistic and sophisticated than any other woman he has ever encountered in New York. She has been educated in Europe, though she is American by birth, and has married into the Polish aristocracy. Indifferent to the taboos of New York society, she offends the matrons who preside over it. Her "European" ideas are somehow dangerous to the solidarity of the tribe. Archer's meager emotional experience leads him to romanticize her as a tragic heroine worthy of the pen of Boucicault. But she liberates him from the provincial prejudices of Old New York. If "there was a time when Archer had definite and rather aggressive opinions" on petty social questions, "and when everything concerning the manners and customs of his little tribe had seemed to him fraught with world-wide significance" (*AI*, 182), Ellen convinces him that love, spontaneity, and openness are more important than social rituals which have hardened and become lifeless. Ellen fulfills Archer's belief that women should be as free as men in order to develop into mature human beings. Archer believes that this is more desirable than May's kind of innocence, "the innocence that seals the mind against imagination and the heart against experience!" (*AI*, 145). But Archer's discovery comes too late: even as he is contemplating whether or not to abandon May and run away with Ellen, the family rallies: "There were certain things that had to be done, and if done at all, done handsomely and thoroughly; and one of these, in the old New York code, was the tribal rally round a kinswoman about to be eliminated from the tribe" (*AI*, 337). Ellen is bloodlessly expelled from the family as May guilelessly announces to Archer that she is "sure" that she is going to have a baby. Trapped by this appeal to decency and his impending fatherhood, Archer "reverts to type," surrenders Ellen, and remains with his wife and unborn child.

If we neglected the final chapter of the novel, we should doubtless suppose that Mrs. Wharton's sole point was the destruction of romantic love by society when its values are threatened. Yet this is not precisely the case. For if Ellen taught Archer an order of values he was too ineffectual to act upon, he teaches her that worth and value can exist beneath conventions that seem stifling to her: " 'At least . . . it was you,' " she tells him, " 'who made me understand that under the dullness there are things so fine and sensitive and delicate that even those I most cared for in my other life look cheap in comparison' " (*AI*, 243). Yet how pitiful a provision was made for the life of the imagination behind those brownstones, Mrs. Wharton once observed. "Beauty, passion and danger were automatically excluded from his [the average well-to-do New Yorker of her childhood] life (for the men were almost as starved as the women); and the average human being deprived of air from the heights is likely to produce other lives equally starved—which was what happened in old New York, where the tepid sameness of the moral atmosphere resulted in a prolonged immaturity of mind."[18]

But Archer does eventually mature through this experience. Though he frankly misses "the flower of life" in not giving all to love and running away with Ellen, he has a rich, rewarding life

with May. In the final chapter he may marvel at the greater openness and spontaneity in turn-of-the-century New York, the greater freedom available to his son Dallas and his fiancée Fanny. But
Archer reaffirms the old, established social and moral traditions
of the 1870s which had already disappeared from New York.
Although they may be as antiquated as "the recovered fragments
of Ilium" in the Metropolitan Museum where Archer and Ellen
have their last interview, he walks away from Ellen's apartment
in Paris, twenty-five years later, reconciled to the traditions of
his youth. In the dignity with which Archer accepts his situation
there is something genuinely admirable, although the irony cannot be missed that the scruples of conscience which marked the
1870s are as meaningless to Dallas and the twentieth century as
the Cesnola antiquities Archer stares at in the Museum—so rapidly
have the foundations of moral life changed in the modern age.
Even so, Archer's decision to stay with his wife is affirmed because it constitutes a recognition that man has institutional, fa-
milial, and social responsibilities which cannot be abandoned
simply for the gratification of a romantic passion. Archer's piety
for the values of the past Mrs. Wharton called "the memorial
manner," a conservative commitment to old, established traditions
which, however relative in the long perspective of man's history,
still enrich, deepen, and intensify the value of the individual's life.

III

Mrs. Wharton's emphasis on the memorial manner, on preserving enduring institutions and values despite the pressures of social
change because they satisfy deep-seated human needs, testifies to
the conservative nature of her mind and art. This conservatism
is most aptly expressed in *French Ways and Their Meaning*
(1919), a manual for American soldiers and tourists in France.
The gist of the book is indicated in the emphasis she gives to
continuity as a value particularly appropriate and necessary to
American society: "In all this, France has a lesson to teach and a
warning to give. It was our English forbears who taught us to
flout tradition and break away from their own great inheritance;
France may teach us that, side by side with the qualities of en-

terprise and innovation that English blood has put in us, we should cultivate the sense of continuity, that 'sense of the past' which enriches the present and binds us up with the world's great stabilising traditions of art and poetry and knowledge."[19]

Hudson River Bracketed (1929) and its sequel *The Gods Arrive* (1932), written at the close of Edith Wharton's career, dramatize the disastrous consequences of cultural deprivation for the American who aspires to become an artist. Born in the culturally barren Middle West, where innovation and continuous change have eclipsed the values of tradition and continuity, Vance Weston (her would-be artist) gets his first glimmering of tradition in New York State, where he is recuperating from an obviously symbolic illness. There he discovers a cultured eastern girl, Halo Spear, and an old house, The Willows, built in the 1830s by A. J. Downing in the style of Hudson River Bracketed. The result of his discovery is *Instead*, a short novel based on the life of Emily Lorburn, a spinster who lived at The Willows in the nineteenth century. In rambling over her old house and imagining what her life must have been like, Vance discovered that a "strange and overwhelming element had entered into his imagination in the guise of these funny turrets and balconies, turgid upholsteries and dangling crystals. Suddenly . . . his mind struck root deep down in accumulated layers of experience, in centuries of struggle, passion and inspiration—so that this absurd house, the joke of Halo's childhood was to him the very emblem of man's long effort, was Chartres, the Parthenon, the Pyramids."[20] Vance's experience of a cultural tradition preserved through history is so meager that this mere nineteenth-century house is sufficient to suggest to him "the idea of a different rhythm, a different time beat: a movement without jerks and breaks, flowing down from ever so far off in the hills, bearing ships to the sea" (*HRB*, 360). And the perception of this mysterious link between the past and the present arouses in Vance a desire to recreate the world in fiction. To bring it to life Vance shapes a style consonant with the idea of continuity—one without jerks and breaks, flowing harmoniously with the thought conceived—a fair statement, incidentally, of what Mrs. Wharton aspired to in her own prose style.

But even with Halo's help in reconstructing the vanished world of Miss Lorburn, Vance's historical romance fails to unravel the mystic meaning. Thus George Frenside, Mrs. Wharton's spokesman, advises Vance to give up the costume romance and to mix in the social life of New York City: " 'A novelist ought to, at one time or another,' Frenside continued. 'Manners are your true material, after all' " (*HRB*, 394). Vance's search for a novelistic form also leads him to consider the documentary novel, by implication a book like *An American Tragedy* (1925). For Vance, this type of novel also turns out to be inadequate because it fails to distinguish between reality and the piling up of details. Unmediated by the selecting faculty of the imagination, the documentary was for Edith Wharton a mere slice of life. The great French writers, she observed, "invented the once-famous *tranche de vie*, the exact photographic reproduction of a situation or an episode, with all its sounds, smells, aspects realistically rendered, but with its deeper relevance and its suggestions of a larger whole either unconsciously missed or purposely left out."[21] If they succeeded, she held, they did so only in spite of their theories.

This is not to say that Edith Wharton admired the Jamesian novel of geometric design. She wrote only one truly Jamesian novel—*The Reef* (1912), an attempt to work out, elaborately, all sides of a central situation (a love affair) involving complex levels of psychological analysis of motive and action. James thought it her finest novel and praised it as a drama of "psychologic Racinian unity, intensity, and gracility."[22] But Edith Wharton had little love for the Jamesian geometry of enclosed relations and could not read the later James with pleasure. "Everything, in the latest novels, had to be fitted into a predestined design," she observed of James's major phase, "and design, in his strict geometrical sense, is to me one of the least important things in fiction."[23] Her natural métier was the expansive chronicle of manners episodically dramatizing "the conflicts . . . produced between the social order and individual appetites."[24]

Vance rejects both the historical romance and the naturalistic documentary and decides, on Frenside's advice, to write a novel of contemporary New York capturing the noise and roar of the city, its range of social experience, and the complexity of its social types. Vance's aim is not "to denounce or to show up, as most of the 'society' novelists did, but to take apart the works of the machine, and find out what all those people behind the splendid house fronts signified in the general scheme of things" (*HRB*, 319–20).

Unfortunately, he does not understand them or their place in the general scheme of things, and he is too poor to live among the rich. In the end, he abandons the novel because his own social experience has been too meager to make use of the manners of the East. In the book he is writing at the end of *Hudson River Bracketed*, Vance Weston's theme is a reflection of his own experience—a tale "about a fellow like himself, about two or three people whose spiritual lives were starved as his own had been" (*HRB*, 511). *Hudson River Bracketed* concludes with Vance struggling to become an artist, to find a form, to overcome the limitations imposed on him by an inadequate American social education.

In *The Gods Arrive* (1932) Mrs. Wharton takes her would-be artist to Europe in further pursuit of the origins of Western culture, in a deeper descent into the self to discover the source of his own creative energies and what is needed to feed them. Halo, now his mistress, goes along. The novel develops three inter-related themes: the vexing problem of love both within and without marriage; the discovery of Europe with its ancient traditions by a young writer excited by the recently discovered concept of continuity; and his search for a novelistic form to express his new vision of the world. Although weaker than *Hudson River Bracketed*, *The Gods Arrive* effectively dramatizes a new kind of subject—the jazz-age international social set made up of the deracinated aristocracies of England, Italy, France, and America. As an aspiring novelist of manners, Vance learns that "in this rushing oblivious world one must jump onto the train in motion, and look about at the passengers afterward."[25] But although he struggles with this seething new social crowd, trying to reduce them to artistic form, he cannot produce the great new international novel of manners. The Bohemian crowd in Paris urges him to write a novel expressing some of the popular literary fads of the day. The Paris crowd argue, like some latter-day critics, that "fiction, as the art of narrative and the portrayal of social groups, had reached its climax, and could produce no more . . .—that unless the arts were renewed they were doomed, and that in fiction the only hope of renewal was in the exploration of the subliminal." But Vance is unwilling to believe that the novel of manners, as a form, is dead. His "robust instinct told him that the surface of life was rich enough to feed the creator's imagination" (*GA*, 112). Mrs. Wharton's opposition to the stream-of-consciousness novel is nowhere more acidulously expressed than here. For like Proust she believed that "the proper study of mankind is man's conscious and purposive behaviour rather than its dim unfathomable sources."[26]

Vance, in fact, is destined to failure until he totally rejects the literary anarchy advocated by the Paris Bohemians, who want to "break the old moulds" and "demolish the old landmarks." They see the artist's genius as an instinct for destruction. Their diatribes against the past—" 'Who ever consulted you and me when the Pyramids were built—or Versailles? Why should we be saddled with all that old dead masonry? Ruins are what we want—more ruins!' " (*GA*, 128)—echo *Of Human Bondage*, where the art students in Paris damn all the great Victorian writers as creators of the bourgeois world and fling their books into the bonfire of oblivion. In exposing this continuing tension between traditional and innovative impulses in art and life, Mrs. Wharton clearly aligns herself with the forces of conservatism. Against the roar of the "discontinuous universe" in the postwar world, Mrs. Wharton posed the tradition of order and continuity embodied in the classical writings of Western literature; in enduring architectural monuments like the cathedrals at Chartres and Cordova—even in New York's Trinity Chapel and The Willows; and in old, established religions like Anglicanism and Catholicism. It is from this tradition that Vance ultimately draws nourishment for his art.

In "The Art of Fiction" Henry James defined experience as a spider web of impressions in the consciousness converted into art through the faculties of conscious observation and inference. He advised the intending fabulist to try to be one of those people on whom nothing is lost. And his novels of the major phase dramatize how extensively he could refine a little lode of experience.

Mrs. Wharton also valued the inferential faculty in the artistic process: "As to experience, intellectual and moral, the creative imagination can make a little go a long way, provided it remains long enough in the mind and is sufficiently brooded on."[27] But her conception of experience was not impressionistic and inward. For Edith Wharton the novelist's subject was the Self in full engagement with the social world. And she did not hesitate to criticize the later James for severing his characters from "that thick nourishing human air in which we all live and move," for stripping them of "all the *human fringes* we necessarily trail after us through life."[28]

IV

The Gods Arrive does not demonstrate Vance Weston's fulfillment as a great American novelist of manners. Though he is already the author of several books, he is still on the threshold of his career. Fundamentally Mrs. Wharton's aim in *Hudson River Bracketed* and *The Gods Arrive* was threefold. First, she wished to point up the thinness of the American social and cultural tradition and its devastating effect on the development of the individual, particularly the would-be artist. The necessity of the individual's getting into creative relationship with his cultural tradition is so pervasive in her fiction that in one way or another it figures in almost all her novels. The marriage of Vance and Halo, daughter of the established traditions of an older American society, symbolically suggests that "only when the energies of the west and the traditions of the old east are brought together can an adequate civilization develop."[29] Only then can the gods arrive. Second, Edith Wharton wished to put on record her conception of that profoundly mysterious process of reason and imagination by which her novels of manners came into being. And finally—through Vance Weston's successive experiments with the autobiographical novel, the historical romance, the naturalistic documentary, and the stream-of-consciousness novel—Edith Wharton wished to defend the novel of social life, the realistic novel of manners, against those critics who were already charging in the twenties that "the art of narrative and the portrayal of social groups" had reached its climax and "could produce no more." Vance's conclusion that the surface of life is ever rich enough to feed the creator's imagination suggests that he has arrived at a full measure of artistic wisdom and may now be expected to realize his potential. His rejection of other forms in favor of the novel of manners is of course a rationalization of Mrs. Wharton's preference and practice. And it implies a rigidity in her conception of the novel that the critic must, finally, deplore. The novel of manners is a significant form, and its appeal has always been more enduring than some of the experimental modes popular with symbol-, archetype-, and myth-oriented critics. But the house of fiction is large, as James remarked, and the autobiographical novel of, say, Thomas Wolfe, the romance parody of John Barth, the naturalistic documentary of Dreiser, and the stream-of-consciousness novel of Joyce or Faulkner—all of these are richly distinguished forms and need, in any case, no defense at this late date.

But what is equally deplorable to the well-tempered critic, it seems to me, is the pervasive assumption that the novel of manners is impossible to write in America or that it is passé because certain writers now popular in the academies are writing in other forms. Since there is clear dissatisfaction with the logic of this avant-garde view—for example, in the critical studies and reviews of W. M. Frohock, John McCormick, John Brooks, Michael Millgate, A. N. Kaul, Hilton Kramer, David Hirsch, Delmore Schwartz, Granville Hicks, Ralph Ellison, and Saul Bellow—we must reconsider the claim that the novel of manners is dead or alien to America and contemplate steadily the novels that demonstrate its vital possibilities. For it is inescapably true, as Arthur Mizener has recently argued, that the realistic novel of manners has survived and will continue to survive because of its "innumerable opportunities beyond those for mere verisimilitude";[30] because it permits an infinite variety in personal vision and expression; and because, as Saul Bellow has recently argued, many living writers feel intensely the existence of social qualities yet unrecognized but demanding "release and expression" in realistic fiction.[31]

Bellow's observation is reminiscent of Mrs. Wharton's hope, expressed in 1914, that "some new theory of form, as adequate to its purpose as those preceding it, will be evolved from the present welter of experiment. . . ."[32] Her own fiction would have been enriched by an intelligent critical dialogue attentive to the full range of fictional forms—for she was an experimentalist herself, in the sense that she tried her own hand at a number of different fictional forms. But by the end of the twenties, formlessness had almost everywhere been praised and substituted for form, and her own form—the novel of manners—was under attack from the Ludwig Lewisohns and Van Wyck Brookses. Mrs. Wharton's defensiveness about the form of fiction made her far too rigid, and the literary criticism in her novels and in *The Writing of Fiction* served only to defend her own preferences, not to renew or enlarge our understanding of the shape of fiction.

On one score, however, Edith Wharton's position still has significance. Hamlin Garland had argued in *Crumbling Idols* (1894) that "the study of evolution" had so "liberated the thought of the individual" that "the power of tradition" was growing "fainter year by year."[33] For Edith Wharton, however, the loss of tradition was no cause for rejoicing. For her, the study of evolution, particularly the evolution of human societies, provided precisely those sanctions for tradition which Garland had repudiated. In a world without absolutes, the traditional provided the only real possibility of stability and civilized living. Passionately committed to a sense of the past, to the value of continuity and tradition (this is, after all, *her* figure in the carpet), Edith Wharton is still relevant today.[34] Her literary conservatism soured leftist critics of the 1930s, who regarded her as hopelessly out of touch with the dynamics of social change. And to a disturbing extent she was. But in the light of the failure of so many liberal dreams, in the context of the apocalyptic rhetoric of the New Left, in the contemporary atmosphere of restless innovation and experiment in arts and society, of "existential freedom" eagerly invoked to create "situational ethics" and ad hoc manners and morals—Edith Wharton's emphasis on the web of cultural connections that define and enrich the self reminds us that we do not create ourselves *ex nihilo* and that the possible good still embedded in some of "the old ways" may deserve, like an archaeological find, to be exhumed, inspected, renovated, and put to creative use.

6

⚹ SINCLAIR LEWIS

The Romantic Comedian as Realist Mimic

Sinclair Lewis had very few theories about the craft of fiction, but on one point he was absolutely adamant. And that was the necessity for the novelist to supply the material furniture of the novel, to give it "solidity of specification." "In the world of the artist," he once wrote, "it is the little, immediate, comprehensible things—jackknives or kisses, bath sponges or children's wails—which illuminate and fix the human spectacle; and for the would-be painter of our Western world a Sears-Roebuck catalogue is (to one who knows how to choose and who has his imagination from living life) a more valuable reference book than a library of economics, poetry, and the lives of the saints."[1] Some years later, more or less to document this view, he wrote an introduction for David L. Cohn's *The Good Old Days: A History of American Morals and Manners as Seen Through the Sears, Roebuck Catalogs 1905 to the Present* (1940). In his introduction he assured the American people that "by your eyebrow pencils, your encyclopedias, and your alarm clocks shall ye be known. The most scrupulous statistics on the increasing acreage of alfalfa and soy beans, the most elevated dissertations on our tendency to chronic philanthropy, could not make us understand that cranky, hysterical, brave, mass-timorous, hard-minded, imaginative Chosen Race, the Americans, half so competently as Mr. Cohn's parade of the wares that we have been buying and paying for and actually lugging into our homes and barns and offices these past fifty years." Lewis took unusual delight in enumerating the Electric Thermostats, Ladies' Percale Sunbonnets, Birth Control Manuals, Imported Fancy Lily Bulbs, Cambric Bust Confiners, Two-Color Bibles, 1939 Model Air Conditioners, Vest Pocket Revolvers, Brewster Sleigh Bells, Fancy Colored Mummy Effect Worsted Round Cut Sack Suits, Clarion Harmonicas in Red Leatherette Cases, *ad infinitum*.[2] Viewed in the light of this statement, Lewis's obsession with the sheer number of things in middle-class American culture becomes more explicable if not more tolerable. His typical character is defined by the things constituting his environment—by the definiteness of his "house, street, city, class of society."[3] It is "this view of the individual imbedded in a matrix of neighborhood, city, and class which constitutes the basis," as Stephen S. Conroy has observed, of what may be called Lewis's "sociological imagination."[4]

I

The publication of *Main Street* (1920), Lewis's first major novel of manners, hit the American public like a bombshell. Judging from the sales history of the book and the outrage in the newspapers, there is no reason to doubt Mark Schorer's claim that it was "the most sensational event in twentieth-century American publishing history."[5] If Lewis was obscure beforehand, he was notorious afterward, and the immediate popularity of *Main Street* and its author fostered the illusion that it was his first book. In a sense it was—and Lewis himself told Alfred Harcourt that *Main Street* was perhaps "the real beginning of my career as a writer."[6] But this beginning had a long foreground in Lewis's youth and in the composition of his early apprenticeship novels.

Much has been written about Lewis's boyhood in Sauk Centre, Minnesota. For the student of Lewis's novels of manners, Sauk Centre is an instance of an environment in the apparent void, engaged in gathering in the preparations, but far from having achieved the amenities. A town of 2,800 people in 1885, when Lewis was born, it had been carved out of the prairie less than thirty years before. Lewis's father, a physician, enjoyed a high social position in the town, thanks to his profession. But his son, an awkward, pimply redhead, grew up uncertain of social forms and deeply contemptuous of them. Later, at Yale, he was a misfit among his sophisticated eastern classmates, and his belligerent radicalism and agnosticism excluded him from college social life. One of his classmates later observed that "Lewis was as different from the correct young types around him as Sauk Center [*sic*] is from Tuxedo,"[7] and one of his teachers, Chauncey Brewster Tinker, observed that "the conventions and restrictions of good society—especially of collegiate society—were offensive to him. His abiding temptation was to undermine them and blow them at the moon."[8] To these experiences is to be added his disastrous marriage to Grace Hegger Lewis in 1914. His "lady from the Upper West Side," who escaped "the trap of shabby gentility" by taking up a career at *Vogue*, had stylish clothes, an English accent, and aristocratic ways—including a French maid, because it pleased her "to give orders in French before guests."[9] Lewis's youth in Sauk Centre, his experience at Yale, and this marriage to a social superior made Lewis hypersensitive to the disparity between the East and the Middle West, the genteel aristocracy and the middle class. His novels of manners, written out of a deep sense of social inferiority and a resentment against polite manners, constituted his means of resolving the deep frustrations of an Outsider-Novelist.

Of all his apprenticeship novels—*Our Mr. Wrenn* (1914), *The Innocents* (1917), *The Job* (1917), and *Free Air* (1919), the latter most clearly illustrates that social insecurity that made Lewis first defend his cultural background and then in *Main Street* attack it. In *Free Air*, the fashionable eastern Boltwoods, visiting in the Middle West, drive to the West Coast in their Gomez-Dep. Milt Daggett, a garage mechanic from Schoenstrom, Minnesota, follows them in his Teal, rescues them from a series of misadventures, and falls in love with the daughter Claire. Although he is not her social equal, Milt wins Claire's love by minding his manners and taking courses in French and engineering at the University of Washington; finally he makes the social grade. As in the previous novels, Lewis sought to overcome a terrible sense of social inferiority by praising the culture and the honest-to-gosh down-rightness of just plain (college-educated) folks: "With Mr. Jones he discussed—no, ye Claires of Brooklyn Heights, this garage man and this threadbare young superintendent of a paint-bare school, talking in a town that was only a comma on the line, did not discuss corn-growing, nor did they reckon to guess that by heck the constabule was carryin' on with Widdy Perkins. They spoke of fish-culture, Elihu Root, the spiritualistic evidences of immortality, government ownership, self-starters for flivvers, and the stories of Irvin Cobb." While the reader may rightly wonder whether these topics are evidence of any real culture, *Free Air* celebrates the manners of the American small town. Claire Bolt-wood has to learn that "what had seemed rudeness in garage men and hotel clerks was often a resentful reflection of her own East-ern attitude that she was necessarily superior to a race she had been trained to call 'common people.' "[10] According to Lewis, "the superiority is all the other way: people who have enjoyed the hereditary advantages of wealth, social position, and educa-tion are ridiculous and contemptible—unless, like Claire, they have the good luck to be regenerated by the Great West." Lewis's intention in the early novels was thus "to bring a warm glow of self-satisfaction to the heart of the great American majority, to strengthen and entrench the folk of Zenith and of Gopher Prairie in their complacency and also in their intolerance of everyone un-like themselves."[11] Advertise the novel as "Milt up against city social complications," Lewis told his publisher Alfred Harcourt, "the small-town garage man going to the opera in his first evening clothes."[12]

Taken together, *Free Air* and the other novels that preceded *Main Street* marked Sinclair Lewis's apprenticeship as a novelist of manners who blended romance and realism in novels dealing with the life of adventure in exotic, faraway places, in aviation, in business, and in the life of the open road; he juxtaposed the social classes in an obvious but effective way, in order to make his Mid-dle West seem just as cultured, just as socially polished as the East. For the Gomez-Dep has imported style to the western provinces, and the "missionaries of business" have taught the backwater merchants how to build up trade and trim windows and "treat customers like human beings," just as they do back East. Lewis implies that businessmen, "as much as the local ministers and doctors and teachers and newspapermen, were the agents of spreading knowledge and justice. It was they . . . who encouraged villagers to rise from scandal and gossip to a perception of the Great World, of politics and sports, and some measure of art and science. And it is through these businessmen and drummers that Milt Daggett gets his first glimpse of the correct clothes and manners that go along with financial success, just as it is through his assiduous cultivation of the arts and sciences, as well as tennis, dancing, and bridge, that he finally becomes acceptable to the belle of Brooklyn Heights."[13]

This conflict of East and West, of provincial and sophisticate, of bourgeois and aristocrat, intensified by his marriage to Grace Hegger Lewis, is the central conflict in Lewis's work. Since it arises out of the circumstances of his own life, little separates Sinclair Lewis from Milt Daggett, Will Kennicott, and Sam Dodsworth. This lonely outsider's effort to prove that he's just as dog-gone good as Claire or Fran—and if he isn't as socially poised, well, he's better off for being a Regular Guy—reflects a cultural conflict developed most effectively in the big novels of the twenties—*Main Street*, *Babbitt*, and *Dodsworth*. In *Main Street*, however, he turned his guns around in order to attack the very village culture he had defended, in *Free Air*, against the eastern Boltwoods.

II

Main Street is a reaction against the conditions of life in small-town America, a novel in what has been called "the revolt from the village." By 1920, as Mark Schorer has observed, "the village as an important unit in capitalist economy had ceased to exist, had become backwash, and, with that life gone from it, its social and moral attitudes had become fixed in the rigidities of the past."[14] No longer was it possible to say that "the history of a nation is only the history of its villages written large,"[15] as Woodrow Wilson had proclaimed in 1900, or to agree with Warren G. Harding that "there is more happiness in the American village than in any other place on the face of the earth."[16] But myths die hard and the view was still prevalent across America that although "cities were evil and even in the farmland there were occasional men of wrath, our villages," as Lewis put it, "were approximately paradise."[17]

In attacking this utopian view of the small town in America, Lewis debunked two illusions of the village then current in America. The first was the stereotype projected in books like Gene Stratton-Porter's *Freckles* (1904), Booth Tarkington's *Penrod* (1914), Meredith Nicholson's *A Hoosier Chronicle* (1912), and Zona Gale's *Friendship Village* (1908). This stereotype held that the American small town is the seat of all values and neighborly virtue. Zona Gale romanticized the homey warmth and the folksiness of Friendship Village. Nicholson claimed that "it's all pretty comfortable and cheerful and busy in Indiana, with lots of old-fashioned human kindness flowing round: and it's getting better all the time. And I guess it's always got to be that way, out here in God's country."[18] Carol Kennicott finds this "first tradition" repeated in "scores of magazines every month"—the idea that "the American village remains the one sure abode of friendship, honest, and clean sweet marriageable girls. Therefore all men who succeed in painting in Paris or in finance in New York at last become weary of smart women, return to their native towns, assert that cities are vicious, marry their childhood sweethearts and, presumably, joyously abide in those towns until death."[19] The other stereotype assumed that "the significant features of all villages are whiskers, iron dogs upon lawns, gold bricks, checkers, jars of gilded cat-tails, and shrewd comic old men who are known as 'hicks' and who ejaculate 'Waal I swan' " (*MS*, 264). This stereotype, Lewis argued, rules "the facetious illustrators, and syndicated newspaper humor, but out of actual life it passed forty years ago." The Gopher Prairie of Carol's day thinks in terms of "cheap motor cars, telephones, ready-made clothes, silos, alfalfa, kodaks, phonographs, leather-upholstered Morris chairs, bridge-prizes, oil-stocks, motion-pictures, land-deals, unread sets of Mark Twain, and a chaste version of national politics."

But while Gopher Prairie may satisfy small-town doctors like Will Kennicott and oldtimers like the Champ Perrys, "the more intelligent young people . . . flee to the cities with agility and, despite the fictional tradition, resolutely stay there, seldom returning even for holidays. The most protesting patriots of the towns leave them in old age, if they can afford it, and go to live in California or in the cities" (*MS*, 265). Why should this be so? Lewis is precise in defining the causes of this grand exodus: "It is an unimaginatively standardized background, a sluggishness of speech and manners, a rigid ruling of the spirit by the desire to appear respectable. It is contentment . . . the contentment of the quiet dead, who are scornful of the living for their restless walking. It is negation canonized as the one positive virtue. It is the prohibition of happiness. It is slavery self-sought and self-defended. It is dullness made God" (*MS*, 265). *Main Street* analyzes the American small town at the precise moment of its disintegration, as young people—refusing to conform to standardized values or be warped into grotesques like Anderson's characters—leave for the cities.

A parallel theme is the plight of the restless, intelligent young woman like Nora in Ibsen's *A Doll's House* (*MS*, 173), who is eager to make something of her life, who rejects the male's immemorial definition of the good life for women: "What's better than making a comfy home and bringing up some cute kids and knowing nice homey people?" (*MS*, 9). Lewis had caught the undercurrent of women's liberation, of rebellion by young women in search of freedom, in search of a conscious life different from that which their mothers and grandmothers had known. Will Kennicott's solution is "lots of children and hard work." Even Guy Pollock thinks that "the darkness of the women" can be lightened by going back "to an age of tranquility and charming manners" in which "good taste" is enthroned. But for Carol, the revolt of the modern woman is merely a facet of the general social revolution: ". . . we're all together, the industrial workers and the women and the farmers and the Negro race and the Asiatic colonies, and even a few of the Respectables. . . . We want our Utopia *now*—" (*MS*, 201-2). Instead of utopia, however, she has Gopher Prairie.

The attack on Gopher Prairie is announced in the foreword to the novel: Ugly, materialistic, business-oriented, dead to art and complacent in its philistine middle-class values, Gopher Prairie is representative of all American small towns, from Ohio to the Carolinas. Implicit in the foreword is Lewis's satire on the American idea of progress (our Ford automobiles); the coercion of public opinion (what Ole Jenson and Ezra Stowbody think is law); the ugliness of small-town architecture; the materialism of the community (Sam Clark's annual hardware turnover); its bourgeois art (the Rosebud Movie Palace); and its complacent faith in its own middle-class values.

In Gopher Prairie, given her passion for village improvement, Carol takes on the coloration of a flaming radical. Her formal parties are abysmal failures, subsiding finally into Dave Dyer's stunt of the Norwegian and the hen. Her dream of Georgian houses turns into a nightmare. The courthouse project collapses, and she herself is virtually ostracized by the narrow townsfolk who see her as an upstart-outsider with highbrow ideas irrelevant to the snappiest burg in the Middle West. Her failure to create a beautiful environment and a satisfying social life in Gopher Prairie infects her with the Village Virus, which nearly destroys her, as it has already destroyed Guy Pollock.

Main Street thus embodies the conflict between the private ideals of Carol Kennicott and the public values of the great American middle class, as expressed in the social structure of the village and its religious, political, and artistic institutions. Although scores of people in Sauk Centre claimed to see themselves and their neighbors in the novel, Lewis's satire was not intended to ridicule specific people but to attack the social institutions that had shaped them.

Among other things *Main Street* provides a comprehensive social analysis of all the interlocking organizations of the town and its people. All of them are condemned as traps or threats to individualism and the free expression of the self. The first of these traps is the Family itself. Lewis capitalizes the term, as Edith Wharton does in *The Custom of the Country*, in order to indicate its power as a corporate structure.[20] Lewis himself was never happy as a "family man," abandoned his wife for weeks at a time, ignored his children, and resented their claims upon him. But the individual trapped here is the woman, who is beginning to rebel against the role created for her by the fact of biology and masculine domination in society. Carol has brains but no useful or rewarding work. She has to beg her husband for money. She is trapped by the babies who limit her to domestic activities. And relatives take liberties with her because, after all, they are "kin." As a consequence, Carol feels imprisoned in her own household. The stale, airless rooms symbolize the stultification of the home as Carol gradually smothers. Because of her entrapment, Carol flees her home—both figuratively and literally—in search of freedom and fulfillment. Many writers have dealt with male resentment against the restrictions of family life, but few before Lewis attacked the fundamental unit of society and the foundation of social morality, the home itself—and from a woman's point of view—as destructive to the development of the individual personality.

Like Cooper, Howells, and Mrs. Wharton, Lewis was also attentive to the meaning of religion in American society. Lewis found American religious life in the village to be narrowing and spiritually stultifying. Though its theology is offensively sanguinary ("Are you washed in the blood of the Lamb?") and irrelevant ("the genealogy of Shamsherai was a valuable ethical problem for children to think about"), it was "still, in Gopher Prairie, the strongest of forces compelling respectability" (MS, 326–32). Lewis's opposition to the fundamentalist church as an enemy of individualism would eventually lead him to attack it in *Elmer Gantry* as an institution composed of fools ministered to by rascals. But here Lewis satisfied himself with a general attack on its hypocrisy and irrelevance. Will "believed in the Christian religion, and never thought about it; he believed in the church and seldom went near it; he was shocked by Carol's lack of faith, and wasn't quite sure what was the nature of the faith that she lacked." Religion, moreover, was for Lewis just the opiate of the underprivileged that Marx claimed it to be. "Sure, religion is a fine influence—got to have it to keep the lower classes in order—fact, it's the only thing that appeals to a lot of those fellows and makes 'em respect the rights of property. And I guess this theology is O.K.," Will goes on, "lot of wise old coots figured it all out, and they knew more about it than we do" (MS, 328). Carol's intuition is right that no church which supports the Reverend Zitterel and has produced the Widow Bogart can minister to her spiritual needs. As a consequence, she flees from the constraints of home life and the irrelevancies of the church to other institutions—like The Jolly Seventeen, "the social cornice of Gopher Prairie" (*MS*, 86).

The Jolly Seventeen was "the country club, the diplomatic set, the St. Cecelia, the Ritz oval room, the Club de Vingt" rolled into one. "To belong," Lewis blandly observed, "was to be 'in' " (*MS*, 86). Carol is "in" by virtue of her social position as the wife of one of the town doctors, but her opinions about the wages to be paid to hired girls, about the beauty of the town, and her "Twin Cities style," eventually result in her being ostracized. Will argues that Gopher Prairie is "an independent town, not like these Eastern holes where you have to watch your step all the time, and live up to fool demands and social customs, and a lot of old tabbies always busy criticizing" (*MS*, 98). But Carol's exclusion from The Jolly Seventeen makes it clear that private opinions are intolerable in the American small town's social life. For The Jolly Seventeen, "bridge is half the fun of life," and the other half is dull parties with repeated stunts and tasty eats. Beyond this limit Carol dare not go.

The Thanatopsis Club, a woman's study group of Gopher Prairie, might have been an instrument for liberalizing the community, for elevating its taste, for carrying on Carol's "campaign against village sloth" (*MS*, 128). But although it is described as a "cozy group" which "puts you in touch with all the intellectual thoughts that are going on everywhere" (*MS*, 124), it turns out to be just a group of aimless matrons with no capacity for impersonal thought. Far from helping Carol to liberalize the culture of the village, they actually defeat her attempts to beautify it.

These institutions might have been fatal to anyone less romantic than Carol Kennicott, but she tries to offset them with an organization of her own—the Gopher Prairie Dramatic Association. Carol and Will see plays by Schnitzler, Shaw, Dunsany, and Yeats performed in Minneapolis, and although Will prefers cowpuncher movies every time to this darn highbrow drama, Carol idealistically believes that Shaw can be performed in Gopher Prairie. But her experiment is bound to fail. The boosting Chautauqua and the Rosebud Movie Palace—with its weekly equivalent of "Mack Schnarken and the Bathing Suit Babes in a comedy of manners entitled 'Right on the Coco' " (*MS*, 194)—

define the artistic standards of the American village in 1920. Carol's Dramatic Association overrules her and insists on staging "The Girl from Kankakee."

These institutions—the religious, social, educational, and artistic—are, of course, largely the creation of the women of the village. American men, as James, Howells, and Mrs. Wharton uniformly complained, are totally involved in business and have no time for culture or polite manners. In Sinclair Lewis's Middle-Class Empire this generalization also holds true. Lewis had praised "business" in *The Job* and *Free Air* as a civilizing influence in small-town America. But in *Main Street*, thanks to the influence of Mencken, Lewis was feeling his way toward *Babbitt* by attacking the Gopher Prairie Commercial Club—a glorified composite of the Rotary Club, Kiwanis, the Jaycees, Elks, and Oddfellows rolled into one. For the men of the town, this Commercial Club satisfies every social, religious, educational, and artistic aspiration. Civic Boosting is, next to high profits and low taxes, the American businessman's Highest Ideal. But all is not sweetness and light in village commerce, for cutthroat competition is commonplace and a sharp deal is the mark of intellect. Even Will cautions Carol to trade with Jenson and Ludelmeyer, rather than Howland & Gould, because (although "Jenson is tricky—give you short weight—and Ludelmeyer is a shiftless old Dutch hog" [*MS*, 99]),Will doesn't want his grocery money indirectly finding its way into the pockets of Dr. Gould, his chief medical competitor.

In one sense, these institutions reflect the organized public lives of the "aristocracy" of Gopher Prairie. (Lewis may seem to be dealing with a homogeneous bourgeoisie, but he felt that enough social discriminations existed in America's small towns to warrant use of the term.) But in this world the "aristocrats" really have no social life. For it cannot be denied that "there is not even the social fabric which must be the basis of social life. There is no social organism, because what should be its members are detached and unrelated, like a heap of pebbles. What is portrayed for us is a social chaos which is singularly standardized and uniform, of which the outstanding qualities are dullness and intolerance, a prying and repressive and negative moralism, and an appearance of hypocrisy which arises from a manifest incongruity between action and professed belief, between cherished sentimental illusions and peccant behavior."[21] Still, Lewis intended the village to be a mock-up of a social organism, and it does have its aristocracy—composed of "all persons engaged in a profession, or earning more than twenty-five hundred dollars a year, or possessed of grandparents born in America" (*MS*, 74).

In general, exponents of the wholesome character of middle western social life have denied that aristocracies of the sort Lewis describes existed in our small towns. Meredith Nicholson argued in *The Valley of Democracy* that "in the smaller Western towns, especially where the American stock is dominant, lines of social demarcation are usually obscure to the vanishing-point."[22] *Main Street* supports this claim as to the leveling character of society, but the "old aristocracy" of Gopher Prairie, built on essentially eastern, Anglo-Saxon foundations, was dying out. A new aristocracy had arisen—an "aristocracy" of shopkeepers, drummers, and salesmen: "The town was as heterogeneous as Chicago. Norwegians and Germans owned stores. The social leaders were common merchants. Selling nails was considered as sacred as banking. These upstarts ... had no dignity" (*MS*, 48). Gradually the older aristocrats are isolated and finally become powerless. Far from having the kind of social power that the van der Luydens exercise in Mrs. Wharton's Old New York, Mr. Stowbody and his class are obsolete; though they are respected as squires of the old school in Gopher Prairie, they are also ignored.

Lewis's jibe at the new class of shopkeepers suggests how ambivalent he felt about the decline of the old American stock, like the friends of Dr. E. J. Lewis. His ambivalence is an instance of the need felt by defenders of the small town in the Middle West to have it both ways—to offer the example of a purely democratic social organization and yet retain the kind of cultural hierarchy traditionally associated with the social organization of "Eastern towns." Meredith Nicholson is again the touchstone of these matters because he reflected unconsciously the contradiction of these social attitudes. In *The Valley of Democracy* he complained that Henry James had ignored the West in his social survey *The American Scene*. Nicholson praised "the dignity and richness" of "polite society" in the West—meaning the aristocracies of the towns—despite the pioneer background of the region: "If an aristocracy is a desirable thing in America [notice that he appeals to the snobbery of those readers who might think it is], the West can, in its cities great and small, produce it, and its quality and tone will be found quite similar to the aristocracy of older communities. We of the West," he went on, deplore fictional characters "whose chief purpose is to illustrate the raw vulgarity of Western civilization. Such persons are no more acceptable socially in Chicago, Minneapolis, or Denver than they are in New York."[23]

Yet the decline of the old American stock and the assimilation of the small-time businessman into the new "aristocracy" of the town left Gopher Prairie virtually two social classes: the "aristocracy" and the "peasants." In part the social classes were divided along occupational lines. The peasants are farmers and immigrants—Scandahoofians, Dutchers, Norskes, and Svenkas, as the townspeople call them.

As Stow Persons has pointed out, it was widely believed by observers of American society during the period of our greatest immigration that "the immigrant must be 'assimilated' in the sense of being absorbed into the population through the loss of his peculiarities; he must successfully undergo a process of 'Americanization' whereby he was made to approximate an ideal American type."[24] Lewis was appalled that such an obligation should be enjoined on the foreigner. He lamented that "Scandinavians Americanize only too quickly" and he regretted that they "permit their traditions to be snatched away."[25] This process deprived our Gopher Prairies of virtually the only color, variety, and charm they possess. Carol saw "Scandinavian women zealously exchanging their spiced puddings and red jackets for fried pork chops and congealed white blouses, trading the ancient Christmas hymns of the fjords for 'She's My Jazzland Cutie,' being Americanized into uniformity, and in less than a generation losing in the grayness whatever pleasant new customs they might have added to the life of the town" (*MS*, 265–66). The children of the immigrants, in ready-made clothes, complete the process, and "sound American customs" absorb another alien invasion without a trace.

But thanks to an economic system that held the farmer in bondage to the town businessmen, even the native-born Yankee farmers belong to this peasant class. Like most other Americans, Carol "had always maintained that there is no American peasantry, and she sought now to defend her faith by seeing imagination and enterprise in the young Swedish farmers, and in a traveling man working over his order-blanks. But the older people, Yankees as well as Norwegians, Germans, Finns, Canucks, had settled into submission to poverty. They were peasants, she groaned" (*MS*, 22). The way out of the peasant class was that taken by thousands of farmers in the early years of the century: they left the farms for the towns and cities and took up a life of business, selling, or industry. As long as they stuck to the farms and tried to grind out a meager living they were despised by the parasitic townspeople. Apparently, Lewis observed, the farmers were ridiculed because they had not "reached the social heights of selling thread and buttons" (*MS*, 57).

It would be a mistake to assume that Sinclair Lewis was wholly sympathetic to the farmers. One of the subjects he explores in *Main Street* is the relevance for the modern age of "pioneer values," as embodied in the struggling farmers. Out on a tramp through the prairie, Carol and Will discover "the bold stone house in which General Sibley, the king of fur-traders, built in 1835, with plaster of river mud, and ropes of twisted grass for laths," a house that "has an air of centuries." In this episode Lewis symbolizes, through an old house, as Mrs. Wharton had done in *Hudson River Bracketed*, the question of a usable history, "a common American past" (*MS*, 16). Carol decides that "the history of the pioneers was the panacea for Gopher Prairie, for all America" (*MS*, 150): a return to the simplicity and heroism of families that teamed it with oxen, lived in sod huts or log cabins, and raised up great fields of wheat and corn. Their values, Carol thinks, must surely provide an answer to the ugliness and dull conformity that characterize Gopher Prairie.

Yet when Carol approaches the Champ Perrys, old-timers who

were among the first settlers in Gopher Prairie, to learn "the principles by which Gopher Prairie should be born again" in the age
of aeroplanes and syndicalism, she is appalled at the pioneer's
system of values:

The Baptist Church (and, somewhat less, the Methodist, Congrega-
tional, and Presbyterian Churches) is the perfect, the divinely or-
dained standard in music, oratory, philanthropy, and ethics. . . . The
Republican Party, the Grand Old Party of Blaine and McKinley, is
the agent of the Lord and of the Baptist Church in temporal affairs.
. . . All socialists ought to be hanged. . . . "Harold Bell Wright is a
lovely writer, and he teaches such good morals in his novels, and
folks say he's made prett' near a million dollars out of 'em. . . ." People who make more than ten thousand a year or less than eight hundred are wicked. . . . Europeans are still wickeder. . . . It doesn't hurt
any to drink a glass of beer on a warm day, but anybody who touches
wine is headed straight for hell. . . . Virgins are not so virginal as they
used to be. . . . Nobody needs drug-store ice cream; pie is good enough
for anybody. . . . The farmers want too much for the salaries they
pay. There would be no more trouble or discontent in the world if
everybody worked as hard as Pa did when he cleared our first farm.
[*MS,* 152–53]

In his satire on the middle western farmer, as embodying a
debasement of pioneer values, Sinclair Lewis touched on one of
the revered myths of the American national consciousness—the
romantic view that a great land, the prairie, makes great men.
Frederick Jackson Turner had advanced the idea in the nineties
that the pioneer experience in the American Middle West had
served to shape the grand social and political institutions of the
real America. If the effete and bloodless East looked toward
Europe and the past, the vigorous Middle West looked westward
to the future. *My Ántonia* and *O Pioneers!* hymned its litany of
greatness and progress and beauty. This is the romantic view
which Carol carries with her to Gopher Prairie. " 'It's a glorious
country; a land to be big in,' she crooned" (*MS,* 25).

Lewis's prose is charged with the sarcasm of a man who believes that, after all, the god that made the prairies taunted the
great land with little men. Carol finally comes to see that " 'it's
one of our favorite American myths that broad plains necessarily
make broad minds, and high mountains make high purpose. I

thought that myself, when I first came to the prairie' " (*MS*, 343). And she advises Erik Valborg to go East and "grow up with the revolution!" (*MS*, 343).

Lewis's preoccupation with the "social revolution," however based on wishful thinking, implies a serious critique of our lip-service to democracy as a social value. The townspeople like to brag about how democratic they are. But when Carol asks Will whether he would go hunting with his barber, he is an accurate index of town sentiment in suggesting that there is "no use running this democracy thing into the ground" (*MS*, 42). Miles Bjornstam, the "Red Swede," is ostracized because he is a socialist, and "pro-Germans"—those with unpopular views— are shamelessly repressed. The seeds of native fascism, Lewis held, are deeply ingrained in the political values of Main Street, and for this reason he espoused a vague radicalism, which took the form of a brief membership in the Socialist party of New York and of prophecies like "The Passing of Capitalism," published by the *Nation* in 1914. Though the rhetoric is exaggerated, the violence of feeling in "aristocrat" Percy Bresnahan's tirade against socialist philosophies is not. Bresnahan defends the Hohenzollern Empire because "the Kaiser and the Junkers keep a firm hand on a lot of these red agitators who'd be worse than a king if they could get control." Bresnahan predicts the return of the czar to power in Russia: "You read a lot about his retiring and about his being killed, but I know he's got a big army back of him, and he'll show these damn agitators, lazy beggars hunting for a soft berth bossing the poor goats that fall for 'em, he'll show 'em where they get off!" (*MS*, 280–81).

The conditions of life in Gopher Prairie place a special pressure on the town's aristocracy: they must set the behavioral standards. Yet the nature of life in Gopher Prairie, where everybody lives in a fishbowl, is repressive, and the frustrations of that life erupt in their sexual behavior. No one has properly remarked, it seems to me, how thoroughly Lewis has described the extent to which the social conditions of life in small-town America are sexually frustrating. (This phenomenon *has* been remarked of Sherwood Anderson's treatment of the village.) " 'There's one thing that's the matter with Gopher Prairie, at least with the ruling-class (there is a ruling-class, despite all our professions of democracy),' " Guy Pollock says. " 'And the penalty we tribal rulers pay is that our subjects watch us every minute. We can't get wholesomely drunk and relax. We have to be so correct about sex morals, and inconspicuous clothes, and doing our commercial trickery only in the traditional ways, that none of us can live up to it, and we become horribly hypocritical' " (*MS*, 158). The sexual implications of this view are borne out in the lives of dozens of the townspeople—Vida Sherwin, Raymie Wutherspoon, the Widow Bogart, her son Cy Bogart, Dave and Maud Dyer, and Will and Carol, who eventually separate, when Carol goes to Washington.

In the end, though she runs away, Carol elects to return to Gopher Prairie and continue asking questions and ridiculing social aberrations. She no longer rages at individuals: "Not individuals but institutions are the enemies," Lewis wrote, "and they most afflict the disciples who the most generously serve them. They insinuate their tyranny under a hundred guises and pompous names," which he enumerated as "Polite Society, the Family, the Church, Sound Business, the Party, the Country, the Superior White Race; and the only defense against them, Carol beheld, is unembittered laughter" (*MS*, 430). She cannot change Gopher Prairie—she looks to the next generation to do that—nor will she admit that a regimen of dish-washing is enough to satisfy the American woman: "I may not have fought the good fight, but I have kept the faith' " (*MS*, 451). She does not save Gopher Prairie, but she does, apparently, save her soul.

I say "apparently" because two issues have since arisen concerning the social significance of *Main Street*, issues not immediately apparent to some readers, including Sinclair Lewis himself. One had to do with the consistency of Lewis's feeling toward Gopher Prairie and the other with his attitude toward his heroine. Carl Van Doren called the novel a document in "the revolt from the village" and emphasized its relationship with *Madame Bovary* and Masters's *The Spoon River Anthology*. Lewis denied that the novel owed anything to these works and rejected Van Doren's claim that he had no love for the villages of America and wanted desperately to escape Sauk Centre. In January 1921

Lewis told William Woodward that, "Mind you, I like G.P., all the G.P.'s; I couldn't write about them so ardently if I didn't."[26] He also told August Derleth that there was nothing to the revolt from the village idea, that he "got out of Sauk Center [*sic*] because there weren't any opportunities for me there. . . . I put into my books what I saw and what I felt, I didn't think it was rebellious then. I don't think it is now, either."[27] This claim reveals how deeply confused were Lewis's feelings toward Sauk Centre and the social institutions there, and how totally he failed to understand the depth of his own bitterness. He was never able to understand why the townspeople, and particularly his father, resented the book so much.

Nor did Lewis fully understand the ambivalence of his portrait of Carol Kennicott in her campaign to beautify and culturally uplift the town. There is no question that he meant her to be an idealistic rebel against the social order. As "The Thesis of Main Street" suggests, Carol was meant to repudiate among other things, "all manner of kings, noblemen, leaders of society, and their paid or unpaid varlets"; she "most energetically & violently believed that the first duty of mankind is to hang, boil, quarter, & bury beside Hohenzollern & the 400, all brisk, spectacled, motor-driving business men who say 'Hell bosh! I don't see any of this poverty you hear these agitators yammering so much about. I tell you I pay my employees only too well.' "[28]

But the Carol in the novel is quite otherwise. Mencken observed that Carol's "superior culture is, after all, chiefly bogus—that the oafish Kennicott, in more ways than one, is actually better than she is. Her dream of converting a Minnesota prairie town into a sort of Long Island suburb, with overtones of Greenwich Village and the Harvard campus, is quite as absurd as his dream of converting it into a second Minneapolis, with overtones of Gary, Ind., and Paterson, N.J."[29] Meredith Nicholson agreed: "The trouble with Mr. Lewis's Carol Kennicott was that she really had nothing to offer Gopher Prairie that sensible self-respecting people anywhere would have welcomed."[30] Harland Hatcher called her "a silly girl, dreamy, naive, impractical, unsettled by her 'culture' like hundreds of other co-eds of her day," and he argued that "it was right and proper for the natives to resent her puerile superiorities and to consider her flip and stuck-up and faintly scarlet when she spoke of legs, silk stockings, high wages for servants, and B.V.D.s in mixed company."[31]

But Lewis hardly regarded her in this way when he wrote the novel, for she represented the best cultural standard he knew at the time. But as people like Mencken ridiculed her, as his marriage to Gracie (the model of Carol) disintegrated, as he came under the wrath of his own father and townsfolk, Lewis's conception of what he had meant shifted. Throughout his career he was to wobble back and forth between the poles represented by Carol and Will, between the cultural values, traditions, and manners of the "East" and the dull but hearty good-fellowship, the mindless but positive optimism and the mannerless informality of the "West." *Main Street* may be a novel about a girl who fails to change Gopher Prairie and ends up struggling for her own faith. But it should not be overlooked that in the clash of cultural values, stodgy old Will has the last word: "Say, did you notice whether the girl put that screw-driver back?" (*MS*, 432).

III

The reaction to *Main Street* was instantaneous and noisy. Scores of women in small towns wrote Lewis to thank him for having understood them. Village Jaycees fumed. Sales soared. Reviewers cheered and howled. *Main Street* was parodied and answered in *Jane Street*, *Ptomaine Street*, Meredith Nicholson's *The Man in the Street*, and Booth Tarkington's *Alice Adams*. Lewis egged his critics on, sponsoring Frazier Hunt's *Sycamore Bend*, a defense of the small town by one of his friends. In the introduction to it he satirized those who pitied the villagers for "not knowing gunmen, burlesque girls, boot-leggers, and gum-chewing stenographers of the cities."[32] Other novelists praised his analysis of the manners of small-town, middle-class American life. Scott Fitzgerald, another Minnesota writer just embarking on his own career as a novelist of jazz-age manners, called *Main Street* "the best American novel."[33] Edith Wharton liked it, and John Galsworthy, whose attack on the Family in *The Forsyte Saga* was as bitter as that in *Main Street*, also praised it—doubtless because, as Grace Lewis pointed out, "the British were charmed to find in this book their cherished belief confirmed that the States were still inhabited by the tobacco-chewing oafs who had horrified Mrs. Trollope in 1853."[34]

In the deliberations for the Pulitzer Prize novel of 1920, Robert Morss Lovett, Stuart Pratt Sherman, and Hamlin Garland, the jury, recommended to the trustees of Columbia University, who administer the prize, that the award be given for *Main Street*. The trustees rejected the recommendation of the jury and awarded the prize instead to Edith Wharton's *The Age of Innocence*. Although it is not generally remembered, the very terms of the Pulitzer Prize are phrased so that the award must be given to a novel of manners, to "the American novel published during the year which shall best present the wholesome atmosphere of American life, and the highest standard of American manners and manhood."

The jury members who had recommended *Main Street* were appalled, and Robert Morss Lovett addressed an open letter to *The New Republic* in which he praised *The Age of Innocence* and declared Mrs. Wharton to be worthy of any distinction Columbia wished to confer on her, but pointed out, for the record, that the committee had chosen *Main Street*. Lewis was outraged at "the *Main Street* burglary," and in 1926, when *Arrowsmith* won the prize, he rejected it—listing as his reasons the mistreatment of *Main Street* and *Babbitt*, the arrogance of any committee in claiming to choose a best novel, and the fact that the jury claimed their award for "*the* in-every-way 'best novel of the year,'" instead of, as the award stated, for the "best portraying the highest standard of American morals and mannners." He also argued that to give a prize "for the American novel published during the year which shall best present the wholesome atmosphere of American life, and the highest standard of American manners and manhood" is essentially to appraise novels not on the basis of "their actual literary merit but in obedience to whatever code of Good Form may chance to be popular at the moment."[35]

Though he felt that he had been robbed, however, on one count he was somewhat satisfied—the choice of *The Age of Innocence*. For Edith Wharton, long a favorite, he considered to be one of the greatest living novelists of manners. So great was his admiration for her, in fact, that he asked her permission to dedicate *Babbitt* to her. From France she wrote him that "when I found the prize sh[oul]d really have been yours, but was withdrawn because your book (I quote from memory) had 'offended a number of prominent persons in the Middle West,' disgust was added to despair.—Hope returns to me, however, with your letter, & with the enclosed article, just received.—Some sort of standard *is* emerging from the welter of cant & Sentimentality," she replied, "& if two or three of us are gathered together, I believe we can still save Fiction in America." She thanked him for his praise of her fiction—"the first sign I have ever had—literally—that 'les jeunes' at home had ever read a word of me." *Main Street* and *Susan Lenox*, she observed, "have been the only things out of America that have made me cease to despair of the republic—of letters; so you can imagine what a pleasure it is to know that you have read *me*, & cared, & understood."[36] The obvious rapport between Lewis and Mrs. Wharton, so evident in his enthusiasm for her fiction and her warmth in reply, led Arthur Mizener, in fact, to call Lewis "the Edith Wharton of the provincial middle class" because, like her, he knew his class from the inside and, like her, he was profoundly alienated from it.[37]

≫⛐ F. SCOTT FITZGERALD

The Romantic Tragedian as Moral Fabulist

When Scott Fitzgerald died in 1940, his novels were little read, very nearly out of print, and he was generally regarded as a literary failure. For many readers Fitzgerald had been dismissed with scorn for "gnawing gin in silver slabs and sniffling about the sham and tinsel of it all." For Westbrook Pegler and his friends, Fitzgerald recalled only "the queer bunch of undisciplined and self-indulgent brats who were determined not to pull their weight in the boat and wanted the world to drop everything and sit down and bawl with them."[1]

So totally has Fitzgerald been identified with the tawdriness of the twenties that recent critics have tried to dissociate him, almost entirely, from the period in which he achieved his greatness and from the flamboyant role he played in his time—the role of Social Historian of the Jazz Age. It is "unfair to Fitzgerald," Weller Embler has objected, "that he should be read always as the spokesman for the febrile gay and the merely sad."[2] A writer in the *Times Literary Supplement* noted that "Fitzgerald's habitual connotation in many people's minds with the 'jazz age' " had "obscured his merits,"[3] and William Goldhurst has recently argued that "Fitzgerald accomplished more than a chronicle of Jazz Age belles and playboys, with whom he has been consistently associated."[4] Even Arthur Mizener has complained that a just evaluation of Fitzgerald's artistry is impeded by the fact that he "began his career with a great popular success" (*This Side of*

Paradise) which "connected him in many people's minds with 'the Jazz Age,' so that he was for them both the historian—'the laureate'—of the post-war generation and its exemplar."[5]

But to dissociate Fitzgerald from the period in which he did his best writing and from the material he drew upon is actually to do a disservice to one of America's finest twentieth-century novelists of manners. For Fitzgerald was intensely aware of period values, of the differences in manners which distinguish generations, and of the demarcations which can signal a new moral era in the national experience. "At certain moments," he wrote in his notes for *The Last Tycoon,* "one man appropriates to himself the total significance of a time and place."[6] Fitzgerald knew himself to be such a man, a man of his time, a representative of the new postwar generation. To preserve his time in the forms of art, he tried hard "to catch the color of every passing year," Malcolm Cowley has noted, "its slang, its dance steps, its songs (he kept making lists of them in his notebooks), its favorite quarterbacks, and the sort of clothes and emotions its people wore."[7] Fitzgerald told Maxwell Perkins that he wanted "to recapture the exact feel of a moment in time and space."[8] And this is exactly what, as a novelist of manners, he did.

In the decade following World War I, which Frederick Lewis Allen has called "the decade of Bad Manners," the United States underwent a social revolution for which F. Scott Fitzgerald provided the clearest mirror in fiction. A "first-class revolt against the accepted American order," it was marked by the emergence of the politically emancipated and economically independent new woman—in rolled hose, rouge, and lipstick; it offered novel kinds of mixed social experience—the cocktail party and the prohibition speakeasy with its bathtub gin and jazz bands; and it was characterized by the moral libertarianism of the Hollywood vamps, of sex and confession magazines, by Ford's rolling bedroom, and the gospel of Freud. And "with the change in manners went an inevitable change in morals," as Allen has noted, a change characterized by greater sexual freedom, tolerance, experimentation, and self-indulgence.[9]

Fitzgerald never understood all of the causes of this revolution in the social and moral traditions of the nation. He was not a historian, philosopher, or sociologist and had no objective ground from which to appraise it. And certainly, as Henry Dan Piper has pointed out, he cannot "be credited with having engineered this revolution in manners single-handedly." But he understood it intuitively, described it, and popularized it. He led the way and became its spokesman. He knew the manners of his Jazz Age contemporaries, and he was able to anticipate the moral gestures of his generation. "The skeptic has only to examine back-files of the *Post*, and other popular magazines," as Piper notes, "to see how quickly the unconventional attitudes and values described in Fitzgerald's early stories were reflected in the magazine advertisements as well as in the pictures illustrating his fiction."[10]

Most of what Fitzgerald wrote was profoundly true of the time and place in which he lived. In his first novel, *This Side of Paradise*, as John O'Hara has observed, "the people were right, the talk was right, the clothes, the cars were real...."[11] Even Arthur Mizener has conceded that "the substance out of which Fitzgerald constructed his stories . . . was American, perhaps more completely American than that of any other writer of his time."[12] To praise Fitzgerald as the Social Historian of the Jazz Age is therefore to pay homage to his powers of observation and intelligence in imaginatively recreating the socially significant detail in the form of art, to praise his gift for appropriating the moral fact and transforming it into the felt experience of his times. Fitzgerald achieves more than a social record, of course, and I would be the last to deny him the high praise he deserves for the subtlety of his emotional sensibility and the lyric prose in which he told the story of his contemporaries. Nor do I wish to slight the obvious power with which his best work rises from fact to satisfying symbolism. The necessity of the artist, Fitzgerald told Dayton Kohler, is continually to revise and polish his style so as to prevent confusion between art and journalism—a lesson Sinclair Lewis might well have heeded in *Main Street*. But in attempting to give his own work permanence through a poetic style, symbolism, and myth, Fitzgerald did not disregard our sense of "the way things really are." He made a serious commitment to a realistic notation of the manners of his social world. So fully realized was his fine achievement, so sparely pruned and

artistically shaped, particularly in *The Great Gatsby*, that Fitzgerald indisputably ranks as one of the great American novelists
of manners in this century.

I

This Side of Paradise (1920) is a quest novel portraying in
Amory Blaine's adventures a generation of young people transforming the society in which they had grown up. "I'm restless,"
Amory tells Jesse Ferrenby's father, "My whole generation is
restless."[13] These youths had begun to question "aloud the institutions that Amory and countless others before him had ques-
tioned so long in secret" (*TSP*, 131). The Princeton social
system, organized religion, the family, capitalism—nothing escaped the criticism of youth in the twenties. Particularly the
morality of society, as reflected in its manners, came under severe
attack. The "terrible speed" who told Amory that she had kissed
dozens of men and supposed she would kiss dozens more was no
different from thousands of her contemporaries who engaged in
"that great current American phenomenon, the 'petting party'"
(*TSP*, 64). One of the values of *This Side of Paradise*, on this
score, is that it dramatizes class attitudes toward sexual promiscuity giving way to generational attitudes. "None of the Victorian mothers—and most of the mothers were Victorian—had
any idea how casually their daughters were accustomed to be
kissed." For these women such behavior was a mark of the lower
class: "'*Servant*-girls are that way,' says Mrs. Huston-Carmelite
to her daughter. 'They are kissed first and proposed to afterward'" (*TSP*, 64). But as the novel makes clear, the Popular
Daughter had undergone a steady descent from "belle" to "flirt"
to "flapper" and "baby vamp": "Amory saw girls doing things
that even in his memory would have been impossible: eating
three-o'clock, after-dance suppers in impossible cafés, talking of
every side of life with an air half of earnestness, half of mockery,
yet with a furtive excitement that Amory considered stood for a
real moral letdown. But he never realized how wide-spread it was
until he saw the cities between New York and Chicago as one
vast juvenile intrigue" (*TSP*, 65).

Fitzgerald's revelation of this juvenile intrigue created a sensation among mothers, ministers, editors, and other public and private moralists. J. W. Aldridge has remarked that "it was an intrigue of manners merely, conducted by glittering children who could hardly bear to be touched. . . .[14] But the facts of our social history suggest that it was a conspiracy to revolutionize manners *and* morals. Fitzgerald later observed that "the first social revelation created a sensation out of all proportion to its novelty. As far back as 1915 the unchaperoned young people of the smaller cities had discovered the mobile privacy of the automobile given to young Bill at sixteen to make him 'self-reliant.' At first petting was a desperate adventure even under such favorable conditions, but presently confidences were exchanged and the old commandment broke down." But petting, "in its more audacious manifestations," Fitzgerald went on, "was confined to the wealthier classes—among other young people the old standard prevailed until after the War, and a kiss meant that a proposal was expected, as young officers in strange cities sometimes discovered to their dismay."[15]

Fitzgerald's distinction between the moral behavior of city and small-town youth confirms the observation that *This Side of Paradise* did in fact introduce to eastern young women "a brand-new kind of heroine—an emancipated American girl whose behavior was quite different from the code of manners to which they were expected to conform." If the western girl was "a product of the more free-and-easy frontier, the Eastern girl was still subject to such old-fashioned European customs as the chaperon, an elaborately formal system of etiquette, and an educational philosophy which advocated the separation of the sexes and the incarceration of the girls into prisonlike boarding schools." Arbiters of manners like Emily Post and Mrs. Frank Learned, author of *Etiquette of New York Today*, might raise their eyebrows at the freedoms permitted unmarried girls in the barbarian West. But Fitzgerald had "naively assumed that, in describing the girls with whom he had grown up in St. Paul, he was describing the behavior of most wealthy American girls. No wonder he was so puzzled by the Boston and Philadelphia ministers and editors who accused him of trying to corrupt their daughters, and puzzled by the daughters themselves who saw his novel as a clarion call to revolt."[16]

In his own copy of Joyce's *Dubliners*, Fitzgerald wrote that he was "interested in the individual only in his rel[ation] to Society."[17] That social interest is reflected in Fitzgerald's essays on the Jazz Age, which clarify the portrait of Amory's generation as it undertook the "greatest, gaudiest spree in history." He had plenty to tell about the Jazz Age—"its splendid generosities, its outrageous corruptions and the tortuous death struggle of the old America in prohibition." And all of his stories "had a touch of disaster in them."[18] He was able to tell the story of the Jazz Age because he stood at the dividing line between two generations—self-consciously drawn to the riotous excesses of youth, but mature enough to think that "living wasn't the reckless, careless business these people thought—this generation just younger than me."[19] He called it "the wildest of all generations, the generation which had been adolescent during the war," and he noted how they "brusquely shouldered my contemporaries out of the way and danced into the limelight." It was a generation of flappers and sheiks bent on corrupting its elders—and succeeding ("people over thirty, the people all the way up to fifty, had joined in the dance"),[20] but it eventually overreached itself, Fitzgerald felt, "less through lack of morals than through lack of taste."[21]

The phenomenon which Fitzgerald witnessed in the twenties was the decline in social authority of the Old New York 400, with its exclusive aristocracy of millionaires, and the formation of a *new* society incorporating elements from all levels in the social hierarchy: "The blending of the bright, gay, vigorous elements began then," he wrote, "and for the first time there appeared a society a little livelier than the solid mahogany dinner parties of Emily Price Post." As a new social phenomenon this group produced, according to Fitzgerald, the cocktail party, Park Avenue wit, and a sophisticated haven for the educated European. And "for just a moment, before it was demonstrated that I was unable to play the role, I, who knew less of New York than any reporter of six months' standing and less of its society than any hall-room boy in a Ritz stag line, was pushed into the position not only of spokesman for the time but of the typical product of that same moment."[22]

So much cash was flowing around in Fitzgerald's crowd during the Jazz Age that "charm, notoriety, mere good manners, weighed more than money as a social asset." But as the decade wore on, "things were getting thinner and thinner as the eternal necessary human values tried to spread over all that expansion." Finally, "the most expensive orgy in history" came to an abrupt end when "the utter confidence which was its essential prop" received "an enormous jolt" on Black Friday in 1929, and the whole "flimsy structure" came crashing down. "It was borrowed time anyhow," Fitzgerald observed, "the whole upper tenth of a nation living with the insouciance of grand ducs and the casualness of chorus girls." Afterwards, during the thirties, in the midst of the depression, it all seemed "rosy and romantic to us who were young then, because we will never feel quite so intensely about our surroundings any more."[23]

There were instantaneous reactions to the extravagance in morals and manners of the Younger Generation, to which Fitzgerald's fiction had alerted the rest of the country. "Mr. Grundy," writing on "Polite Society" in the *Atlantic Monthly* in 1920, argued that even though customs change, every generation and nationality had always produced the two flowers of civilization—the Lady and Gentleman. But thanks to the mores of flaming youth, feminine modesty and manly chivalry were dead.[24] Katherine Fullerton Gerould, consistently paired with Edith Wharton as a Jamesian novelist of manners, sustained Mr. Grundy's attack in "Reflections of a Grundy Cousin," also published that year in the *Atlantic*. She cited the causes of the revolution in manners and morals as the motorcar, the movies, the war, the extreme opinions of radical intellectuals, the corrupting luxuries possible to the nouveaux riches, prohibition, and the collapse of religious values. Ultimately, she found "the lack of religion more responsible than war or movies or motor-cars for the vulgarity of our manners and the laxity of our morals. . . ."[25]

But the Younger Generation would not be lectured by the genteel Grundy tribe. John F. Carter rose to their defense in "These Wild Young People—By One of Them." Complaining that "hardly a week goes by that I do not read some indignant treatise depicting our extravagance, the corruptions of our manners, the futility of our existence," Carter enumerated what to him were the *real* causes of the social revolution. The older generation, he argued, ruined the world before handing it on. The idealism of the generation of the 1890s was phony, and older people resented the frankness with which it was exposed by the youngsters. The Younger Generation, he argued, had seen history accelerated, had witnessed man's beastliness and were no longer babes in the woods. We are too busy, he told the Grundyists, for "the noble procrastinations of modesty or for the elaborate rigmarole of chivalry. . . ."[26] Carter was joined almost immediately by his feminine counterpart, "A Last Year's Débutante," who ended the series of charges and countercharges with "Good-Bye, Dear Mr. Grundy." Sizing up the generational gap, she argued that "we are at war, and we may as well acknowledge it. We are just as different in language and customs as if we belonged to different nations instead of different ages. We are foreordained enemies, and we youngsters are not ready to appeal to a court of arbitration, even when justice is administered by so neutral a judge as you try to be."[27] The moral unity of the "civilized" world had so deteriorated, it seemed, that Cornelia James Cannon was moved to ask "Can Our Civilization Maintain Itself?"[28] How contemporary these arguments sound in the 1970s!

Throughout the acrimonious skirmishing between the younger and older generations in the 1920s, Fitzgerald's position was somewhat anomalous. He was, whether he wanted to be or not, the spokesman for youth. His public life with Zelda seemed a sordid justification of the oldsters' worst fears. But Fitzgerald saw with dazzling precision that "a whole race" was "going hedonistic, deciding on pleasure,"[29] and he knew that they were riding for a fall, that a real moral letdown was in store for them. He loved the flamboyant style of the young people, and he also recognized how false were some of the accusations against them. Fitzgerald "knew the absurdity of confusing its trivial manners and its serious morals, of supposing that a particular way of dancing was 'an offense against womanly purity' and rolled stockings identical with sexual promiscuity. He knew from experience that within the emerging system of manners the old distinctions still held, that among his contemporaries there were still the wise and the foolish, the brave and the cowardly, the good and the bad."[30]

But Fitzgerald could not help admiring what he saw, particularly when the new libertarianism asserted itself in an atmosphere of wealth, sophistication, and aristocratic taste. He was divided by "the conflict between Fitzgerald the snob and the worshipper of dazzle, and Fitzgerald the judge and moralist."[31] What flawed *This Side of Paradise* was Fitzgerald's failure to achieve adequate artistic detachment from his subject. His notation of the new mores was precise and detailed but Fitzgerald simply could not distance himself enough to criticize them. Years later the mature artist recognized this defect of the novel and said that although it still contained "very real and living" pages, it was marked by an "utter spuriousness."[32]

II

Fitzgerald's natural subject was the sensibility of the good-looking, intelligent, and talented but poor boy among the amoral, insensitive rich. "That was always my experience," he observed in the thirties, "a poor boy in a rich town; a poor boy in a rich boy's school; a poor boy in a rich man's club at Princeton. . . . I have never been able to forgive the rich for being rich, and it has colored my entire life and works."[33] But in the mid-twenties and throughout the depression, critics were less interested in the drama of class mobility than in the social morality of proletarian fiction. Edith Wharton complained that critics tolerated only novels about "the man with the dinner pail." And Fitzgerald resented "the Barnyard Boys" who were "merrily at work getting together epics of the American soil in time for the next publishing season."[34] And when Burton Rascoe criticized *Gatsby* for being isolated from the social reality of American life, Fitzgerald facetiously promised Gilbert Seldes a "serious" novel about "the Great Struggle the American Peasant has with the Soil" with Rascoe as the hero—"as I'm going to try to go to 'life' for my material from now on."[35]

But *The Great Gatsby* (1925) was related to the social reality of American life in two important ways. It was a clear reflection of Fitzgerald's experience as a poor boy on the make, and it held up a very mirror to the moral nature of America in that fascinating decade, the twenties. In addition, the novel was informed with artistic seriousness of a high order. (In this respect, it differs from his play *The Vegetable* of the year before, which contradicted Fitzgerald's democratic beliefs by implying that simple postmen like Jerry Frost are happiest if they accept their modest "social station" and abandon grandiose aspirations to the presidency. The play so reeked of the Baltimore sage that John F. Carter, the *Atlantic* defender of the Younger Generation, argued in the *New York Post* that "the spirit of the play is an obvious act of deference to Mencken's virulent contempt for the American people.")[36] *The Great Gatsby* embodied Fitzgerald's deepest social convictions and reaffirmed his belief that, as a writer, he could be "in this game seriously and for something besides money." He told his aunt and uncle that "if it's necessary to bootlick the pet delusions of the inhabitants of *Main Street* (Have you read it? It's fine!) to make money I'd rather live on less and preserve the one duty of a sincere writer—to set down life as he sees it as gracefully as he knows how."[37]

Reflecting "purely creative work—not trashy imaginings as in my stories but the sustained imagination of a sincere yet radiant world," *The Great Gatsby* was composed with the compression, precision, and subtlety of poetry. Never before had he tried "to keep his artistic conscience as pure as during the ten months put into doing it."[38] He told Max Perkins that it would be "a consciously artistic achievement and must depend on that as the first books did not."[39] By August of 1924 he felt bold enough to call *Gatsby* "about the best American novel ever written,"[40] and he described himself as "much better than any of the young Americans *without exception.*" His only fear for the novel was that "people who are perhaps weary of assertive jazz and society novels might . . . dismiss it as 'just another book like his others.'" Fitzgerald asked Perkins to find some appropriate way to advertise the novel, but he warned him to "avoid such phrases [as] 'a picture of New York life,' or 'modern society'—though as that is exactly what the book is it's hard to avoid them. The trouble is so much superficial trash has sailed under those banners."[41]

As a novel of manners *Gatsby* develops two interrelated themes: Jay Gatsby's dream of recapturing a lost love in the inaccessible world of the fashionable rich—its development and disintegration; and the growth of Nick Carraway's moral sensibility as he pieces together Gatsby's story and unravels its meaning. Out of the interrelation of the two emerges a third theme implied in the symbolism of the last page of the novel—a critique of the American dream of romantic wonder. On the literal level the first two themes are interwoven with structural mastery and grace; the third theme is a perfect symbolic fusion of the two. And, as many readers have noted, the point of view—Nick Carraway as interpreter-critic of Gatsby's history—permits Fitzgerald to objectify and divide between two characters his ambivalent feelings about the fascinating but sinister rich and the talented but excluded outsider. In its way the novel resembles James's *Daisy Miller*, in which a young man much like Nick, Ralph Winterbourne, witnesses a tragedy of manners in which a nouveau riche young woman is expelled from the society of the American colony in Rome. And it offers a variation on the theme of *The American*, which James described as a story of a new man "insidiously beguiled and betrayed" at the hands of persons "pretending to the highest civilization and to be of an order in every way superior to his own."[42] But if James's novel is a comic study of the ill-mannered American, Fitzgerald's is a tragic witness to the destruction of an innocent by sophisticated "aristocrats" who prey upon his dreams.

Although it is tragic, there are tones of classical satire in *Gatsby* that ought not to be overlooked. At one point Nick speaks of Gatsby's "career as Trimalchio,"[43] and we are reminded that Fitzgerald seriously considered naming the novel *Trimalchio* or *Trimalchio in West Egg*. Tragedy, mystery, and glamour attach to Gatsby in the novel, but it is still instructive to think of him in terms of the comic portrait of Trimalchio in the *Satyricon* of Petronius. A parvenu vulgarian, Trimalchio is a vehicle for Petronian satire on the follies of the nouveau riche—his pride despite humble origins, his lavish but tasteless display of wealth, and his casual assumption that money can buy anything. Like Trimalchio, Gatsby appears from nowhere, squanders his wealth in staging one stupendous party after another, serves up mountains of food and drink, and is the object of ridicule among his guests, none of whom know him.[44]

Gatsby provokes endless speculation and rumor as to his origins and "business gonnegtions." The riddle of his background is solved for us by Nick in a series of carefully suspended revelations which identify his lower-class origin and the immensity of his social ambition. Who Gatsby is—this "elegant young roughneck" whose "elaborate formality of speech just missed being absurd," whose hypercorrect manners jar with his "gorgeous pink rag of a suit," and whose crudities clash with the style of East Egg —is the central question of the novel. What revelation will deliver him from "the womb of his purposeless splendor"; will explain the apparently pointless cocktail parties where Gatsby is a stranger among his guests; will account for his enormous mansion, built during a "period craze" by a brewer who wanted all his neighbors' cottages to have straw-thatched roofs but who was defeated in his ambitions because "Americans, while occasionally willing to be serfs, have always been obstinate about being peasantry"? Nick Carraway could have "accepted without question the information that Gatsby sprang from the swamps of Louisiana or from the lower East Side of New York." Among the patterns of American social mobility these are familiar and comprehensible. But young men did not "drift coolly out of nowhere and buy a palace on Long Island Sound."[45]

What explains Gatsby's splendor is symbolized by the green light at Daisy's dock on East Egg, and at bottom it involves a familiar tragedy of love frustrated by class barriers. Fitzgerald told one of his friends that "the whole idea of Gatsby is the unfairness of a poor young man not being able to marry a girl with money. This theme comes up again and again because I lived it."[46] When, as a young lieutenant, Gatsby falls in love with Daisy, the first "nice" girl that he had ever known, she interposed none of the "indiscernible barbed wire" (*GG*, 149) which always separated him from girls of her class. Though "a penniless young man without a past," Gatsby had been temporarily given social status by an officer's uniform. His lieutenancy gave Daisy "a sense of security," and he "let her believe that he was a person from much the same stratum as herself—that he was able to take care of her." But "he had no such facilities—he had no comfortable family standing behind him." Because she lived in an "artificial world . . . redolent of orchids and pleasant, cheerful snobbery and orchestras which set the rhythm of the year," her style made Gatsby "overwhelmingly aware of the youth and mystery that wealth imprisons and preserves, of the freshness of many clothes, and of Daisy, gleaming like silver, safe and proud above the hot struggles of the poor" (*GG*, 150). He wanted her, and one October night he took her, "because he had no real right to touch her hand" (*GG*, 149).

As Nick interprets Gatsby, there is "something gorgeous about him, some heightened sensitivity to the promises of life," an "extraordinary gift for hope," and a "romantic readiness" (*GG*, 2) for experience that make it quite plausible that he should transform his identity and amass wealth in order to regain the love of the rich girl. Given his romantic idealism, how natural that he should spring from "his Platonic conception of himself," invent "just the sort of Jay Gatsby that a seventeen-year-old boy would be likely to invent" (*GG*, 99) and to be faithful to it until the end. The end *is* tragic because it is only by following the example of Dan Cody in transporting "the savage violence of the frontier brothel and saloon" (*GG*, 101) to his business in the East that Gatsby can accumulate wealth and create the "universe of ineffable gaudiness" (*GG*, 99) which he hopes will draw Daisy back to him. Situated on unfashionable West Egg, his Palace of Lights does not "naturally" attract the Buchanans from East Egg, and Gatsby is forced to arrange an "assignation." It is a mark of his "purity of heart," his "innocence of mere sex," and of his deference to the canons of etiquette governing "introductions" that the assignation is so formal, so "properly chaperoned" and roundabout in its arrangement. His manners are so hypercorrect that he has Nick invite Daisy to his cottage and then he just "drops in": " 'I don't want to do anything out of the way!' he kept saying. 'I want to see her right next door' " (*GG*, 80). Not even Emily Post could have raised an eyebrow.

Gatsby's death is partly the consequence of his own idealism in believing that the past can be retrieved and relived to fulfill one's dreams, and partly the consequence of his failure to see Daisy and Tom for the corrupt spoilers that they are. Gatsby cannot turn back the clock; money will not redeem the time, and Daisy cannot confess that she never loved Tom. Sophisticated but cynical, empty of feeling, she is an unfit object of Gatsby's dream of great wealth, eternal youth, and love. Corrupted by the melody of money, by the materialism of her class, Daisy destroys Gatsby's dream, virtually murders Myrtle Wilson, lies to Tom, escapes justice, and leaves Gatsby to take the rap. But such is the "colossal vitality" of Gatsby's illusion that he hardly thinks of her as an individual; "Daisy" is another Platonic ideal of which the actual woman is merely an imperfect representation. When she visits Gatsby's mansion, sees his estate, weeps over his silk shirts—while Klipspringer plays "The Love Nest" and "Ain't We Got Fun?"—her presence is unreal to Gatsby, and Nick speculates that "there must have been moments even that afternoon when Daisy tumbled short of his dreams . . ." (*GG*, 97). Later, after the Plaza Hotel room argument—staged to the melody of Mendelssohn's Wedding March, which is drifting up from the ballroom below—Gatsby, struggling to hold on to the dying dream, tells Nick that Daisy's love for Tom meant nothing, that it was "just personal" (*GG*, 152).

Fitzgerald's characterization of Tom Buchanan, one of the best portraits in the novel, is, like the portrait of Daisy, an objectification of Fitzgerald's sense of the decline of manners and the decay of civilization. The theme of civilization in decline was a commonplace of the fin de siècle and of the years of Fitzgerald's youth and appeared in works as diverse as Max Nordau's *Degeneration* (1892), Spengler's *The Decline of the West* (1918), the poetry of Pound and Yeats, and in Eliot's *The Waste Land* (1922). Political events such as World War I, the Bolshevik Revolution, and the Greco-Turkish war reinforced the idea that a cycle of civilization was coming to an end. The most significant influence on the theme of social decay in *The Great Gatsby*, according to Fitzgerald, was Spengler's *The Decline of the West*. "I read him [Spengler] the same summer I was writing *The Great Gatsby*," he later wrote, "and I don't think I ever quite recovered from him." Even as late as the eve of World War II Fitzgerald believed that Spengler and Marx were "the only modern philosophers that still manage to make sense in this horrible mess. . . ."[47] Although Fitzgerald's recollection of just when he first read Spengler was probably inaccurate, Spengler argued that every civilization or culture is subject to a cycle of birth, development, and decay predetermined by "historical destiny." Western civilization, he argued, has passed its apogee and is dying; the future belongs to the emerging colored races. What strikes the modern reader is how skillfully Fitzgerald has sketched in the story of Gatsby against the background of a disintegrating American gentry and how his social aspiration is destroyed by a gang of millionaires like the Buchanans—who almost perfectly fulfill Spengler's prophecy of the rise of the "new Caesars" or "monied thugs" who are given to "gang rule," "young peoples hungry for spoil" with "a dominant supercessive idea" of "the world as spoil."[48]

How seriously Fitzgerald believed Spengler's theory is hard to say. *The Decline of the West* was not translated into English until 1926, and Fitzgerald could not read German. But he picked up ideas in the air, as well as in books like Lothrop Stoddard's *The Rising Tide of Color* (1920), and worked them into the novel. In any event, Fitzgerald did subscribe to the general idea that society is threatened by the emergence of insincere, careless, and morally irresponsible rich people who "smashed up things and creatures and then retreated back into their money or their vast carelessness, or whatever it was that kept them together, and let other people clean up the mess they had made . . ." (*GG*, 180–81). On the other hand, Fitzgerald satirized some of Stoddard's views—particularly in Tom Buchanan's wild claim that civilization is threatened by the rise of the colored races: " 'Civilization's going to pieces,' broke out Tom violently. 'I've gotten to be a terrible pessimist about things. Have you read "The Rise of the Colored Empires" by this man Goddard? . . . Well, it's a fine book, and everybody ought to read it. The idea is if we don't look out the white race will be—will be utterly submerged. It's all scientific stuff; it's been proved' " (*GG*, 13). Later, in the Plaza Hotel, though an adulterer, he sees himself as "standing alone on the last barrier of civilization": " 'I suppose the latest thing is to sit back and let Mr. Nobody from Nowhere make love to your wife. Well, if that's the idea you can count me out. . . . Nowadays people begin by sneering at family life and family institutions, and next they'll throw everything overboard and have intermarriage between black and white.' " Nick's judgment on this outburst is correct—"impassioned gibberish" (*GG*, 130). It is the Buchanans and their morally rotten class who constitute the real threat to society. Daisy runs down Myrtle Wilson and Tom virtually murders Gatsby. Their blackest crime, however, is the violation of Gatsby's dream, their desecration of the single ideal to which the whole of his innocence had been sacrificed. (Still, one of the ambiguous episodes in the novel is Nick's glimpse of a limousine crossing Blackwell's Island with "three modish negroes, two bucks and a girl" driven by "a white chauffeur"—a vision suggestive of "the haughty rivalry" [*GG*, 69] between the declining white and emergent Negro races prophesied in *The Decline of the West*.)

The portrait of Meyer Wolfsheim also suggests Fitzgerald's anxiety over the rise of an alien class threatening to the social order. Edith Wharton praised Wolfsheim as a *"perfect* Jew" because he symbolized, like her own Sim Rosedale in *The House of Mirth*, the assault on traditional social standards by aliens of no social background, of no manners. Gatsby *might* have been tolerated in traditional society because he tried to conform, with exaggerated deference, to the already established social norm. But not Wolfsheim; for him there could be no assimilation. Not only does Wolfsheim disgust us by speaking in "the idiom of the social climber," as William Goldhurst has noted, but Fitzgerald invests him with "the character and appearance of the typical alien outsider of the period" and "the morals of a crook."[49] The decline of the solidarity of the home and the continuity of the family as the repository of social values, the enfeeblement of formal religion as a bulwark against the decay of morals, and the disappearance of a clearly defined, heirarchically stratified society with a system of intelligibly differentiated manners (all middle-class social values) frankly distressed Fitzgerald. If the Wolfsheims and Buchanans were to inherit the earth, he preferred the old values. In fact, the moral norm affirmed in the novel, which Nick Carraway expresses, is a middle-class moral norm.

The social judgments in his essays on the Jazz Age are implied in *The Great Gatsby* through the devices of point of view, structure, symbolism, and style. Principally in the spectatorial point of view of Nick Carraway, Fitzgerald was able to get adequate distance to evaluate the society in which Gatsby's history was worked out, the preposterousness of his dream, and the vulgarity of the Buchanans, who destroy it. Carraway is admirably fitted to narrate and interpret Gatsby's story. An ex-soldier who has abandoned his native Middle West, which he calls "the ragged edge of the universe" (*GG*, 3), Nick has come East looking for kicks, for the speed, thrills, and excitement of the war years. Like Conrad's Marlow, he is sympathetic to the romantic figure whose story only he is perceptive enough to interpret. What makes him so effective a narrator is the tolerance and sympathy which lead people to show him "privileged glimpses into the human heart." For, above all, his father has taught him to be "inclined to reserve all judgments" (*GG*, 1–2).

It is worth criticizing the novel on the grounds that Nick Carraway is *too* sympathetic to Gatsby, too dazzled. But if Nick is too sympathetic to Gatsby it is because Fitzgerald admired Gatsby's "heightened sensitivity to the promises of life." "That's the whole burden of this novel," he told Ludlow Fowler in 1924, "the loss of those illusions that give such color to the world that you don't care whether things are true or false as long as they partake of the magical glory."[50]

Yet for all his tolerance of Gatsby's transcendent romanticism, Nick has nothing but scorn for the social values of Gatsby and the Buchanans. Witnessing the mess they make revives the fundamentally moral attitude toward life he learned in his midwestern childhood. Born of "prominent, well-to-do people . . . for three generations," Nick Carraway has been shaped by the values of a middle-class family living in a city where "dwellings are still called through decades by a family's name" (*GG*, 177). Because the family is rooted in time and place, it is able to retain in the postwar chaos "a sense of the fundamental decencies" which, his father wisely counsels him, is not parcelled out equally at birth. But although he is tolerant because not everyone in the world has had his "advantages," Nick is no latitudinarian. He is self-disciplined, full of "interior rules" (*GG*, 59) which act as brakes on his desires. Witnessing the desecration of Gatsby's dream and the carnage which follows leads him to abandon his habit of reserving judgment: the novel is his unreserved condemnation of the very rich. Wishing "the world to be in uniform and at a sort of moral attention forever" (*GG*, 2), Nick returns in the end to the Middle West.

Nick's Middle West is not the Middle West of Sinclair Lewis —not the world of Main Streets. It is rather a condition of the heart. When Nick says "I see now that this has been a story of the West, after all—Tom and Gatsby, Daisy and Jordan and I, were all Westerners, and perhaps we possessed some deficiency in common which made us unadaptable to Eastern life" (*GG*, 177), he is suggesting that their attempt to cast off "interior rules" has led to social disaster. Nick's return to the Midwest is a return to the origins of his existence, to the wisdom of his father, to those middle-class "fundamental decencies" marked by the inner check, by the family continuously rooted through the generations in the same place, by social stability. The disintegration of society in the Jazz Age, Fitzgerald suggests, is curable by a return to the moral foundations, to the simpler middle-class virtues.

III

The Great Gatsby achieved the acclaim Fitzgerald had hoped for, and having written the novel, nothing else ever seemed as important to him as the creative process. He was so certain that he had written a nearly perfect novel of manners that he later said that he wished he had "*never* relaxed or looked back—but said at the end of *The Great Gatsby*: 'I've found my line—from now on this comes first. This is my immediate duty—without this I am nothing.' "[51] Gertrude Stein praised him for "creating the contemporary world much as Thackeray did his in *Pendennis* and *Vanity Fair*."[52] Her choice of a literary model for the novel of manners was shrewd, for Fitzgerald had read Thackeray "over and over by the time I was sixteen."[53] He himself spoke of *Gatsby* as "shooting at something like *Henry Esmond*" while *Tender Is the Night* "was shooting at something like *Vanity Fair*."[54]

T. S. Eliot, who read the novel three times, told Fitzgerald that it was "the first step that American fiction has taken since Henry James."[55] What Eliot meant was that Fitzgerald's novel offered a fresh analysis of American social experience reflecting the theme of a civilization in decay through a masterly use of objective correlatives expressing despair over the human condition and the need of moral regeneration. It offered a transposition into prose of thematic and poetic techniques which marked his own poem *The Waste Land*.

The most thrilling praise came from Edith Wharton, "a remote and awful figure to the young rebels of Paris"[56] and a novelist of manners whom Fitzgerald desperately admired. Writing from Pavillon Colombe, she said that she was touched at his sending her *Gatsby* because she felt that "to your generation, which has taken such a flying leap into the future, I must represent the literary equivalent of tufted furniture & gas chandeliers." She felt that *Gatsby* made a great advance upon his previous work, that Wolfsheim and Wilson were triumphs of characterization, and that the "seedy orgy in the Buchanan flat" was a masterly piece of scene construction.[57]

What is noteworthy about the episode in the Buchanan flat is how concisely it serves as a paradigm of the whole social order reflecting the prejudice of all the classes in American society. The scene features the bogus aristocrat Tom Buchanan with his lower-class mistress and his fear of the rising colored races; Myrtle Wilson, the wife of the garage attendant who puts on high-class airs with her cream-colored chiffon dress and who complains at "the shiftlessness of the lower orders" (*GG*, 32) because the elevator boy is not prompt with the ice; and Mrs. McKee, who "almost married a little kike who'd been after me for years. I knew he was below me" (*GG*, 34). Gilbert Seldes observed that *Gatsby* was composed as "a series of scenes, a method which Fitzgerald derived from Henry James through Mrs. Wharton."[58] This is no doubt the case. Seldes was thoroughly familiar with the tradition of the novel of manners, was a great admirer of Mrs. Wharton, and talked about her themes and techniques to Fitzgerald while he was writing *Gatsby*.

The praise of these writers was justified by Fitzgerald's achievement. But during the next decade his ambivalence about the glamour of the rich, particularly in the short stories, aroused the scorn of many of his critics—particularly Hemingway, who reduced the complex causes of Fitzgerald's crack-up to an alleged disillusionment with the rich. In "The Snows of Kilimanjaro," which was published in 1936 in *Esquire*, Hemingway's hero thinks: "The rich were dull and they drank too much, or they played too much backgammon. They were dull and they were repetitious. He remembered poor Scott Fitzgerald and his romantic awe of them and how he had started a story once that began, 'The very rich are different from you and me.' And how someone had said to Scott, Yes, they have more money. But that was not humorous to Scott. He thought they were a special glamorous race and when he found they weren't it wrecked him just as much as any other thing that wrecked him."[59]

Hemingway was in part perfectly accurate—and, in part, obtuse. Fitzgerald did believe that the rich were a special race, that they were different from you and me. Stories like "The Diamond as Big as the Ritz," "Winter Dreams," and "The Rich Boy" *do* assert that poverty is dingy and degrading, that wealth can create the elegance and distinction absent from middle-class life, that there is a blessed moral freedom, grace, and mobility that wealth can confer. If Gatsby was "overwhelmingly aware of the youth and mystery that wealth imprisons and preserves..." (*GG*, 150), so too was Fitzgerald. But in ridiculing the notion that the rich constituted a special race, Hemingway was denying the reality of class differences in American society and therefore the reality of differences in American manners. And in this presumption lies a limitation of Hemingway's insight. For "the novelist of a certain kind, if he is to write about social life, may not brush away the reality of differences of class, even though to do so may have the momentary appearance of a virtuous social avowal."[60]

If we look at "The Rich Boy" to see *why* the rich actually differ from you and me, it is clear that—far from idealizing them—Fitzgerald deplored their softness and cynicism and the presumed superiority induced in them by their money. These he regarded as alien to his own values, and although he wanted to share that "mobility and grace that some of them brought into their lives,"[61] he distrusted them. What he believed in, he once said, was the dignity of work, "the rewards for virtue" and "the *punishments for not fulfilling your duties*,"[62] and testing human values by their conformity to "the strictest and most unflinching rationality."[63] Consequently, he resented John Peale Bishop's claim that "in the Midwest where Fitzgerald grew up, it was the common dream that riches made the superior person."[64] He also complained to Edmund Wilson against the frequent charge that he was "a suck around the rich": "I've had this before," Fitzgerald remarked, "but nobody seems able to name these rich."[65] What these remarks suggest—even more so, what the portraits of the very rich suggest —is that Fitzgerald was disillusioned with the exclusiveness of the rich, on the one hand, and with their moral imperfections, on the other. There is no question that Fitzgerald was attracted by money. Money meant power and magnificence and the "disciplined distinction of personal existence" which for him was the mark of a real aristocracy.[66] But Fitzgerald's treatment of the rich is never informed with the sympathy and understanding with which he invests Jay Gatsby, Dick Diver, Monroe Stahr—all poor boys struggling to make good. "When Fitzgerald writes about the rich, it is always as an outsider. He either endows them from a distance with romantic glamour or, moving closer, judges them by the standards of a disillusioned member of the middle class."[67] "Riches," he told Hemingway, "have *never* fascinated me, unless combined with the greatest charm or distinction."[68]

Elements of this charm, this distinction, are evident in *Gatsby*. But it was his sense of "the old virtues of work and courage and the old graces of courtesy and politeness,"[69] that gave Fitzgerald the orientation from which he could write some of the most interesting studies of manners in American fiction. In noting his contribution to a tradition shared by James, Wharton, and Lewis, we do no injustice to the uniqueness of his achievement in *Gatsby*. It is one of the triumphs of American fiction. Yet the reluctance of some critics to acknowledge the form of this triumph is surprising. Kenneth Eble grudgingly concedes that "we could restrict its [*Gatsby's*] scope to that of the novel of manners and still find the novel an admirable achievement."[70] And Lionel Trilling observes that *The Great Gatsby* "has its interest as a record of contemporary manners" although "this might only have served

to date it, did not Fitzgerald take the given moment of history as
something more than a mere circumstance, did he not, in the manner of the great French novelist of the nineteenth century, seize
the given moment as a moral fact."[71] But every successful novel
of manners—French, English *or* American—appropriates the given
moment as a moral fact and elevates it above mere journalism. No
doubt, as Arthur Mizener has observed, "the perfect novel of
manners will never be written. There are rigidities in the Jamesian
'given' in both of the worlds the novelist must unite [interior and
exterior] which probably can never be wholly reduced. But a
reasonable solution of these difficulties is nonetheless the task the
20th Century novelist has to face, and along with him the critic.
The possibility for such a solution is always present in writers like
Fitzgerald. . . ."[72]

8

✖ JOHN O'HARA
Class Hatred and Sexuality

John O'Hara's realistic notation of the character of American social life is perhaps the most striking feature of his compendious body of fiction. Few writers of the twentieth century since Dreiser have documented as massively and as realistically as O'Hara, during a career that spanned more than thirty years, "the way it was" between the 1920s and the 1960s. Unlike Fitzgerald, who tried to capture the precise sense of how it felt, subjectively, to be alive at a given moment, O'Hara's method, in writing about what he called "the most interesting subject in the world—the human being,"[1] was almost wholly objective and reportorial. He believed that what makes a human being distinctive is the way his sensibility is impinged upon by the pressures of the external world. For O'Hara, as for most of the writers whom we have discussed, the material properties of existence do not merely express character; in a special sense they "constitute" character. Virginia Woolf attacked this theory of characterization in *Mr. Bennett and Mrs. Brown* (1924). In criticizing Wells, Galsworthy, and Bennett, Mrs. Woolf argued that they were "never interested in character itself"; instead, to make the reality of, for example, Hilda Lessways believable, Bennett began "by describing accurately and minutely the sort of house Hilda lived in, and the sort of house she saw from the window. House property," she observed, "was the common ground from which the Edwardians found it easy to proceed to intimacy. Indirect as it seems to us, the convention worked admirably, and thousands of Hilda Lessways were launched upon the world by this means. For that age and generation, the convention was a good one." But for the modern writer, she argues, such techniques are not only outmoded but "the wrong ones to use." The Edwardian novelists (and by Edwardian we may understand her to mean the realistic novelist of any generation) "laid an enormous stress upon the fabric of things. They have given us a house in the hope that we may be able to deduce the human beings who live there. . . . But if you hold that novels are in the first place about people, and only in the second place about the houses they live in, that is the wrong way to set about it."[2]

The material properties of existence, however, are endemic to the novel, and for O'Hara—as for Balzac, the early James, Wharton, and Lewis—they are necessary for more than mere verisimilitude. Each believed that character is the product of external pressures represented by houses, streets, towns, professions, habits, and opinions. For all of them, a character is what he is because of the vocation he takes up, the kind of house he lives in, the social role he wants to play. As Mrs. Wharton put it in discussing Balzac and Stendhal, the French novelists of manners were first to discover that "the bounds of personality are not reproducible by a sharp black line, but that each of us flows imperceptibly into people and things."[3] O'Hara's stress on the fabric of things, therefore, is not an outmoded *convention of fiction* but rather the expression of a behavioristic conception of character—a Lockean conception incompatible with the psychological impressionism that underlies Virginia Woolf's criticism.

The novelist of manners, in other words, rejects character (or human nature or personality) as an abstraction with any objective significance. Character for him does not exist apart from the actualities that shape human beings. Psychological novelists like Virginia Woolf, on the other hand, do not believe that material properties can truly affect character. For her, houses and furniture and clothes are "alien and external" to "the luminous halo of consciousness," to what she called "the semi-transparent envelope surrounding us from the beginning of consciousness to the end"— which, she claimed, it is the novelist's task to portray. But this notion few novelists of manners will accept. As Mrs. Wharton pointed out in "The Great American Novel," little of "human nature" is left "when it is separated from the web of customs, manners, culture it has elaborately spun about itself."[4] O'Hara held that "the bloodless profundities of social philosophers and historians are often due . . . to the fact that writers forget that they are writing about men and fall into the error of writing about Man. It is perfectly all right to write about Man if you want to, but when you do you cease to write about men."[5] Real men are distinguished and defined by the *things* they surround themselves with; from these ego-extensions, in relation to the events that happen to them, the novelist forms psychology and character. As O'Hara once put it: "My characters have two patterns. One is superficial—clothes, schools, social positions, jobs. The other is psychological."[6]

O'Hara's novels illustrate as fully as those of his predecessors the extent to which houses, clothes, furniture, and the externals of social existence serve to define "human nature." If O'Hara begins *Elizabeth Appleton*, *Ten North Frederick*, and *Ourselves to Know* with a carefully detailed description of a house or what can be seen from it and *The Lockwood Concern* with the motivations that have gone into the building of a house, he is not mindlessly adhering to an obsolete convention of fiction; he is expressing a persistent proposition of behavioristic psychology. This technique may risk a confusion of life and art, but as Wellek and Warren observe in *Theory of Literature*, "A man's house is an extension of himself. Describe it and you have described him." What they remark of Balzac's detailed specifications of the house of the miser Grandet or the Pension Vauquer is true of O'Hara's exhaustive description of 10 North Frederick, with its three brownstone steps, front door four inches thick, and engraved brass nameplate attached exactly sixty-eight inches from the porch floor. Details like these are "neither irrelevant nor wasteful. These houses express their owners; they affect, as atmosphere, those . . . who must live in them."[7]

I

The power of environment to shape character is thus the chief assumption at work in O'Hara's fiction. None of his characters is ever as absolute as Marquand's George Apley in attributing his behavior to the determinism of environment—"I am the sort of man I am, because environment prevented my being anything else." But since O'Hara intended us to see behavior as a function of the conventions of time and place, his novels are not "arranged" like works of art that create a new reality. Instead they are wholly mimetic representations of "life," freed as much as possible of artifice, including—on the plane of style—figurative language. "My fiction writing depends almost completely on characterization, situation, locale, dialogue," he once conceded, "and practically not at all on plot or plot devices."[8] In documenting the effect of convention on character, O'Hara composed seven "Lantenengo County novels" or "Gibbsville novels" (after the county seat). The value of the setting is not merely that O'Hara grew up in Pennsylvania and knew the environs, but also that it constituted a whole world available for social analysis: "The small town, like my invention Gibbsville, has it all; the entrenched, the strivers, the climbers, the rebellious."[9] He documented nearly all of it in *Appointment in Samarra* (1934), *A Rage to Live* (1949), *Ten North Frederick* (1955), *From the Terrace* (1958), *Ourselves to Know* (1960), *Elizabeth Appleton* (1963), and *The Lockwood Concern* (1965).

If, as O'Hara once argued, "everything an author does, everything, can be made useful,"[10] much that happened to him was incorporated into the Lantenengo County novels. They suggest reflections of his own "experience" as man and boy in Pottsville, a town of about 25,000 people (the county seat of Schuylkill County) some ninety miles northwest of Philadelphia. In his Lantenengo County saga—which compares with Faulkner's Yoknapatawpha chronicle in social density and historical scope, though not in artistic excellence—O'Hara's principal method is to integrate a more or less full-length biography of a major character (plus, perhaps, a series of shorter biographies of other Gibbsville residents) into the social history of the town itself. This method often requires O'Hara to do a three- or four-generation panorama in order to show us the forces that produced his protagonist and to reveal the agencies of social change at work in the community during his lifetime. So totally are his biographies integrated into the sociological history that his novels constitute a dramatized record of the community life of southeastern Pennsylvania.

Sequence novels are often an annoyance to critics who like to think of a novel as an autonomous artifact to be judged on the basis of its own "inner laws." For such critics, a novel has little or nothing to do with the "real world" which it is said to imitate or with other novels which may repeat the "same" characters and setting. But the sequence novel is a popular mode with the great novelists of manners—Balzac, Cooper, Wharton, Proust, Zola, for example. O'Hara's social history, involving the interrelation of a large group of local families over a period of generations and portrayed in a series of sequential novels, was suggested to him in 1936 by F. Scott Fitzgerald, who advised him to "undertake something more ambitious" than individual novels: "Invent a system Zolaesque (see the appendix to Josephson's *Life of Zola* in which he gives Zola's plan for the first Rougon-Macquart book), but buy a file. On the first page of the file put down the outline of a novel of your times enormous in scale (don't worry, it will contract by itself) and work on the plan for two months. Take the central point of the file as your big climax and follow your plan backward and forward from that for another three months. Then draw up something as complicated as a continuity from what you have and set yourself a schedule."[11]

Establishing literary influences is at best a tenuous business. O'Hara expressed admiration for writers as diverse as Hemingway, Cozzens, Steinbeck, Fitzgerald, Sinclair Lewis, Galsworthy, Tarkington, and Owen Johnson, "but chiefly Fitzgerald and Lewis."[12] (They are all, it is worth insisting, novelists of manners preoccupied with the configurations of British or American social experience.) O'Hara's master plan does not closely follow Zola's pattern of the history of a single family under the Second Empire. But using *Appointment in Samarra* as the center of a comprehensive cross-section of Gibbsville life, O'Hara filled in the history of Lantenengo County from its earliest settlement by English, Irish, and German immigrants. Taken together, the Lantenengo

County novels suggest the density of an interrelated social world comprehensively imagined and precisely planned.

II

"I guess I know as much about Society as any author today," O'Hara once immodestly admitted. He particularly felt that he knew more than the "social authorities" (Cleveland Amory, for example) who claim that Society no longer exists in the United States. For O'Hara, Society is still here, but it is not as conspicuous as it used to be: "The disappearance of the stately homes of Newport, the razing of the Fifth Avenue town houses, and the popularity of the rather more simple life than that of forty years ago have been taken as proof that Society itself went bye-bye. The truth of the matter is that it is slightly more difficult for the outsider to identify Society, but Society is, if anything, more there than ever." In fact, "it is now possible for a family to be very, very Society without having to build a ten-foot wall to advertise the fact. The Society people nowadays may prefer to live in a house that's smaller than the porter's lodge on Grandfather's estate, but the smaller house is if anything harder to get invited to."[13]

O'Hara's entrée into the social life of the eastern cities—Providence, New York, Philadelphia, Wilmington, and Baltimore—gave him a length's lead on other contemporary novelists of manners. After the death of Marquand, the social life of the cities had few authentic interpreters besides O'Hara. "Aside from Louis Auchincloss," O'Hara once noted, "I can't think of any Insider who has dared to risk ostracism by slipping out messages to the Outside." O'Hara is of course no Insider, but his fiction may be taken as a message slipped out to the rest of us describing exactly *how* different the rich are from you and me: "The Auchinclosses do interest me, and I have abundant information on their habits and tribal customs," he noted; in fact, "they interest me so much that it's hard for me to know when to stop."[14] O'Hara did not think much of Louis Auchincloss as a novelist of manners, however, because he staked out a territory O'Hara liked to call his own and because Auchincloss was a severe O'Hara critic in "Marquand and O'Hara: The Novel of Manners."[15] Besides, he thought Auchincloss a snob—"he went to Groton, and don't you forget it."[16]

Society has not disappeared, but O'Hara felt that it might vanish if some of the "liberal" political tendencies were not reversed. As a political conservative O'Hara wanted to keep High Society and its Exclusive Institutions because their disappearance would impoverish the American novelist. In modern society "an author who has not been born social has a better chance of observing the upper crust than he would have in Grandpa's day." This is not the same thing as getting into society. But the modern writer who "makes a good score, who observes ordinary rules of cleanliness and politeness, and doesn't dress like a Texan or a Broadway sharpie, will get invited to some Society homes." There is a distinct boundary between People in Society and Talented Outsiders, however, which presumably O'Hara was in a position to know about. A writer may get invited to social occasions, but there are "more or less subtle ways of letting him know how far he can go, how much a part of Society life he can become, but if he is a good writer he will know what to expect, how much and how little, because in order to have made that good score professionally he will have had to be a sensitive man in the first place. The authors who have trouble and for whom the Society kick is a swift one in the pants are the ones who were not subtle enough, not sensitive enough."[17]

O'Hara is interested in the established rich like the Chapins, Tates, and Eatons because they offer opportunities for discovering the private hells that exist beneath the conventional exterior. "You see a large band of them assembling at a wedding, for instance, and there is a wholesale display of politeness, a fair uniformity of attire among the men, and an exhibition of fashion among the women. You observe that they are clean, that they have appetites for food and drink, that they love sport or despise it. That's the big picture. If you, like me, are an outsider, for you they start conventional. But then you see a little more of them and then still a little more, and then you begin to see the holes in the lining. Pretty soon you realize that the moths have been really industrious—and it's time you got so yourself, if you are a novelist."[18] O'Hara's studies of people like Lex Porter of *From the Terrace*, the Jarvis Websters of *Elizabeth Appleton*, and the Lockwood clan expose personal despair all the more moving for being discreetly concealed beneath conventional manners. He offers a little middle-class consolation—the knowledge that "all that money" does not really make any difference: everybody has his own private hell. "But the writer who affects an attraction to sharecroppers out of some progressive social theory (or because a Faulkner has invested them with interest) is fated to miss one of the most varied, colorful, and stimulating worlds of novelistic material left in the United States." For a writer to "deprive himself of Society's society because, well for any reason," O'Hara argued, "is a mistake." Money, he pointed out, "makes a difference between Society people and the rest of us, but it should not make the big difference to a writer."[19]

O'Hara is more conscious of the polite manners of this aristocracy than almost any other American novelist of manners.[20] Some of his characters are sensitive to the point of morbidity about the class proprieties expected of them. Arthur Mizener has suggested that Julian English is intended to represent "the true American gentleman, refined, aware, instinctively gallant, whose bad behavior is a result of his sensitive nature's being driven beyond restraint by the crudeness of the people around him."[21] But Julian's bad manners in throwing a drink in Harry Reilly's face exclude him from the class of real O'Hara gentlemen, like Joe Chapin ("His manners were exquisite even in a day when good manners were the rule"), Alfred Eaton ("Beautiful manners . . . the thoughtful type . . . quite aristocratic-looking . . ."), and Sidney Tate ("He had good manners, and he seemed to me sincerely, genuinely respectful").[22] Hence, it is more than a little surprising that Norman Podhoretz claims that "O'Hara is not a 'novelist of manners' in the sense in which literary critics have used that term," that "manners in O'Hara refer to nothing outside themselves or deeper than themselves," and that they are "neither an index of sensibility nor the expression of moral impulses: O'Hara is no disciple of Henry James. Nor does he share in the same tradition as Fitzgerald."[23] If anything, the precise opposite is true. While the manners of some of O'Hara's characters may be "Chesterfieldian," O'Hara usually manipulates manners to express individual sensibility and a moral view toward the world. The manners of Sidney Tate, for example, are a perfect expression of his belief that "in this world you learn a set of rules, *or* you *don't* learn them. But assuming you learn them, you stick by them. They may be no damn good, but you're who you are and what you are because they're your rules and you stick by them. And of course when it's easy to stick by them, that's no test. It's when it's hard to obey the rules, that's when they mean something" (*RL*, 245).

The good manners of Sidney Tate are remarkable because most people do not learn any moral rules in this world and do not have a code to express the principles they live by. Or, if they have learned any rules, they cannot keep them and continually fail the test. Those who have a code of manners are remarkable because of the decline, if not disappearance, of polite manners in American society. The informality of social life in the twentieth century has caused a serious loss to the novelist of manners, who is deprived of nuances of form as an index to a wide variety of phenomena—including manners as the expression of moral sensibility, emotional turmoil, absentmindedness, and so on. Edith Wharton suggests the emotional turmoil of a young woman in *Madame de Treymes* (1907) who emerged into a Paris Street *without yet having put on her gloves*. O'Hara knows that such slight deviations from an accepted norm of manners can be a highly significant index to complex inward matters. But such is the loss of form in our time that the meaning of manners is harder for the modern writer to suggest, and the novelist runs the risk of losing his audience if his use of polite manners is too technical. O'Hara ended one of his stories with the protagonist walking out of a room with the bow of his hat on the wrong side of his head. O'Hara meant this obvious lapse to indicate inner agitation. But his readers' letters to the editor were angry and baffled. This attention to subtleties in the social sphere has led critics like Chester E. Eisinger to call O'Hara one of the children (albeit "illegitimate") of Henry James.[24] I am not sure that O'Hara appreciated being thought of as the bastard son of Henry James, but they *are* in the same tradition, although what was easy for the father is more difficult for the son: "The decline of good manners is fairly universal," O'Hara once lamented, "and not limited to great nations or teenagers."[25]

III

O'Hara must be criticized for the failure of his novels to embody significant generalizations. He does not penetrate very deeply the surfaces of American life, and in committing himself to the significance of the "insignificant" O'Hara was preoccupied too much with the things of this world. But the absence of ideas in his writing is also the consequence of an indirect method that has often confused and irritated his readers. O'Hara follows Fitzgerald and Lewis in concerning himself with the life of society, but he loved Hemingway's kind of understatement. He does not generalize because he does not want to be caught making a statement. But his Lantenengo County novels are informed by one overriding idea: America is a "spurious democracy" marked by the intense hatred of its rival social classes.

The phrase "spurious democracy" first appears in *Appointment in Samarra* (1934). It suggests that, for all our egalitarian claims, ours is essentially a society of antagonistic classes defined by money, family, occupation, region, religion, education, and ethnic background. The only democrats in *Appointment in Samarra* are Ed Charney and Whitney Hofman—Charney because he has the noblesse oblige of a powerful gangland killer and Hofman because he has fourteen million dollars and can *afford* to be democratic. "The ones with the dough, the big dough, they're always democratic (*APS*, 169), Lute Fliegler tells his wife. If you don't have money, you don't have to be democratic; nobody pays any attention to how you act. The very rich are set apart by their wealth; to get any kind of cooperation from others they have to dramatize their egalitarianism. Being "just one of the boys, a democratic guy," may be a form of condescension, but it works better than insolence or force. Though lip service is paid to the democratic ideal, O'Hara exposes with deft precision the antagonism among the various classes and the envy and hatred that separate those who have Arrived from those who are still Climbers. Polite manners often the expression of this studied egalitarianism. Manners do not simply oil the social machinery; they constitute a white flag declaring the truce between warring factions that need each other to survive.

The metaphor which expresses the idea that democracy is a spurious "union of equals" is the Christiana Street gang. In *Appointment in Samarra*, the rich live within two or three blocks of the middle and lower classes. Because there are not enough rich children to make up a football team, they have to go down to Christiana Street to play with the sons of the less affluent. "Consequently, from the time he was out of kindergarten until he was ready to go away to prep school, Julian's friends were not all from Lantenengo Street" (*APS*, 183). The Christiana Street gang—which is a symbol of the social "contract"—is composed of the sons of a butcher, a motorman, a surveyor, a freight clerk, two bookkeepers for the coal company, a Baptist minister, a neighborhood saloonkeeper, a garage mechanic, and a neighborhood convict. Because of the diversity of religious, occupational, and social backgrounds in the gang, a rule of decorum prevailed: you could not talk about jail because the father of one of the boys was in the pen. You could not talk about drunks because of the saloonkeeper's son. Talk about Catholics was forbidden because of the motorman's son. And Julian could not talk about doctors because of his father's profession. These topics are, of course, talked over—and O'Hara's ear for nuances of class in dialogue is exceptionally accurate—but only behind the back of the boy involved. Despite the social differences that separate them, these Gibbsville boys have developed a code of manners which permits them to get along together well enough to "play the game." Common need and the proximity of rich and poor in the American small town thus make for a "spurious democracy, especially among boys," O'Hara observes, "which may or may not be better than no democracy at all" (*APS*, 183). At least, none of them is deceived by the arrangement. The notion of American society as a "spurious democracy" is not complex, but so adequately does it express O'Hara's skepticism of "equality as the basis of good society," to use Howells's term, that it characterizes all of his social portraits and even reappears thirty years later in describing St. Bartholomew's School in *The Lockwood Concern*.

Democracy presumes a willingness to subordinate private need to the common good and the brotherhood of man expressed in fraternal respect and fellow-feeling. But O'Hara distrusts human nature and calls "the brotherhood of man" "a term that is usually invoked when someone is making a pitch."[26] His portraits of the social process show men and women driven by ungovernable desires—greed, lust, ambition, and savage egotism. Democracy is hardly viable in such a world, and the Lantenengo County novels —with their atmosphere of anger and hatred—chronicle the failure of this egalitarian dream. Jealousy, envy, and hostility separate the classes, irritations are produced by social climbing, frustrations grow out of the arbitrary codes which imprison people in a social class—these are the origins of the hatred that O'Hara sees as the infected core of American social experience. John Portz has noted how thoroughly O'Hara has dealt with the theme of war in *Appointment in Samarra*.[27] *From the Terrace* concludes that conflict is the natural condition among men: "The sad truth I guess," Alfred Eaton remarks, "is that the human race is made up of people who don't get along very well together" (*FT*, 882). Nothing, apparently, can be done to remedy the evils of social life. For it is "basic to the human condition" for men to "find something to quarrel over." O'Hara's youthful Irish Catholicism was not a determinant in his mature view of the world, but there is a clear and inescapable secularization of the doctrine of fallen humanity in his belief that "while the soul of man remains, the need to do something naughty will linger on."[28]

O'Hara's method of organizing his novels around the twin focus of character and community, in relation to the idea of our "spurious democracy," is aptly illustrated in *Appointment in Samarra*. The period is the 1920s, the community is Gibbsville, and the character is Julian English. The conflict in Gibbsville is revealed in O'Hara's notation of the manners of the various social groups in the town—the aristocracy, the solid respectable middle class, and the underworld of racketeers, bootleggers, prostitutes, and pimps. The aristocrats of Lantenengo County are an upper-middle-class commercial oligarchy composed of families like the Englishes, Ogdens, the McHenrys, the Chapins, the Caldwells, the Stokeses, and the Hofmans. They live on streets like Lantenengo or North Frederick, belong to the Lantenengo County Country Club, are generally graduates of Pennsylvania, Princeton, or another "Ivy League" university. The middle class, more or less excluded from the social life of the rich, is made up of families like the Luther Flieglers, the Dutch Snyders, the Dewey Hartensteins, the Kleins, the Reichelderfers, the Harvey Ziegenfusses, the Rothermels, Benzigers, Fenstermachers, Gormans, Reillys, and Millhousers. This class is constituted of small businessmen, skilled craftsmen, and tradesmen. If college men at all, they have gone to less prestigious schools like Lafayette, Penn State, Muhlenberg, or Lebanon Valley. (O'Hara is sensitive to the social significance of not merely *whether* an individual goes to college but *where* he gets his degree. Some of his characters are permanently scarred by not having gone to the "right" prep school or college. His preoccupation with this badge of status and class and his residence in Princeton were attempts to experience vicariously the college life he was denied as a youth. He wrote at great length about the college experience and revealed detailed knowledge of college degree requirements, dormitory life, and fraternity rituals. He read *This Side of Paradise* every year after its appearance in 1920 because Fitzgerald portrayed most excitingly what it was like for a poor boy to be thrown among the snobbish sons of the eastern rich. In describing his fascination with "the small-town boy in the Ivy League world,"[29] O'Hara gave away his own admiration for the forms of prestige and power that always dazzle the kid from Pottsville or St. Paul.)

If the aristocrats have their exclusive clubs and hotels like the John Gibb and the Nesquehela, the middle class has its own social haunts—like the Stage Coach Inn. The climactic scene in *Appointment in Samarra*, in fact, occurs at this road house, where O'Hara brings together the major classes of the town to dramatize and test the manners of each group. O'Hara's novels are full of such public rituals—weddings, funerals, county fairs, and festivals—where the various classes of the community are brought together in a dramatic confrontation. In his treatment of the special underworld class created by prohibition, O'Hara also documents what it feels like to live at a flophouse like Gorney's Hotel, to eat at a greasy spoon like the Apollo Restaurant, and to guard the boss's girlfriend to make sure that she is not playing around. Though beyond the law, this class has conventions of its own expressed in the interior monologues of Al Grecco and the style of Loving Cup, Packy McGovern, and Foxie Lebrix.

These classes are not rigidly separated. As with the Christiana Street gang, there is enough interaction to permit the desire for social mobility that aggravates class hatred, which O'Hara sees as paramount in the social experience of communities like Lantenengo County. There is a good deal of incidental ridicule of minorities like the Italians, Poles, and Jews—some of whom, like the Brombergs, have "invaded" Lantenengo Street. But the major ethnic tensions occur among the Anglo-Saxon aristocrats and the Irish and Pennsylvania Dutch middle class.

The central action of *Appointment in Samarra* is Julian English's throwing a drink in the face of an unpleasant Irish social climber. As Delmore Schwartz has observed, "It was probably neither accident nor intention which made O'Hara call the scapegoat hero of his first novel, Julian English; for English is an Anglo-Saxon, he resents the Irish, he belongs to what is supposed to be the upper class, and the tragic action which leads to his suicide is his throwing a drink in the face of a man with the choice name of Harry Reilly. It might as well have been Murphy, O'Mara, or Parnell."[30] A number of Irish Catholics in Gibbsville take it as an insult to their religion, and Pat Quilty, the town undertaker, transfers his automobile business to Julian's rival, Larry O'Dowd of the Gibbsville Buick Company. In *A Rage to Live*, when Brock Caldwell's article criticizing a Jesuit explorer offends the Catholic townspeople of Fort Penn, within a week—although nothing is ever said from the pulpits—the newspaper loses four thousand subscribers and a dozen advertising accounts—enough to bankrupt the paper.

In one sense, O'Hara's novels may thus be seen as the means by which he worked out his own ethnic resentment against the high and mighty in southeastern Pennsylvania.[31] This is especially true of *Ten North Frederick*, in which Joe Chapin tries to engineer a political appointment, without taking into account the local political machine. A gentleman with perfect manners, aristocratic self-confidence, honor and integrity, the Prince of Gibbsville whose hauteur earned him the college nickname of "M'lord," Joe Chapin has one ambition—to be president of the United States. When Joe goes over the head of Mike Slattery, the local party boss, to try to get a federal appointment from which to launch his presidential bid and then offers the Republican party bosses $100,000 for the lieutenant governor's nomination, Slattery takes the money and directs the party to nominate someone else.

Few of O'Hara's contemporary novelists understand as well as he that events are arbitrary and can never be fully anticipated. The central question of *Appointment in Samarra* is why Julian English committed suicide, and it is possible to adduce half a dozen good reasons to explain the mystery. But the title of the novel and the epigraph, with its parable of Death seeking the servant, suggest that none of the presumed reasons is quite relevant: it was simply *time* for Julian to die and nothing could avert the fate awaiting him. John Appleton has every reason to expect to be appointed president of Spring Valley College, but the trustees absurdly decide that Appleton is "too logical" a choice and select someone else. What Joe Chapin never knows is that, for all her unobtrusiveness, Peg Slattery controls Mike's decisions. Because she "hated Roosevelt" as a "Protestant, an aristocrat, a charm-boy, a socialist, a liar, a warmonger, a double-crosser, and the husband of Eleanor Roosevelt" (*TNF*, 14), Joe Chapin, who wants to be a Republican version of FDR, does not have a chance. He has no idea of the class hatred he is up against. And when his ambitions are casually wiped out by the party bosses, he spends his final years in dignified alcoholism.

The hatred of the Pennsylvania Dutch for these aristocrats is equally intense. There is a paradox in this since a number of Pennsylvania Dutch families like the Reichelderfers go back to the early days of the Revolutionary War, and some of them—like Charlotte Chapin in *Ten North Frederick*—are descended from the German nobility. But the aristocrat's view of them is that they are stodgy middle-class Germans, and despite how rich and established they become, no one ever called them aristocratic. The consequence of their bourgeois stolidity is that the aristocrats ridicule them as "dumb Dutch bastards" and mimic their funny accents. Even Sidney Tate, O'Hara's most nearly perfect gentleman, cannot escape the prejudice of his class.

One of the functions of O'Hara's three-generation panoramas of American social life is to explore the meaning of heredity in defining character. The notion of hereditary recurrence is invoked in *Appointment in Samarra, The Lockwood Concern,* and *From the Terrace* in order to suggest the psychological power it has over those who believe that the sins of the fathers will be visited on the sons. In *Appointment in Samarra* Julian English's desire to evade the consequences of his behavior is associated with his grandfather's embezzlement and suicide. When Julian steals a flashlight as a boy and periodically overdraws his account at college, his mother cautions him to be more careful in money matters because his father "thinks it's in the blood, because of Grandfather English" (*APS*, 196). And when Julian commits suicide, Dr. English hopes that people will notice "how the suicide strain had skipped one generation to come out in the next. So long as they saw that it was all right. You had to expect things" (*APS*, 288).

But the notion that heredity explains Julian's behavior produces some serious problems. Suicide is not "in the blood" or "hereditary." But the psychological pressures on Julian created by his father's belief that thievery and suicide *are* hereditary do provide a credible motivation for his suicide—although this is, in fact, an environmental factor. Socially conditioned beliefs *about* heredity are thus one of the elements of naturalistic force affecting men's lives in O'Hara's world. But a more important "cause" of Julian's death is the social antagonism which arises out of class differences in small-town American society. Mary Klein, Julian's secretary in *Appointment in Samarra*, most satisfactorily suggests how the psychology of suicide was created in Julian.

Mary Klein could make Julian feel like "a thief, a lecher (although God knows he never had made a pass at her), a drunkard, a no-good bum. She represented precisely what she came from: solid, respectable, Pennsylvania Dutch, Lutheran middle class; and when he thought about her, when she made her existence felt, when she actively represented what she stood for, he could feel the little office suddenly becoming overcrowded with a delegation of all the honest clerks and mechanics and housewives and Sunday School teachers and widows and orphans—all the Christiana Street kind of people who he knew secretly hated him and all Lantenengo Street people." It makes no difference that the Pennsylvania Dutch have "their illegitimate babies, their incest, their paresis, their marital bestiality, their cruelty to animals, their horrible treatment of their children"—as other ethnic groups do. The point is their class solidarity, against which Julian is helpless: ". . . collectively they presented a solid front of sound Pennsylvania Dutch and all that that implied, or was supposed to imply." Julian cannot help realizing that "they were thinking what a pity it was that this wonderful business wasn't in the hands of one of their own men, instead of being driven into the ground by a Lantenengo Street—wastrel" (*APS*, 218–19). And, at the end of the novel, their wishes, as Julian imagines them, are realized: his Cadillac agency is in sound middle-class hands—virtually owned by Harry Reilly and managed by Luther Fliegler. Although Julian may overreact to the Mary Kleins of Gibbsville, such is the intensity of their presumed disapproval that it becomes a part of the mysterious motivation of his suicide.

A second way of defining this hatred among rival ethnic groups is to see it as a struggle between rich and poor. This may or may not amount to the same thing since the poor are often Irish, Pennsylvania Dutch, or another minority. Roger Bannon, the Irish contractor in *A Rage to Live*, runs afoul of the rich Caldwell clan and is virtually driven out of Fort Penn. A part of his hatred for the Caldwells is class structured. The son of a father known for radicalism, Bannon grows up thinking that benevolent local squires like William Penn Caldwell are a greater danger to the workingman than J. J. Morgan and should be combatted by any means, so he seduces Grace Tate. O'Hara's study of Tom Rothermel in *From the Terrace* suggests that envy of the rich may become the energy behind socialist radicalism. In Port Johnson Alfred Eaton grows up in a household where it is bad taste to talk about money and is thus unequipped, in a sense, to handle the fortune he later inherits. Thomas Rothermel, the poor boy with nice manners who grows up holding two or three jobs at once, knows everything about money by the age of eleven. In later years Rothermel argues that the capitalistic system stinks because it deprived him of his childhood. As a union official sympathetic to communism, Rothermel sees World War II as a contest between fascism and capitalism.

In the study of Rothermel's "violent hatred of the rich," some of O'Hara's finest social insights are dramatized. Rothermel knows enough about the very rich not to look for "the thin, cruel aristocrat who would delight in starving the tenantry." And he knows that the Port Johnson Eatons and Van Peltzes are "spurious aristocrats" not really in the same class with New York millionaires. But he has seen the Eatons put on "the airs of the gentry with their coachmen and their condescension as they did their shopping in Lower Montgomery Street," and he hates them doubly for assuming a superiority not even justified by their wealth. Jean and Creighton Duffy, very rich New Dealers in Washington, puzzle Rothermel because they seem to be aristocrats, although they ought to be Irish Catholic outsiders. The episode which crystallizes Rothermel's hatred of the Duffys occurs at a party one evening when he observes Duffy and his butler Barrett in relaxed conversation. Characteristically, the insight involves an expression of manners. Although Rothermel tries to break the butler of his deferential manner, Barrett is coldly precise and impersonally polite toward Tom—"colder than any snub Tom had ever received from one of the society men" (*FT*, 687). Gradually Rothermel comes to understand that in such relaxed moments Duffy and his servant are showing their respect for each other: "The man with the money and the man saying 'sir' understood each other, liked each other, and observed rules that kept the relationship successful." The precise distance they keep is a measure of their respect for each other. With the discovery that Duffy is "at ease with a servant and therefore, in Tom's view, a member of the ruling class," he decides that "in the crisis that he was doing everything he could to hasten" he "would have liquidated both Duffys" (*FT*, 688).

What is remarkable about O'Hara's treatment of the rich and poor is his identification with the values of both. Not a little of Rothermel's hatred for aristocrats reflects O'Hara himself, the

Outsider from Pottsville. Yet more than any other twentieth-century novelist of manners, O'Hara admired the capacity of the rich to command power. Joe Chapin and Alfred Eaton are about as far removed from O'Hara's middle-class world as they can be, yet O'Hara's understanding of their observable manners is more informed and sympathetic than we are accustomed to find in an Outsider. "The study of enormously rich men is more than a hobby with me," O'Hara once acknowledged. "It is an occupation that can be almost as entertaining as girl-watching, and in a surprisingly large number of cases you can do both at the same time."[32] O'Hara loved Hemingway this side idolatry, but he had to admit that Hemingway's response to Fitzgerald—Yes, the rich have more money—"rated better as flippancy than as observation." O'Hara realized that quantity of money may make a profound difference in quality of behavior and manners: "You do not, in the United States of America in the 20th Century, so casually disregard [as Hemingway did] a man's power to put his hands on a billion dollars."[33]

A third way to see the hostility pervasive in O'Hara's Gibbsville chronicle is to visualize it as a contest between the established and the intruder. Fort Penn regards Grace Caldwell's husband with suspicion because he is a New Yorker—not a local boy. He never escapes their disapprobation. In *The Lockwood Concern*, Abraham Lockwood's "concern" (in Quaker usage the term refers to an obsession of a religious nature) is to form a dynasty, to raise his sons to be gentlemen.[34] The Lockwood plan requires Abraham to overcome the stigma of his father's being a murderer and to establish himself as "a man of business and leading citizen." His sons George and Penrose are to become "gentlemen, men of affairs, patrons of the arts, third-generation leaders of their community and the first generation upon which the national public would bestow the title, Lockwood of Swedish Haven" (*LC*, 118). Although "murder never disqualified a family from a position in history; it was the method by which kings became kings, barons became dukes," Abraham's scheme founders because Lantenengo County never accepts the Lockwood outsiders from Swedish Haven. It is crucial that Abraham marry his son George into one of the first families of Lebanon Valley. But Eulalie

Fenstermacher's father blocks the marriage because George "did not talk like a Pennsylvanian, he dressed too old for a college senior, he had artificial manners" (*LC*, 202). And when George marries a woman undistinguished in social station, the dynastic dream slides over into nightmare: Penrose winds up a murderer and suicide and George an ineffectual candy manufacturer. Great-grandson Bing becomes a penny-ante whoremaster in the West, and great-granddaughter Ernestine Lockwood, a syphilitic, sterile nymphomaniac, marries an impotent New England homosexual. The causes which destroy the Lockwood dream of an American aristocracy are complex. But one inescapable cause is the opposition of Lantenengo County society to the Swedish Haven Lockwoods.

The reason that Outsiders are excluded, O'Hara suggests, is often based on the illusion of status rather than upon status itself. Middle-class Irma Fliegler in *Appointment in Samarra* hates not only the Jewish Brombergs who have "lowered" Lantenengo Street property values, but a good many aristocrats as well. Her reasons for feeling superior are wholly irrational: "Her family had been in Gibbsville a lot longer than the great majority of the people who lived on Lantenengo Street. She was a Doane, and Grandfather Doane had been a drummer boy in the Mexican War and had a Congressional Medal of Honor from the Civil War. Grandfather Doane had been a member of the School Board for close to thirty years, before he died, and he was the only man in this part of the state who had the Congressional Medal of Honor" (*APS*, 5–6). No different from most Gibbsville residents, Irma Fliegler is typical of her fellow townsmen in desperately clinging to "some family tradition, some membership in a select organization, some personal association with the famous," from which she tries to derive social distinction.[35]

The theme of hatred, in relation to the "spurious democracy" that constitutes American social relations, is given ironic expression in the Ralph Barton cover of *The New Yorker* described in *Appointment in Samarra*—a picture of "a lot of shoppers, all with horribly angry or stern faces, hating each other and themselves and their packages, and above the figures of the shoppers was a wreath and the legend: Merry Xmas." The perfect motto for the whole Lantenengo County series is given at the end of chapter 1 of *Appointment in Samarra*, where Al Grecco, the bootlegger, follows Julian English home on Christmas night, and, as he drives down Lantenengo Street, rolls down his window and yells out at the darkened houses: "Merry Christmas, you stuck-up bastards! Merry Christmas from Al Grecco!" (*APS*, 26).

IV

O'Hara is notorious for the cynical and "hard-boiled" treatment of sex in his novels. A survey of his work suggests the fullness of his notation of sexual phenomena—incest, homosexuality, lesbianism, transvestitism, voyeurism, and pederasty, not to speak of the more "normal" sexual pastimes, usually fornication and adultery. The sex drive is the most important naturalistic force, besides environment, operating in O'Hara's universe. If he gives us extensive flashbacks outlining the sexual experience of his personae it is because the individual's sexual history partly makes him what he is in his destructive social relations.

In general, O'Hara presents American society as an arena of competition for social position in which sex means athletic diversion, self-gratification, a means of alleviating boredom, and a method of social revenge. Inevitably sex means trouble. His modest understanding of the emotions, his anti-intellectualism, and his too-ready dependence upon lust to explain his characters tend to weaken the authority of his fiction. His treatment of sex is most troublesome, I believe, when sexual maladjustment is casually explained as the consequence of class antagonism. Jim Roper's homosexuality, for example, is presented to us as the consequence of being jilted by Mary Eaton when "a rich bastard with a big car came along, and I got the gate." His seduction of Mary is the only revenge he can relish. Lloyd Williams has a brief affair with Edith Chapin simply because she is an aristocrat's wife and he is just a colliery "patch lad." In *A Rage to Live* Grace Tate is the victim of an elaborately planned seduction by a psychopathic Irishman who resents her upper-class snobbery. When she snubs Roger Bannon publicly in the streets of Fort Penn, there is no other way he can get "satisfaction." "Doing it to the rich man's daughter" may be precious little consolation to the snubbed outsider—and a perversion of the act of love—but it is Bannon's mode of revenge. Bannon, Parker Wells, and Larry Von Elm of *From the Terrace*, and George Lockwood of *The Lockwood Concern* all go after the women of the very rich because of hatred—as revenge for the social ostracism they have suffered. As George Lockwood meditates, "it was not . . . merely a question of seducing a girl of good family, but an attractive girl of good family." Agnes Wynne is all of these: "She was desirable, and it would be a real triumph to seduce her," to "take her down a few pegs" (*LC*, 221). The clearest symbol of the sexual assault motivated by class antagonism in *Appointment in Samarra* occurs when an eleven-year-old boy at the Gibbsville Mission, where Caroline English is teaching, reaches under her skirt and touches her. Characteristically, he is a redheaded Irish brat.

Brendan Gill has noted that "O'Hara like Dr. Kinsey has an interest in determining the extent to which the various classes in our society can be distinguished from one another in terms of what they do about sex and then in terms of what they *think* about what they do about sex."[36] But aside from the motive of revenge I cannot see that class makes too much difference in affecting what O'Hara's characters do and what they think about sex: they think about it all the time and indulge as often as they can get away with it. Elizabeth Appleton admits, "we're caught, trapped, by something that happens to our glands. . . ."[37] Sex is rarely the expression of love in O'Hara's world, and love rarely survives in marriage. Many of O'Hara's violent death scenes—murders, accidents, and suicides—reflect how the glands degrade men to the level of animals. Penrose Lockwood and Marian Strademeyer, Peter Van Peltz and Victoria Dockwiler, Norma Budd and Joseph Waterford, Julian English, Gloria Wandrous, Anson Chatworth, George Lockwood, and Hedwig Millhauser suggest in their deaths that love is inevitably doomed by the nature of our sexuality. In the parable from which *Appointment in Samarra* takes its name, Death is a woman; in O'Hara's world sex means not life but death.

Norman Podhoretz has observed that O'Hara "draws no conclusions from class."[38] O'Hara draws conclusions, but they are implied in the experience of his characters. Nothing can be done about heredity and fate. But what can achieve the redemption of society, his novels suggest, is freedom from the antagonisms of class that make American society an arena of social warfare. In short, redemption through love. If goodwill obtained more widely, there would be no social barriers obstructing the fulfillment of love. A Julian English could love his Polish Mary, a George Lockwood could marry his Eulalie Fenstermacher, and an Ann Chapin could marry her Charlie Bongiorno, even if he is an Italian accordion player. But O'Hara knows only too well that love fails because people withhold themselves from each other. His novels therefore suggest no way that love can transform the social order. His skepticism continually thwarted his own effort to visualize redemption through love. His portraits of "great love"— Alfred Eaton and Natalie Benziger, Joe Chapin and Kate Drummond—usually turn out to be simplistic, for when O'Hara moves from the physiology of sex to the emotion of love he tends to fall back on romantic sentimentalism. But as Leslie Fiedler has noted, "only a dedication to imaginative truth" is sufficient protection against a "sentimental falsification" of love,[39] and O'Hara's belief in the reality of the imagination, as against the world of the fact, was less than absolute. Still, O'Hara was right without doubt in believing that people would be a little less miserable and contemptible and the social order a little more humane if the cruel realities and illusions of caste did not keep them from loving each other.

9

✄ JOHN P. MARQUAND

Stasis and Change

It is often said that Marquand is an American Balzac or Thackeray.[1] Oddly enough, Marquand felt himself to be a part of the tradition of New England letters—Cotton Mather, Hawthorne, Emerson, Thoreau, Melville.[2] But his interest in these writers was antiquarian rather than derivative, and there is little evidence—aside from a recognition of the relief nature offers from the oppression of society—of their influence on his work. Among his contemporaries Marquand expressed admiration for Fitzgerald, Dos Passos, Dreiser, Sherwood Anderson, Hemingway, and Faulkner. But of the author of *Main Street* he confessed: "I would hesitate to rank myself with Lewis. I don't think I have nearly the same stature. But I am working in his vineyard."[3]

That vineyard is of course the novel of character defining itself in relation to society—through manners. Above all, it is a realistic novel. "A novel is great and good," Marquand once observed, "in direct proportion to the illusion it gives of life and a sense of living. It is great in direct proportion to the degree it enfolds the reader and permits him to walk in imagination with the people of an artificial but very real world, sharing their joys and sorrows, understanding their perplexities."[4] In ironically depicting the life of the American *haute bourgeoisie*, Marquand focuses on "money, property, and manners, the chief concerns of the middle class."[5] His subtle social perception, his almost effortless studies of the helpless individual caught in the cogs of the social machine, and the agreeableness of his prose style compel assent to the view Edward Wagenknecht expressed in 1950—that at mid-century Marquand was "our foremost practitioner of the social novel as Edith Wharton, F. Scott Fitzgerald, and Sinclair Lewis all understood the term."[6]

What these American writers understood by the term is markedly different from what Thackeray or Balzac meant by it. The difference lies in the relative impermanence of our social conventions as the material for fiction. Instead of a fixity of social types and social stability, the American novel is obliged to dramatize the impermanent and the evanescent. As C. Hugh Holman has observed: "The American novelist who would test his characters against a static social order or fixed conventions must ultimately despair of his native land as a subject for his art, as Cooper, Hawthorne, and James had done. The impact which democracy makes on manners converts the novelist from being a tester of character by established standards to a portrayer of character under the persistent impact of change. The social novelist's subject becomes mutability rather than order, and his testing cruxes occur when change rather than stasis puts stress on the moral values of his characters. 'Social mobility,' a term which he borrowed from the social anthropologists, thus becomes a recurrent condition, even in Boston, in Marquand's novels. The problems of caste, class, and social movement he knew intimately, and found fascinating."[7]

The changes which have occurred "since the horse and wagon days"—specifically the revolution in American social and moral standards—Marquand once called "the only thing that really interested me...."[8] They interested him enough to inspire nine novels documenting the impact of change on people conditioned to a belief in stability and order. His aim was a *Comédie humaine*: "I would like, before I'm through...to have a series of novels that would give a picture of a segment of America during the past fifty years."[9] His work constitutes a social history of the upper middle class in America, from the horse and wagon days to the mid-twentieth century, a social history rivaled in scope only by the Yoknapatawpha novels of William Faulkner and the Lantenengo County novels of John O'Hara. Marquand's settings range from the small town like Newburyport, Massachusetts, to the cities of Boston, New York, Washington, and Hollywood. His major characters include writers, businessmen, industrialists, radio personalities, lawyers, bankers, investment counselors, journalists, generals, and the idle rich (and not so rich). The books in which Marquand carries on the tradition are *The Late George Apley* (1937), *Wickford Point* (1939), *H. M. Pulham, Esquire* (1941), *So Little Time* (1943), *B. F.'s Daughter* (1946), *Point of No Return* (1949), *Melville Goodwin, U.S.A.* (1951), *Sincerely, Willis Wayde* (1955), and *Women and Thomas Harrow* (1958).

In giving us his vision of the American scene in these novels of manners, Marquand's method, like O'Hara's, was generally to compose a loosely plotted biography of a major character (usually the title character) struggling against the pressures of his society. Nearly all of the novels involve a flashback (or interwoven scenes presenting the past and present), in which the middle-aged protagonist, faced with a crucial decision, returns to the past—either through reminiscence or by physically returning to the scenes of his youth—and then solves his problem. "I like to begin with a man facing the crisis of his life," Marquand observed, "and then show how he got there."[10] On this "high-level" formula Marquand played some fascinating variations which are not too troublesome unless his novels are read in rapid succession.[11] The pattern expresses Marquand's recognition that the individual is fated to suffer, to be "caught in a pattern of social change, usually tragically."[12] Marquand's mastery of the flashback structure, his satisfying point-of-view technique, his command of dialogue, his believable characters, and his immense knowledge of the manners of the class he portrays led Nathan Glick in 1950 to call Marquand "our most accomplished novelist of manners."[13] It is difficult to see, then, why Marquand has never received the attention that some of his lesser contemporaries have enjoyed.

I

Although Marquand is identified with New England, he was born in Wilmington, Delaware, in 1893. His father, Philip Marquand, a well-to-do civil engineer and broker, lived in New York

City and Rye, where young Marquand grew up with the graces that wealth and an old family tradition can provide. The first Marquands settled in Newburyport, Massachusetts, in 1732 and over a period of nearly three hundred years distinguished themselves in shipping, privateering, and the China trade. Marquand claimed descent from the Dudleys who governed colonial Massachusetts; from Edward Everett Hale (author of "The Man Without A Country"); from great-aunt Elizabeth Curzon Hoxie (who cast her lot with Ripley and Hawthorne at Brook Farm); from great-aunt Mary Curzon (who was courted by both John Greenleaf Whittier and William Ellery Channing); and from great-aunt Margaret Fuller (whom one recent journalist soberly described as the Dorothy Thompson of the nineteenth century).

Supported by family tradition and wealth, Marquand was slated for Groton or St. Mark's and Harvard. But because of his father's bad luck on the stock exchange, the Marquands lost everything they had. Fifteen-year-old John was sent to live with three maiden aunts in Newburyport, and his parents went to Central America to work on the Panama Canal. "I can remember distinctly how I felt when we didn't have any more money [after the crash of 1901]," Marquand later reminisced. "I could feel myself becoming what [anthropologist W. L.] Warner calls 'mobilized downward.' Of course, I had read Horatio Alger and I was ready to face this change in circumstance in a sportsmanlike manner."[14] But instead of Groton, Marquand went to Newburyport High School, where he was the only boy whose parents were listed in the New York *Social Register*. Marquand did not have the money for Harvard when the time came, and he was forced to matriculate in 1911 as a Scholarship Boy in Chemistry, a subject in which he had no interest whatsoever. At Harvard he made none of the clubs, knew very few people, and was miserable. "Harvard is a subject which I still face with mixed emotions," he later confessed. "I brought away from it a number of frustrations and illusions which have handicapped me throughout my life."[15] Nevertheless, he stuck it out and graduated with the Class of 1915.

It is difficult to overestimate the significance of these experiences on Marquand's development as a novelist of manners. Like

Fitzgerald and O'Hara, he had a father whose financial failure affected him profoundly, particularly in relation to his education. Like them, he brooded on the gradations of class and status, on his exclusion from the center of things, on the manifestations of snobbery which told him just what his place was. Fortunately, the decline of the family fortune introduced him to his New England heritage and provided him, in *Wickford Point*, with a charming model of an aristocratic family gone to seed in the twentieth century, and there can be little question that the portraits of John Gray of *Point of No Return*, George Tasmin of *B. F.'s Daughter*, and Alf Wayde of *Sincerely, Willis Wayde* are based on his improvident father.

In 1922 he married Christina Sedgwick of Stockbridge, Massachusetts. New England patricians, the Sedgwicks reinforced Marquand's sense of social inferiority. Ellery Sedgwick, Christina's uncle and editor of the *Atlantic Monthly*, was an *arbiter elegantarium* of Boston Literature. Henry Dwight Sedgwick, another uncle and one of the last of the true Brahmins, spoke for the family in *In Praise of Gentlemen* (1935), which celebrated urbanity, tact, manners, elegance, the proprieties and traditional standards—as opposed to the vulgar forces in America which threatened his class—science, democracy, business, and like related ills. The old virtues of "manners, style, modesty, taste, privacy, and love of traditional values," he lamented, "have gone down hopelessly before the assaults of democracy."[16]

This marriage into the wealthy Sedgwicks forced Marquand to spend his time writing for the high-paying "smooth" magazines, as he blandly called them—*Saturday Evening Post*, *Collier's*, *Ladies' Home Journal*, and *Good Housekeeping*. Only the *Atlantic* measured up to the Sedgwick standard of taste, but it was a luxury Marquand could not afford. Christina "didn't realize that my Uncle Ellery would have given me a nice silver inkwell or a hundred dollars, and that wouldn't pay the bills."[17] Out of this need for money Marquand wrote exclusively slick fiction during the early years of his career. His critics have consequently underestimated Marquand's powers as a writer. Yet he never dismissed these works as easily as his critics because of his respect for the consistently high craftsmanship such writing required.

II

In 1935, Marquand rebelled against the Sedgwicks and, financially "in a position to write something which [he] really wanted to write," he unleashed "a savage attack on the old water side of Beacon Street."[18]   Christina warned him that they would have to leave Boston, but in this aristocracy Marquand had his subject, and he went ahead with the novel. The product of this rebellion against the Sedgwicks and their class was *The Late George Apley* (1937). Besides a divorce, it won for him the 1938 Pulitzer Prize.

Bostonians have always believed themselves to be a chosen people, as Howells's *Lapham* and *A Chance Acquaintance* suggest. "More and more," as Barrett Wendell reminded Mrs. Gardner in 1902, "it seems to me that the future of our New England must depend on the standards of culture which we maintain and preserve here."[19] The "we" of whom Wendell spoke were the Brahmins, whom Oliver Wendell Holmes first distinguished from the merely rich, on the ground that the "trivial and fugitive fact of personal wealth does not create a permanent class." *Elsie Venner* defines the Brahmin caste in terms of "the repetition of the same influences, generation after generation," which had produced "a class organization and physiognomy." The hereditary Brahmin could be easily recognized by his frank physiognomy, delicate features, clear eye, graceful and ready articulation, and quick intelligence. The Brahmin's felicitous refinement, aptitude for learning, his feeling for the life of the mind and for the "finer instincts," Holmes argued, characterize this "harmless, inoffensive, untitled aristocracy."[20]

Holmes knew little enough of the economics of New England industrialism or of the shrewd practices by which the fortunes of the ancestral Brahmins were amassed, not to speak of the nature of hereditary transmission.[21] But Marquand understood the values of Holmes and his descendants. He knew the tacit importance of money to the Brahmin caste and the power of the family in shaping its tone, attitudes, and values. *The Late George Apley* exposes with dazzling clarity the characteristics of the caste in perpetuating its conventions virtually unchanged during one of the most turbulent eras of American history. Marquand's method in the novel was to parody the authorized life and letters of a famous Bostonian, the kind of biography produced by John P. Morse, Jr., and M. A. DeWolfe Howe. Of the organization of the book and its point of view, Marquand once noted: "I conceived the idea for its structure after having read several volumes of collected letters of V.I.P.'s in Boston (and elsewhere) throughout which were scattered numerous biographical interpolations prepared by an often unduly sympathetic editor."[22] It is subtitled "A Novel in the Form of a Memoir," an invitation to think of it in terms of George Santayana's *The Last Puritan* (1935), which was subtitled "A Memoir in the Form of a Novel." George Apley is revealed to us by his letters to family and friends and by the interpolations of the vain and easily deceived fictitious biographer, Horatio Willing. Marquand believed that Willing's "long-winded pomposity" was "not a bad device for setting the tone of this novel, since Mr. Apley himself was a carefully nurtured product of a pompous self-conscious provincial environment, whatever may have been its virtues."[23]

Its virtues are of course considerable, and they are suggested in great detail—"the essential undeviating discipline of background," tradition and continuity, civic responsibility, the wise and prudent stewardship of great wealth, the avoidance of ostentation, noblesse oblige, the reconciliation of inclination with obligation, family solidarity, conscientiousness, and conscience. But Marquand shows Brahmin Boston to suffer the defects of its virtues—reactionary opposition to change, clannishness, snobbery, an exaggerated reverence for respectability, and the repression of the individual. The crucial episode in Apley's life is falling in love with an Irish girl from South Boston, a defection from the standards of his class which gets him shipped off to Europe. In part his defection is what Marquand saw as "the perpetual revolt of youth from tradition."[24] But this aborted rebellion is also the chief illustration of the massive power of the environment to conform the individual to the group will: "I am the sort of man I am," Apley says of himself, "because environment prevented my being anything else" (*LGA*, 3).

Few individuals, Marquand noted in *Timothy Dexter Revisited*, "are important in themselves. The environment that produced and tolerated Dexter," like the environment that produced Apley, "is far more interesting than the man."[25] If Apley goes to Europe, London is simply a larger Boston—because only Bostonians are worth knowing abroad. If he wants to go into business he finds that his inheritance has been bequeathed in trust—because the Apley family distrust his business acumen. If he has romantic inclinations, they are nipped in the bud and a sensible marriage—based on property and a community of tastes—is "arranged" for him. To Horatio Willing there is nothing remarkable in Apley's surrender to the "quiet world of mind and order" which was Boston:

> To those of us who know it and are a part of it there is nothing unnatural in the preoccupation of a Bostonian with his environment; for order—so lamentably lacking in other cities—tends to make him so completely at home and so contented with his social group that he is unhappy in any other. Starting with the nucleus of the family and its immediate friends, and next to it the school attended by these same contemporaries, he finally reaches the dancing class, and then the Thursday afternoons, and next the Friday evenings. A young girl will be introduced into society and will join the Sewing Circle of her year; a boy will be taken into his father's Club at Harvard. There is a simplicity in this procedure which emanates, I think, from the laudable similarity of ideas which makes up Boston life. These ideas have their foundation on the firm substratum of common sense which runs back to the beginnings of our colonial founders. This common sense, combined with an appreciation of what is truly fine, has given us a stability and a genuine society in a chaotic, nervous nation. If this society has moulded an individual in conformation to its principles, I, for one, cannot see why this is a deplorable situation, as every human being must conform to the social demands of his group, whatever that group may be. [*LGA*, 41–42]

This passage is a useful illustration of the ambivalence of Marquand's satire. For it would be hard to deny that individuals *do* seek out their counterparts, that they *do* want to integrate themselves into the social lives of their groups, whatever they are. But this desire is especially characteristic of Apley's world. For Boston, as Marquand once noted, "is a complex of intricately developed manners and of delicately balanced values that make it not only a city but also a state of mind which demands constant association if it is to be fully comprehended."[26]

Apley's capitulation to the values of his class is full of genuine pathos because, as we soon discover, it is paid for by the utter loss of his individuality and spontaneity. Eventually Apley will drill into his son John what his father Thomas has drilled into him—that "family is more important than the individual" (*LGA*, 231): "I know well that it is hard always to be conventional, for one rather struggles against convention at your age. On the whole you will find this struggle is a mistake and really a great waste of time. Do not try to be different from what you are because in the end you will find that you cannot be different" (*LGA*, 217). John, like a large number of Brahmin youth, revolts and goes off to New York to work. In urging his son to return to Boston, Apley expresses a reverence for tradition that Edith Wharton would warmly have approved: "I cannot think that you do not love this place as I love it. It is impossible for me to believe that you can fit anywhere else. I am so sure of it that I have a hope that in a year or two you will reconsider. If you do not, who will look after Hillcrest when I am gone? I am older than you and the older I grow the more convinced I am that there must be some sort of continuity in this changing world, something to which one must hold fast. It is something which we have here." Apley goes on to say, "I know you have laughed at many people and at many customs, as I have in my time, but I hope that you have laughed kindly as I have. At any rate, when the jest is over, continuity remains. You will find, as I have, a solace in background and tradition. It will always be waiting for you here" (*LGA*, 280). At Apley's death, John *does* return to Boston, reenacting his father's abortive revolt from and return to the tradition. Since the sense of freedom is illusory in Marquand's world, he finally submits to the obligations of class and status. There never is an opportunity for an Apley to walk up any road alone.

The conventions of New England society are so fully and inflexibly spelled out, so omnipotent, that instead of saying You Can't Go Home Again, Marquand's fiction suggests that You Can't Ever Leave. The return of George and John Apley is paralleled in the submission of Harry Pulham to the magnetism of Boston and in Jim Calder's recognition that he will never be able to escape the Brills and Wickford Point. Bostonians, Marquand once observed, "have all been molded by environment and they have all reacted to a sequence of common experience which has sharpened their capacity of adjustment until they are more at home in Boston than in any other place."[27]

Marquand's chief objection to the narrow social world of New England, as portrayed in *Apley*, *Pulham*, and *Wickford Point*, is that excessive deference to convention frustrates the emotional life of man. Apley's love for Mary Monahan is the most important fact in his life, yet such is the power of convention that it is never realized. New England society is rocky soil for the seed of love: Apley is estranged from Catherine, his son rebels, and his daughter rejects him altogether. Social conventions are affirmed by the men of Apley's world, but Marquand's fiction consistently suggests that wives are responsible for the repression of feelings and emotions. Most of his novels deal with a man torn between Wife (representing obligation, convention, and social responsibility) and the Ideal Woman (representing freedom, spontaneity, and love). Catherine Bosworth represents the obligation of class Apley must accept and defend; Mary Monahan represents freedom from obligations and institutions: "Darling, I love you more than anything in the world," he writes to Mary Monahan. "You give me something that makes me feel free for the first time in my life. Nothing, dear, has made me so happy as this sense of freedom" (*LGA*, 89). The freedom may be ultimately illusory, but the happiness is real. Man may still be defeated by society, but Marquand suggests that love mitigates the power of necessity by creating an illusion of freedom and happiness.

Marquand once complained that "it is a reflection on the American male of the twentieth century that only his secretary is really good to him. Not his wife. The American wife in the upper brackets," he observed, "is aggressive, arrogant, domineering, not conditioned to the school that English, French or Italian wives are. She is invariably difficult. Therefore American men turn elsewhere frantically and in every direction. Every American in all the fiction I have read—from Sinclair Lewis down the line—is seeking a sympathetic woman. He can seldom find her in his own social echelon."[28] This observation doubtless grew out of the failure of his first two marriages, the second to Adelaide Hooker, a relative of the Rockefellers. But it offers a revealing insight into the origin of American novels of manners. If we contemplate the love-triangles of some of the writers we have so far considered (May-Archer-Ellen in *The Age of Innocence*; Daisy-Tom-Myrtle in *Gatsby*; Myra-Babbitt-Tanis in *Babbitt*; Mary-Alfred-Natalie in *From the Terrace*; and Catherine-Apley-Mary Monahan in *The Late George Apley*) the pattern Marquand defines is valid. The novel of manners may thus dramatize the resentment American men feel at the social demands of the women of their class. To cope with it they turn to sympathetic women of a lower social station who give them a sense of freedom and fulfillment not expressed in the manners of their own social world. The dilemma of such protagonists is this: either find the sympathetic woman or find some way of escaping from society through creating a masculine world.

Marquand's fiction employs both patterns. The conflict between Obligation and Desire—symbolized by the Wife vs. the Ideal Woman—is found in many of Marquand's novels. Harry Pulham wants to leave his wife Kay for Marvin Myles in New York. Jeff Wilson wants to abandon Madge for the glamorous Marianna Miller in *So Little Time*. Bob Tasmin is torn between Polly Fulton and his wife Mildred in *B. F.'s Daughter*, Melville Goodwin between Helen and Dottie Peale. *Women and Thomas Harrow* bristles with resentment against the destruction a wife may inflict on a sensitive man. As wives, Marquand's women aggressively manipulate the power of convention, inhibit spontaneity, and frustrate feeling; their function in Marquand's novels is to embody the social and institutional pressures which make of men's lives a human bondage. In this respect, Marquand's resentment of the feminine world and its rules resembles Sinclair Lewis's and, like Lewis's battles with Gracie and Dorothy Thompson, probably grew out of his own relationships with Christina Sedgwick and Adelaide Hooker.

The other alternative—creating a masculine world—also reflects male hostility to convention. Babbitt's Maine hunting trip with Paul Riesling is an effort to escape social pressures associated with Myra and Zilla. Marquand's characters also seek this escape. The idea of nature generally has no function in American novels of manners except to offer a foil to society, as a place of solitude where the single individual may find himself. Charles Gray wants to go off on an anthropological expedition to the Orinoco in *Point of No Return*; Jim Calder retreats down the Wickford River in his canoe when things are too much for him. Tom Brett, Jeff Wilson, and Melville Goodwin use their clubs, the war, or the army as an excuse to get away from women and the life of society. George Apley creates a hunting camp on Pequod Island as "a haven for men, since he was under the illusion that its facilities were of too rough and ready a nature to appeal to the fairer sex." But, as Horatio Willing blandly notes, "He was soon cheerfully to admit his error" (*LGA*, 172). Within a short time Catherine Apley, Amelia Simmings, and other Brahmin women invade the sanctuary and take it over. They impose a schedule on the camp, organize all the activities, and import those Boston proprieties that Apley has tried vainly to escape. So totally do they overrun the camp that, to get any solitude, Apley is forced to organize a group within the group—known as the "camping crowd," composed entirely of men. "I had thought on first coming to Pequod Island," he writes to Dr. Sewell, "that we might have a moment's breathing space, a respite from what we know so well and love so much. I suppose that this was rather too much to hope for. It sometimes seems to me that Boston has come to Pequod Island. I suppose we cannot escape from it entirely, nor do we really wish to, but I know what you and I like: the dripping water from a canoe paddle, the scent of balsam, the sweet smell of pond lilies, and the mud, the weariness of a long carry. These things are still on tap at Pequod Island" (*LGA*, 175).

But in Marquand's world there is no escape from society or from the manners and conventions it imposes because there is no escape from the self that society has shaped. "Given certain qualities, you've either got to take to the woods or get in there and play by the rules that are laid down," Marquand once observed in another connection. Apley is one of those who have to get in there and play by the rules. "I wish I were not always resting beneath the umbrella of my own personality" (*LGA*, 176), Apley says. It is a vain wish. But Apley is no straw man, for "like anyone in any *rentier* class," he "had many admirable sides to his character"; these ruled out too savage a caricature.[29] So carefully controlled and qualified by affection is Marquand's kindly satire, it is often impossible to separate the voice of Willing and Apley from that of Marquand. Certainly Marquand disliked in equal measure some of the things Apley deplores—like the ill-digested Freudianism of the twenties, the inanities of New York café society, the corruption of machine politics, and the vulgarization of public life by the advertising world. "Boston has been shaken by impacts that may well make strong men weep,"[30] Marquand once observed, and Apley's attempts to save Boston from *some* of these degrading forces are rendered with rare sympathy. No one can disagree with Apley's observation that "we have evolved a fine variety of flushing toilets but not a very good world." And it is hard to fault his hope that the generation of his grandson would return to a sense of civic obligations, realize their duty to the community, and comport themselves responsibly: "I hope he will see what so many of you have forgotten," Apley says to John of his grandson, "that there must be certain standards, that there must be certain formulae in art and thought and manners," that there must be "a class which sets a tone, not for its own pleasure, but because of the responsibility which it owes to others" (*LGA*, 329). A privileged class yes, but a class that knows how to pay for its privilege through service.

Always in Marquand's world, however, it is the individual who must pay for the conventions of society. And the poignancy of Apley's sacrifice is his knowledge of what it has cost him. Shortly before his death he reads Emerson and reexamines his life objectively: "I have always been faced from childhood by the obligation of convention," he confesses to John, "and all of these conventions have been made by others, formed from the fabric of the past. In some ways these have stepped in between me and life. I had to realize that they were designed to do just that. They were designed to promote stability and inheritance. Perhaps they have gone a little bit too far" (*LGA*, 343–44). Apley missed love, a life of action, the pleasures of the sensual life, and the satisfaction induced by the contemplation of nature. But in perceiving how repeatedly (though futilely) Apley struggled with his world, we come to concede and appreciate Apley's sense of honor, courage, and truth. As John Apley admits, "Father and guts."

III

Wickford Point (1939) and *H. M. Pulham, Esquire* (1941) complete Marquand's early tryptich of American life in nineteenth- and twentieth-century New England. They seemed to type him as a New England regionalist—a classification he always resented. The pattern of revolt from convention and submission to it, Marquand felt, was a universal pattern. If Apley has any value today, he said in 1956, "I believe it is because Mr. Apley still has his own sort of universality. Wherever a few generations of leisure combine with inherited security, there will develop a pattern of manners, attitudes, and politenesses."[31] The point was the pattern, not the region. But so few readers have cared to separate Marquand from his New England milieu that he complained that "ever since *The Late George Apley* my novels, no matter what their characters or locale, are known in advance to be about wealthy and snobbish citizens who live in the vicinity of Boston."[32] What makes *So Little Time* (1943) and *B. F.'s Daughter* (1946) interesting, however, is not the New York, Hollywood, or Washington settings but a perceptible change in Marquand's view of the relationship of the individual to society. The World War II years posed the question of whether *society itself* could survive the stresses being put on it. Marquand was terrified by the slogan: "Everything before the war is out." This attitude promised a disorientation in manners and morals comparable to that which followed World War I.

The best of Marquand's postwar novels was *Point of No Return* (1949), a study in what he called "the badgered American male—and that includes me—fighting for a little happiness and always being crushed by the problems of his environment."[33] Charles Gray, like Apley and Pulham, suffers a quiet desperation comparable to the *angst* of modern philosophy. Its origin, though, is less existential than social. Charles responds to social pressure by keeping a stiff upper lip and carrying on, but this postwar novel suggests that no longer is society, with its elaborate conventions and manners, the enemy of the individual. From this point on in Marquand's career the enemy is Time itself—in its sociological dimension as the continuum in which communities like Clyde and Boston suffer change, and in the psychological sense as the fluid present where the consciousness preserves the past unchanged. As always with Marquand, *Point of No Return* deals with the defeat of the individual.

The framework within which Marquand explores the defeat of Charles Gray, by the impact of time upon him and his environment, is the personal crisis posed in the first chapter of the novel: Will he be promoted to the vacant vice-presidency of the Stuyvesant Bank in New York City and receive all the advantages such an advancement confers—a larger house in a better suburb with a new car and a more affluent way of life? If the novel explores some of the same issues of philistine corporation morality dealt with in William H. Whyte's *The Organization Man*, Riesman's *The Lonely Crowd*, and Sloan Wilson's *The Man in the Gray Flannel Suit*, Marquand invests them with real emotional power by showing the pattern of events which lead the middle-aged protagonist to where he is—at the point of no return. The novel employs a three-part envelope structure involving the beginning and end set in contemporary New York and Clyde, Massachusetts, and the middle set in the Clyde of Charles's boyhood. In developing this structure, Marquand tests some widely held American values subsumed under the phrase "The American Dream": success and failure, money and ambition, gambling and "the system," the relation of happiness to liberty, and the question of whether it is worth it all.

At the same time, *Point of No Return* presents a superb portrait of the social history of two groups of people in two widely dissimilar regions. This social history is necessary to our understanding of the significance of the crisis that faces Charles Gray, for New York is characterized by a high degree of social mobility, Clyde by a high degree of stability. They become symbolic of the dichotomies that Marquand wished to work out— order vs. chaos, and flux vs. permanence. The novel begins in Sycamore Park, the businessman's bedroom-suburb of New York, where Charles and Nancy live with their children; it ends in Roger's Point, at the Long Island mansion of the president of the bank, a symbol of what Charles Gray is working to achieve. The arena where upward social mobility is to be achieved in Charles's world is the floor of the Stuyvesant Bank where Charles and Roger Blakesley compete for the vacancy caused by the death of a colleague.

The most memorable scenes in the novel, however, are set in Clyde, the old New England village thirty-five miles north of Boston, for Marquand's imagination functioned best when he dealt with his native Newburyport. The Clyde Historical Society with its layers and layers of the past in which Charles's roots are sunk; the Lovell House on Johnson Street, with its old Federalist architecture and its Hepplewhite and Chippendale furniture; the large house of John Gray on Spruce Street; the Clyde Inn, the Shore Club, Dock Street—all of these settings create the web of Clyde in which Charles Gray, long after he leaves, is psychologically imprisoned. The extensive flashback is not irrelevant to Charles's crisis at the Stuyvesant Bank, for Charles's story is "a small-town story": "It's the difference between Spruce Street and Johnson Street. I should have remembered we [the Grays] were Spruce Streeters."[34]

The signals of status and social gradation are in part suggested by these settings—the differences between Sycamore Park and Roger's Point, between the Oak Knoll and the Hawthorn Hill country clubs, and between the residences on Spruce Street and Johnson Street. In New York City money confers status. At the bank, Charles reflects, "your social status was obvious from the position of your desk" on the bank floor, from the commuter train you took (those on the make take the 8:02, while the "executive aristocracy," who have a "margin of leisure," take the 8:30). When status changes, it is signalled by subtleties which only an observer like Marquand could suggest. In Clyde status is conferred not by money but by family position. When Charles Gray proposes to Jessica Lovell on the basis of the $45,000 he has won on the stock market, Mr. Lovell tells him that inherited money is one thing and stock market money another. The Lovell grandfathers were shipowners; the Grays were merely ship captains. Again and again, Marquand suggests the rigidity of a social order as tightly organized as a beehive: "Everyone had a place in that plan and everyone instinctively seemed to know where he belonged. Its completeness reminded Charles of what his Aunt Jane said once when she was arranging the flat silver in the sideboard of her dining room—everything in its place and a place for everything. The Irish, for instance, had their place, and so had the French-Canadians and the new immigrants, like the Italians and the Poles, who naturally belonged close to the Wright-Sherwin factory and the shoe-shops. There was a place for the North Enders, too. They lived in the North End and went to the North End Congregational Church and even if they lived in other parts of Clyde they were still North Enders." Few observers have known an American small town well enough to perceive the inflexibility of such class lines despite their invisibility. Growing up in Clyde, Charles learned that "certain people who lived on Johnson Street were not Johnson Street people, hence, because you knew, their living on Johnson Street did not disturb the plan" (PNR, 166). He discovers that whether one belonged to the Monday Club, the Thursday Club, the Confessional Club, the Clyde Fund, or the Board of the Dock Street Bank told a great deal about where he fitted into the complex social hierarchy of Clyde. "Probably no other American novelist since Sinclair Lewis," as Hugh Holman rightly observes, "has examined the class structure of a small American city with the accuracy and illuminating insight that Marquand employed in this novel."[35]

In dealing with these signs of social gradation, Marquand also explores the problem of stability and change in society itself. By this I mean not the upward or downward mobility of the individual but what the passage of time does to the social order itself. Old timers like John Gray and Miss Sarah may complain that Clyde is much changed from what it was in the "old days," but Clyde is fundamentally a changeless world—or so at least it seems. During the twenty years Charles lives in New York it abides for him as the one changeless frame in a fluid and shifting world. Mark Twain observed that "custom is custom; it is built of brass, boiler iron, granite; facts, reasonings, arguments have no more effect upon it than the idle winds have on Gibraltar."[36] But there is one thing that does change communities and their customs—time. Charles does not sufficiently anticipate how Clyde will have

changed in his twenty-year absence. When he returns in 1947, he
finds it so altered that Jackie Mason has risen to the top of Clyde
society and intends to marry Jessica Lovell. Jessica and Mr. Lovell are pathetic shadows of the powerful forces Charles has been
subjectively struggling with for twenty years. As Louis Auchincloss suggests, when status and conventions are shown to be
largely illusory and sustained only by the imagination and memory, the novel of manners has passed over into the psychological
novel.[37]

   Change for Marquand then was not merely a sociological phenomenon; it was also a metaphysical datum affecting the consciousness. Marquand saw change as an existential feature of the
human condition which continuously compromised the authen-
ticity of values: "They were all caught in a current that jostled
them and interfered with normal existence," Charles thinks to
himself. "All anyone could do was to try to adjust his life within
the limits of a constantly changing frame." But the difficulty for
the Marquand hero is that "even the limits were continually
changing" (*PNR*, 129). Jeff Wilson's conclusion in *So Little
Time* that nothing was going to be permanent, that he could see
the whole thing going, is similarly pessimistic. Polly Fulton ac-
knowledges in *B. F.'s Daughter* that "everything that had been a
constant quality was lost" and that "there was no continuity any
longer in the way people materialized."[38] The idea of a life as a
constantly changing frame is presented in the image of an aquar-
ium: "It's gone . . . and I don't know when it went, and what's
more, I can't entirely remember what it was although we all lived
in it. We're like fish being moved from one body of water, and
now we're in another, but everything is moving so fast I can't
remember what it used to be like" (*BFD*, 75). Things are so
complicated, Sid Skelton observes in *Melville Goodwin, USA*,
that no one ever had a chance to know what he was made for.
And Thomas Harrow is obsessed by the continuous transformations of the New York world he has grown up in: "You lived
for decades in New York, but the time inevitably arrived when
you retreated to a small area of it. You finally could not adjust
yourself to its constant changes. You were more aware of impermanence there than anywhere else in the world." "In every-

one there was a lurking desire for permanence," Harrow thinks to himself, "and most of life was pursuit of it." That is why Harrow takes refuge in Clyde: although he does not belong to the "elastic but undeviating social order" of Clyde, it is the nearest thing life offers to satisfy the desire for permanence.[39]

The novelist of manners has a fairly constant theme in *O tempora, O mores*, as I have indicated. Marquand's point is that you cannot understand the mores unless you understand the past out of which they emerge. Marquand's flashbacks are thus not sterile formulae but the means of making visible the mysterious relation between the present and the past. If literature is a form of knowledge, it is because techniques like this give us an understanding of an event in the totality of its impact on a character. We are what we are, Marquand insists, because of the way the past has shaped us, and that shaping is the effect of external forces: "Everybody says 'life is what you make it,'" Marquand once observed, "and it seems to me, by God, it's mostly environment you're coping with and you have mighty little chance to make it yourself. I don't see that many people are particularly captains of their fate. They bat it out," Marquand continued, "but do they really get what they want? I'm damned if I think so."[40]

Marquand's admiration of Sinclair Lewis is evident in the satire in *Point of No Return*, particularly the spiel of Mr. Forbush about the Oak Knoll Country Club and Tony Burton's "Banking as an Art," a speech which reduces all values to a matter of money and all history to a clay tablet preserving ancient errors in arithmetic. But the most trenchant satire in the novel, in all of Marquand's novels in fact, is reserved for the coldly impersonal analysis of Clyde by Malcolm Bryant, a social anthropologist. Bryant sees Clyde as "a complex of instinctive forces and behavior" resembling a beehive or the Spartan world under King Lycurgus. He brings to his study of Clyde the same methods he uses to study the Zambesis of Africa or the headhunters of Borneo. "Man is essentially the same, whether he's in G-strings or plus fours" (*PNR*, 409), Bryant tells Charles Gray. The Fireman's Muster is a sacred ritual and the Confessional Club is a gathering of the Old Men of the tribe, keeping the women hidden.[41] And to define the social stratification of Clyde, he slices it up into social classes—the upper-upper, the middle-upper, and the lower-upper; the upper-middle, the middle-middle, and the lower middle; and the same divisions for the lower class. Everybody is fixed in Bryant's little system.

Point of No Return thus satirizes the multivolume sociological analysis of Newburyport, Massachusetts, undertaken by W. Lloyd Warner and his staff of thirty field workers between 1930 and 1934 and abridged in one volume entitled *Yankee City*. Warner had been studying Stone Age aborigines in Australia when he decided to study the "whole man" in his sociological and cultural milieu in a modern American town. Working on the basis of a six-level social hierarchy, "and with the aid of such additional testimony as the area lived in, the type of house, kind of education, manners, and other symbols of class," Warner sought to determine "the approximate place of any individual in the society."[42] Warner's object was to define the facts of social class and social mobility and to relate them to what he called the American dream of " a great democracy trying to remain or become democratic and equalitarian while solving the problems of unifying vast populations and diverse enterprises."[43] There can be no question that Marquand disliked the pedantry of social anthropologists who were "pampered, preposterous creatures," "who lived an artificial life," "who did not want to understand or be liked by other people," and who represented "the unskillful ignorance of most dwellers in ivory towers."

But Marquand was in fact strongly sympathetic to a systematized study of social phenomena. He believed that man is "a nexus of institutions,"[44] that everyone has a place in one frame or another, and that happiness and contentment may be a by-product of one's integration into the social order. When Charles gets over his personal resentment of Bryant and reads his *Yankee Persepolis* (so named because New England villagers, like ancient Persians, revere the past and worship memories), Charles begins to see Clyde as it was in his youth: "There was the individual's unknowing surrender to the group, the unthinking desire for order. He could see the Grays on Spruce Street and the Lovells on Johnson Street through Malcolm Bryant's eyes, and it was hard to believe that he could have lived in this arbitrary frame, illustrated by curves and diagrams, and now he was living in another. He could almost see the Stuyvesant Bank and that evening at Oak Knoll in a new revealing light—almost, but not entirely" (*PNR*, 147–48). But the way really to learn about Clyde, Marquand held, was not from the outside like Bryant and his team of social anthropologists, but from *within*—by being brought up there. Warner was not the model of Malcolm Bryant, but, as Granville Hicks has pointed out, Marquand had the right to satirize *Yankee City* because he had "a better understanding of the class structure of contemporary American society than Lloyd Warner and all his advisers, colleagues and assistants put together."[45]

In *Point of No Return* Marquand's analogy for the environmental force which crushes the individual is simply "they" or "the system." In the course of the novel, several careers are studied in terms of "the system." Burt J. Selig, for example, achieves rapid upward social mobility. But if he is not dishonest, he is a Jew; his ascent is blocked by an economic establishment dominated by WASPs. In the banking world Walter Gibbs and Roger Blakesley are also studied. Gibbs fails because he does not have a Dale Carnegie personality. Blakesley has superficial advantages, like a degree from the Harvard Business School, but he too has the wrong personality; he is too eager, too extravagant, too imprudent and flippant when he should be dignified. The "ideal" type is Tony Burton, the bank president, with his conservative double-breasted suit, square wristwatch, and managerial bearing.

Marquand also tests the careers of several Clyde men in terms of the "system." Although he has more money than anyone else in town, Mr. Stanley counts for nothing with upper-uppers like Mr. Lovell, who thinks it has come to a fine pass in Clyde when a *nouveau* like Stanley can ask for his daughter's hand in marriage. Jackie Mason is a more interesting study of the upward mobility of the successful businessman. Grandson of a druggist (not even a ship captain, much less an owner), Jackie Mason seems limited by his middle-middle-class background. Yet he is aware of his limitations and attentive to appearances. He knows that he cannot afford to be eccentric because of his grandfather's occupation. As a boy he reads magazine stories about successful men, and he comes to believe that "it didn't matter where you started—even if your grandfather had been a druggist—it was a question of working hard, Jack said, and of meeting the right people" (*PNR*, 199). Jackie plays his cards very carefully, and when Charles Gray returns to Clyde after an absence of twenty years, he finds that Jackie heads up the accounting department at Wright-Sherwin, has been elected to all the best local societies, and is even engaged to marry Jessica Lovell. Remaining at home, he has become the first man in Ostia, while Charles has become the second in Rome. Yet as Charles studies him, it is clear that Jackie—with his loud, sedulously knotted tie and his unfashionable brown suit—is and always will be a small-town boy. His success is an almost perfect illustration of the possibilities of the American Dream. But the significance of Jackie's rise is sharply undercut by our realization that he would never have become successful if people like Charles Gray had stayed in Clyde. The moral of Jackie Mason's rise is that the social order is disintegrating. As in Lewis's *Main Street*, the village is dying.

The major studies of success and failure are John Gray and his son Charles. John Gray is a man generally loved by the townspeople for his generous and liberal spirit, but he is bitterly ashamed of his financial failures. His obsession with money is a critique of the very dream that Jackie Mason cherishes, and Charles comes to wonder whether all human behaviorism is perhaps somehow mixed up with money. John Gray is the dreamer who wanted to get something for nothing, to beat the system. When the Grays inherit Aunt Jane's money and John Gray conspicuously puts a $100 gold treasury note into the collection plate; when he buys a brand new Cadillac phaeton they cannot really afford; and when he gambles on the stock market to make a million dollars, it is more than vulgar ostentation. It is intended to erase at one stroke all his previous failures and to establish himself and his family as the social equal of the Lovells and the Johnson Street people. As they stand on the porch looking at the new Cadillac, Charles thinks to himself, "It was all like a dream, the Great American Dream." "Don't worry, Esther," John tells his wife, "we really need a car." "Somehow it was inevitable,"

Charles reflects, "somehow the Great American Dream was not tawdry" (*PNR*, 376).

But the system is rigged, of course; the stock market crashes in 1929, and John Gray is wiped out. Aunt Jane's money, the "product of self-denial and planning, something which had been saved and earned, something to be treated with decent respect" (*PNR*, 356), is squandered in John Gray's foolish speculation. But his gambling on the stock market is more than just an attempt to "make it" in terms of the American dream of wealth and success. The stock market is symbolic of the human condition itself. All life is a desperate gamble on a rigged exchange, or in what Marquand once called "the great crap game of life."[46] And the bequest of Aunt Jane's money represents John Gray's first chance to beat the system—to pit himself totally against the conditions of life that have made him the "failure" that he is. He wants everything or nothing out of life and when he fails—mastered and betrayed by his dreams—he commits suicide.

To cover his father's market losses and to prove to Mr. Lovell that he was wrong to reject him as a prospective son-in-law, Charles goes to New York determined to triumph over the system that defeated his father. The image which expresses Charles's ambition is the hay: "There's always the bundle of hay out ahead, for any ass who wants to get on," John tells him, "and They make it look like a very pleasant bundle" (*PNR*, 220). He warns his son not to be too ambitious about the bundle of hay. But Charles ignores his father's advice. And in working up through the ranks at the Stuyvesant Bank he discovers that "They" have involved him in various kinds of systems from which there is no escape. Clyde involves him in one system, the bank involves him in another, and the army is just like the bank—another system with other rules. All of the systems of the world make up the Environmental Force that wears down the individual. Charles and his wife are just like his father—trying to beat the system, but in another way. "It was always himself and Nancy against the world and against all the systems in it, against Tony Burton and the Stuyvesant Bank and American Tel & Tel, against the furnace and the doctors and the bills. It was always himself and Nancy striving for security . . ." (*PNR*, 473). The system is the world, which stands in hostile opposition to the desire of the individual for security and happiness. In various ways, it defeats John and Charles Gray, Jessica Lovell and her father, Roger Blakesley and even Jackie Mason.

The trouble with trying to beat the system is that in a value-less universe the basis for happiness, like everything else, is also constantly changing. The quotations from *Rasselas* reinforce Charles's discovery of the vanity of human wishes; the more you get the more you want, nothing seems to bring real happiness. As Charles tells Jackie, when you pursue happiness, "you usually lose your liberty . . . and the best part of your life. Maybe that's what everything's about" (*PNR*, 516). Playing the system in search of happiness leads to apple-polishing your superiors, stifling your ideas and emotions, knifing friends and acquaintances, neglecting wife and family, and inventing a public-relations personality to front for Them, the system itself. Maybe it's best not to try too hard for happiness, Apley counsels his son John. Maybe, as Malcolm Bryant suggests, happiness is merely the consequence of the individual's integration into a perfectly ordered social world.

Several times the novel asks whether it is all worth while, whether life has any values that justify trying to beat the system. When Charles mistakenly believes that he has lost the vice-presidency, he is flooded with relief, a sense of freedom, and momentary happiness. But this freedom is illusory, the happiness a chimera. Charles *is* the choice for the vice-presidency and has been all along. When he is *told* that he is, he is disillusioned by the recognition that he long ago passed the point of no return and that there is no turning back. His promotion was fated to happen by the nature of things. Nathan Glick and others have objected that none of Marquand's protagonists ever truly rebels against the system.[47] But the opportunity for rebellion occurred long ago in another country, and, besides, the hero never recognized the moment. What is the good of rebellion when the illusion of freedom is bondage, when what happens is determined? This overriding determinism is indicated in the title of the last chapter of the novel—"Fate gave, what chance shall not control," a line from Arnold suggesting that everything is written in the stars: "There was a weight on Charles again, the same old weight, and it was heavier after that brief moment of freedom. In spite of all those years, in spite of all his striving, it was remarkable how little pleasure he took in final fulfillment. He was a vice-president of the Stuyvesant Bank. It was what he had dreamed of long ago and yet it was not the true texture of early dreams. The whole thing was contrived, as he had said to Nancy, an inevitable result, a strangely hollow climax. It had obviously been written in the stars, bound to happen, and he could not have changed a line of it, being what he was, and Nancy would be pleased, but it was not what he had dreamed" (*PNR*, 557). Charles discovers, in other words, that the hay is not worth the struggle.[48] What matters in Marquand's world is knowledge of the self's predicament, stoic resignation at the fact that in the great crap game of life the dice are loaded, and the love of individuals—Charles and Nancy against the world, against all the systems. If there is any freedom from necessity, it lies in this recognition, which may itself be an illusion.

IV

After *Point of No Return* (1949) Marquand continued to write about Clyde and New York in *Melville Goodwin, USA* (1951), *Sincerely, Willis Wayde* (1955), and *Women and Thomas Harrow* (1958). They suggest that the world was becoming more kaleidoscopic, contradictory, and confusing. Like Rhonda in *Harrow*, Marquand was distressed that "everything is beginning to move so fast that we'll have to run to keep up with it." Like her, Marquand yearned for the earlier period of more settled stability: "I like things so I know where they'll be tomorrow." But nothing had a place any longer; nobody knew where he belonged, what he belonged to, or what he was made for. Quality, style, and form were giving way to vulgarity, cheapness, and the commonplace. The banality of the Eisenhower years was too much for Marquand, who reflected through Harrow that the "national life was approaching an average that expressed itself in gastronomical and in spiritual mediocrity." The flood of public vulgarity, he believed, would soon engulf the individual in a "wave of the commonplace."

With the publication of *Women and Thomas Harrow* (1958), Marquand announced the end of his career as a novelist because he was "out of the tempo of the times." "Unless I go mad, I'm not going to write another novel." He admired the way Edith Wharton kept "completely in touch with her times up to her death," but he saw in Sinclair Lewis a cautionary example of the writer who did not stop in time.[49] He did not want to be such a writer, but he recognized that a new generation of writers and critics, with its own unique literary preoccupations, was trying to invalidate the subjects and the narrative traditions he had inherited from the great European and American novelists of manners.

Like Harry Pulham and Tom Harrow, Marquand was educated for life in an older period. Thackeray and Trollope established the angles from which he viewed the world. The essential aspects of society, Marquand once argued in an introduction to *Vanity Fair*, "have not changed one iota, and its characters, like parts of a good internal combustion engine, are always interchangeable. You might put the small people from Thackeray's puppet box into the café society of New York . . . and with hardly a blink of the eye, they would adjust themselves to a century of change and recognize their friends."[50] *Vanity Fair* was a model of satirical social analysis, a model of the high level of art which the novel of manners could attain. It was a book worth remembering; it was a *kind* of book still worth writing, still worth defending against avant-garde writers and critics.

Women and Thomas Harrow is the portrait of the successful writer as middling artist and spiritual failure—like all of Marquand's protagonists a man defeated, here by the increasing tawdriness of American life. The novel ends with Harrow driving down the highway alone in a chromium-plated luxury car, contemplating the effect of the "juke-box civilization" of mid-century America on his own life. A mediocre product of a mediocre society who has failed with all of his wives and whose other human relationships have also been a mess, he deliberately drives his "fin-tail car of distinction, beloved by those who really cared," off the road into the concrete posts and cables lining the highway. Harrow does not kill himself; in fact, he pulls himself together, stiffens his upper lip, shoulders again his burden of responsibility, and drives the wrecked car away. In Marquand's first novel, George Apley—hedged around by a tightly knit society of family and friends, all with the same conventions and manners—wonders whether he will ever go down any road alone. In Marquand's last novel, Harrow gets back into his car with the reflection that "in the end, no matter how many were in the car, you always drove alone" (*WTH*, 497).

Harrow is the representative victim of the vulgarity of American life which during Marquand's lifetime seemed rapidly to lose the last vestiges of form and ceremony, ritual and order. The novel was Marquand's valedictory to a society adrift, a society which had cut itself off from the past, from tradition, and from the conventions and loyalties that had once ordered the civilized world. For Harrow and other contemporary Americans the past exists only as collectors' items which have lost their function in the modern world—Chippendale tables, George the Second candlesticks, Crown Derby china, three-pronged forks, pistol-handled knives. Obviously the past exerts a force in modern life, but it is incomprehensible; it works invisibly like a puppetmaster pulling the strings. "The past in his [Harrow's] experience was in a tangled mess like ticker tape, unwinding from the staccato recording machines and pouring in sinuous coils into wastebaskets that stood beside them. The past was twisted and slithered. Instead of being instructive and nostalgic, it interfered with the definitiveness of the present, forever impeding and very seldom helping present logic or decision" (*WTH*, 153).

Women and Thomas Harrow brings Marquand's career full circle by making in its indirect way a plea for the very conventions which once organized the social experience of the country but which have been destroyed under the pressures of change in a technological society. Thomas Harrow, as Alfred Kazin has noted, "is fighting not for freedom *from* conventions, as George Apley did, but *for* conventions—standards of belief and behavior —that will allow him to function as a human being again in a world where beliefs are shared."[51] Marquand knew that the values of the Apleys were not absolute, and he saw how ridiculous was their certainty that some values would never change. He saw how a tightly knit social order could frustrate the happiness of the individual. But he could not help admiring the loyalties, the sense of responsibility and duty, the courage, and the feeling for disciplined conduct that obtained in the older world America was leaving behind. In particular, he could not help valuing the protection against absurd and meaningless change offered by a traditional society which expressed itself through form, convention, and ritual. The ambivalence of his critique of manners and morals is thus one of his strengths, not weaknesses. And the loss of conventions did not really invalidate his subject. Men, he understood, were oppressed whether there were conventions or not. He would have agreed with John Welch's observation in Ellen Glasgow's *The Sheltered Life*: "The trouble is we imagine we can change ourselves by changing our scenery. I feel that way, though I ought to have learned better. I'd like to go away and be free, and I know perfectly well the kind of freedom I am looking for has not yet been invented. After all, Queensborough is only a small patch in the world. It is the same everywhere. People who have tradition are oppressed by tradition, and people who are without it are oppressed by the lack of it—or by whatever else they have put in its place. You want to go to New York and pretend to be unconventional, but nothing is more cramping than the effort to be unconventional when you weren't born so."[52]

Marquand's mastery of the surfaces of life, his grasp of the American scene, his understanding of the invisible boundaries of class—all of these strengths serve to account for his immense popularity with the public. If he did not plumb the depths explored by the Melvilles, the Hawthornes, the Faulkners—those whom Alfred Kazin has called "the theoreticians and visionaries who have always stood for American literature"[53]—it was because he had other work to do in dramatizing the plight of the badgered American male trapped by his own social experience. He was not one of the best novelists "of this or any other time,"[54] as Herschel Brickell once called him. That is saying too much. But he did render the realities of American social experience during his time with close observation, the charm of a clear style, and the compassion of a humane man who saw the individual as yearning for happiness but defeated by the world. His was no mean achievement.

10

❧ COZZENS AND AUCHINCLOSS

The Legacy of Form

In spite of Marquand's unhappiness, toward the close of his life, because his detractors were calling the novel of manners passé, the attractions of the form have continued to fascinate our writers. Edward Newhouse, John Phillips, Stephen Birmingham, Josephine Pinckney, Richard Powell, Struthers Burt, William Wetmore, Christopher LaFarge, Gerald Warner Brace, Evan S. Connell, John Cheever, John Brooks, and John Updike have all produced significant novels of manners, since World War II, which extend and enlarge the traditions shared by Fitzgerald, Lewis, Marquand, and O'Hara.

John Brooks—author of *The Big Wheel* (1949), *A Pride of Lions* (1954), and *The Man Who Broke Things* (1958) and one of the more interesting of the inheritors of this tradition—has replied to those critics who so irritated Marquand as he wrote *Women and Thomas Harrow*. Brooks's novels are written out of what he calls "a passion to record": "That nothing should be lost, that the essences of one's time as well as its facts and figures should be set down, that the timeless struggles of the human heart should be seen exactly as they existed under a certain set of conditions—such is the aim and also the motive for writing one type of contemporary novel." Brooks concedes that this kind of fiction may aim at "smaller game than those whose target is to discover and enunciate new human truths." He frankly confesses that his kind of fiction has primarily a journalistic intention—to filter through an individual sensibility the facts and phenomena of his own time. But chief among the premises of the novelist of manners is that "social behavior, as well as individual behavior, is an aspect of the human heart, and an interesting one; and that the uniformity of the many presents a dramatic background against which to project the individuality of a few." Although Brooks is dissatisfied with the various names for the form and prefers to call it "the recording novel," it is clear that he is talking about the novel of manners. The form, as he conceives it, is "a vision of a certain place at a certain time, taken out of the author's experience." It is not a naturalistic or a morally neutral portrait of the age: "To the extent that it is concerned with manners, the recording novel is concerned with morals. For what are most manners but a conscientious effort to do the right thing, and what is that but morality, however misdirected?" What he means by this is that the novelist who satirizes bad manners is fundamentally expressing a judgment on his characters: "Descriptions of manners are without life and color unless the writer has, and has the skill to imply, an attitude toward the manners; he must think they are ridiculous or commendable or contemptible or merely human, or combinations of these. Otherwise, he presents nothing but a tape recording—material for a novel by somebody who has the necessary passion."[1]

I

One attitude clearly implied in the postwar novels criticizes the causes of unhappiness in the social life of the American people. Toward the end of his life John P. Marquand, noting that most people never grow up, observed that "the thing we've got to do in our institutions is try to build up more maturity. Mature people are happier." At least, "they can rationalize the world in such a way that they are not going to beat their heads against a wall. I certainly think that an understanding of other people and of your environment makes for happiness—at least it makes for repose."[2] This antiromantic, skeptical assessment of unhappiness and the means of achieving at least repose is shared by James Gould Cozzens. Neglected as a novelist of manners, even though he had been publishing since 1924 and although he had even won a Pulitzer Prize in 1948, Cozzens suddenly achieved national attention in 1955 with the publication of *By Love Possessed*. (The neglect suffered by American novelists of manners is nowhere more clearly evident than in the career of Cozzens. When *By Love Possessed* was published no one had yet written a full-length study of his work and few articles of literary criticism had yet appeared.)

The major novels of James Gould Cozzens are *The Last Adam* (1933), *Men and Brethren* (1936), *The Just and the Unjust* (1942), *Guard of Honor* (1948), *By Love Possessed* (1957), and *Morning Noon and Night* (1968). An unusually varied group of books, they document in close detail the lives of men in diverse professions—medicine, the ministry, the military, and the law. The realism with which these professions are presented rivals the verisimilitude of Lewis's portraits of the doctor, the realtor, the clergyman, and the businessman. *Guard of Honor*, set on an Air Force base and populated by a large gallery of military characters of all ranks and backgrounds, was submitted to an Air Force general who reportedly found no inaccuracies in it. Zechariah Chafee, Jr., who reviewed *The Just and the Unjust* for the *Harvard Law Review*, urged every beginning law student to read it for its picture of the operation of the legal profession and observed that "it is extraordinary that an author who is not a lawyer could have written this book."[3] Only Louis Auchincloss has matched Cozzens in portraying the legal profession—and Auchincloss *is* a lawyer.

But Cozzens's realism is more than sociological; it is a moral realism as well. The intention of his fiction has been to define just how free man is to act on moral questions, how bound he is by the necessities of his social existence. Like James and Edith Wharton, Cozzens restricts himself to the kind of people capable of analyzing the moral dramas of which they are participants—people like Abner Coates, Ernest Cudlipp, Colonel Ross, Julius Penrose, and Arthur Winner, Jr. In general they are of the *finer grain*. Well-educated and highly intelligent professionals, mature men of sensibility, taste, and discrimination, they are "natural aristocrats" capable of acting with rational authority in a significant way. Cozzens, as Malcolm Cowley has observed, "seems most interested in the inner lives of prosperous old-line Americans, particularly if they are conscious of their standing in society and the duties it involves. Today Cozzens is one of the very few serious novelists who speak for this still powerful group."[4]

Cozzens's novels dramatize the hierarchies of authority and power in society and the responsibilities attendant upon those whose backgrounds have fitted them to command. The necessity for action involves his characters in the problem of trying to understand the complexities of moral experience—"the inner meaning that lies in the simultaneous occurrence of diverse things."[5] But rational understanding in Cozzens's world is thwarted by the power of feeling. This dilemma is signified by the old gilt clock on the mantel in *By Love Possessed* with its motto *omnia vincit amor*—love conquers all. And the often disastrous effect of feeling is acted out in the histories of Noah Tuttle, Helen Detweiler, Arthur Winner, Jr., and a host of other characters in the novel. *By Love Possessed* dramatizes the power of love, from *eros* to *agape*. But never is love accorded the sentimental value it has for most people in American society. For Cozzens "love" is a comprehensive term signifying all of the varieties of feeling, emotion, and sentiment which confuse and disorient the individual, a species of the irrational which deflects, misleads, and betrays men from the path of duty—a life devoted to reason and intelligence operating on the moral and social problems that arise out of human experience. To be "possessed" by love is to be afflicted with a kind of madness; to be guided by feeling is to become a fool. As Julius Penrose declares:

"We're in an age pre-eminently of capital F Feeling—a century of the gulp, the lump in the throat, the good cry. We can't be said to have invented sentimentality; but in other ages sentimentality seems to have been mostly peripheral, a despised pleasure of the underwitted. We've made sentimentality of the respected essence. If I believe my eyes and ears, and I do, sentimentality is now nearly everyone's at least private indulgence. The grave and learned are no whit behind the cheap and stupid in their love of it. Snuffling after every trace, eagerly rooting everywhere, the newspapers stop their presses, the broadcasters interrupt their broadcasts, so it may be more immediately available. In professional entertainment, in plays and motion pictures, it is the whole mode. In much of what I'm told is our most seriously regarded contemporary literature, I find it, scarcely disguised, standing in puddles. . . ."[6]

Cozzens holds no brief for the adequacy of the intellect to solve the problems of life. Man is not perfectible; society can never become utopian. Reason is the glory of man but man, Cozzens insists, is but a thinking reed—condemned to error and limited, finally, by circumstance and his ineradicable capacity for evil. To some extent, these are determining characteristics in Cozzens's world. In *The Last Adam* May reflects that "facts were facts, and May didn't mean to do anything but face them and make the best of whatever misfortunes they implied. Still, she couldn't help seeing—the same turn of mind which made her patient in reading so many books made her patient in reflection—that there had been a point in every course of events (and usually countless points) at which the littlest, most incidental change in any one of a hundred interlocking details of time, place, or human whim, would have turned the whole present into something entirely different."[7]

But May's is the wisdom of hindsight: the present is what it is because of the conjunction of specific particularities, and whatever accidents might have altered the design of the present are fundamentally irrelevant because of the necessity to act in terms of what is, not what might have been. Fred Dealey in *By Love Possessed* presents this aspect of Cozzens's moral realism most intelligibly: "This may sound like a lot of words. I just notice how often, afterward, you think: If only I'd done this, if only I'd known that! But, observe: You *didn't* do this, and you *didn't* know that. Make you think of anything? *Quare*: Could you ever have changed what's going to happen? You know this much: Whatever happens, happens because a lot of other things have happened already. When it gets to where you come in—well, it's bound to be pretty late in the day. Things have been fixing for whatever this is for a long time; and that includes you—whether you know it or not, what you're going to do or not do has been fixing for a long time, too. Freedom, I read at college, is the knowledge of necessity" (*BLP*, 118).

II

The problem of choice in a world where freedom is the knowledge of necessity leads the Cozzens hero into the search for order and for the ceremonies and social forms by which the anarchy of experience can be reduced to form. This is why, as Harry John Mooney, Jr., has observed, "forms and codes of behavior play such an important part in his work, and it is also the reason concepts of honor and manners loom large in his analysis and presentation of his characters."[8] Cozzens is most successful when his novels of manners juxtapose feeling and emotion against the framework of the profession of law. In *The Just and the Unjust*, *Guard of Honor* (Colonel Ross is a former judge whose task is to thread his moral way between the necessities of the "regs" and the practical situations confronting him), and *By Love Possessed*, the law is a system of reason codifying man's relationship to society itself. It seeks to establish the intersection of freedom and necessity and to circumscribe the arena within which a man may exercise his liberty. The law is that fund of pragmatic wisdom which the rational mind has evolved over the centuries to deal with the anarchy of the world. The epigraph of *The Just and the Unjust*, a quotation from Lord Hardwicke, is "Certainty is the mother of repose; and therefore the law aims at certainty." Cozzens's assent to this proposition identifies him as one who seeks to understand and perhaps even to defend the repose of the status quo and as a realist who recognizes that happiness may not be possible, as Marquand put it, in a world where desire is frustrated by the walls of the impossible. For Cozzens, an intelligent acceptance of the necessity to limit desire in terms of the possible helps us to avoid pointlessly beating our heads against that wall. Accepting limits may not lead an individual to happiness, he would say, but it may lead at least to serenity.

The conditions created by necessity—the interlocking of past events and conditions—constitute the framework of limitations within which Cozzens's characters must act. The limitations deny any romantic enthusiasm about the possibilities of radical change in the forms of society. As Cerise d'Atree asserts in *Confusion*, "I don't believe this world can ever be changed. . . . I think everything will go on pretty much as it used to."[9] This skepticism has led many critics to discover in Cozzens's portraits of various disadvantaged groups—the Negro officers in *Guard of Honor*, the criminal in *The Just and the Unjust*, the poor in *Men and Breth-*

ren—an apparent lack of human sympathy. Cozzens is certainly
no reformer. In his view there are limits to human endeavor,
"boundaries of the possible whose precise determining was . . .
the problem" to solve. As Colonel Ross reflects in *Guard of
Honor*, one has to know how much can be done with other men,
how much can be done with circumstance, and how much can be
done with oneself. And if not a great deal can be done, if events
shape themselves in no intelligible pattern, still the Man of Reason
must exercise his intelligence and will to understand the social
pattern: "Downheartedness was no man's part. A man must stand
up and do the best he can with what there is. If the thing he la-
bored to uncover now seemed in danger of stultifying him, could
a rational being find nothing to do? If mind failed you, seeing no
pattern; and heart failed you, seeing no point, the stout, stubborn
will must be up and doing. A pattern should be found; a point
should be imposed. Was that too much?"[10]

It is not too much for Cozzens. One of the conclusions suggested by his novels is that the effort to impose order on the
world may require of the Man of Reason a concession of principle, a compromise with reality, an accommodation of desire
and hope to the freedom-limiting circumstances which bind us.
Men and Brethren, for example, suggests that Dr. Lamb is right
not to have patience "with people who demanded extreme mea-
sures or drastic stands. The making of concessions he regarded
as a part of charity and a proof of good faith and will. He would
make them himself to anyone whose position of difference
seemed to him morally tenable."[11] Again, in *By Love Possessed*,
Julius Penrose urges Arthur Winner, Jr., to "conspire" with him
in concealing the malfeasance of their partner Noah Tuttle from
the authorities by pointing out that the circumstances are so complex that any other course than silence would be irrational:
"Principle must sometimes be shelved" (*BLP*, 556). Winner's
dilemma is that for the first time he finds himself faced with
having to do what he would prefer not to. The conclusion of
By Love Possessed suggests, however, that such concessions are
not evil; they reflect the reasonable man's acquiescence in the
facts of the real world. The test of the Man of Reason is his
capacity to accept philosophically the persistence of the irra-

tional and the necessity it occasionally imposes on one to adjust himself to its imperatives; if passion and reason are self-division's cause, victory "is not in reaching certainties or solving mysteries; victory is in making do with uncertainties, in supporting mysteries" (*BLP*, 569). Arthur Winner's decision represents a triumph over the emotional impulse needlessly to expose Noah Tuttle. In his emphasis on the rational intelligence as the only trustworthy guide, Cozzens's fiction echoes the claim, advanced by Spinoza, that we can make experience valuable when, by the use of imagination and reason, we turn experience into foresight. If we do so, Spinoza reasoned, we can shape our own future and cease to be a slave of the past. Submission to passion is human bondage, he argued, but the exercise of reason is human liberty. Freed of "possession" by irrational and emotional impulses, Cozzens's characters are thus able to formulate pragmatic moral principles to live by.

Cozzens's tone in treating "the observable inequality of men in every known human society" (*BLP*, 518) has led his critics to call him unsympathetic to our egalitarian social ideals. This charge is partly just. Cozzens is an aggressive proponent of the fundamental rightness of the system, even though it manifests visible weaknesses. He takes the long view and finds ultimately irrelevant many of the issues out of which the American novel of manners arises. He finds less drama in social climbing than Fitzgerald, less outrage in snobbery than O'Hara, and less agony in the impact of time on manners and values than Marquand. Cozzens is a conservative whose skepticism of the utopian aspirations of liberal visionaries is profound. He doubts whether real social progress is possible because he sees evil as moral rather than sociological, a feature of the human condition rather than an environmentally created phenomenon. Since men are evil and imperfect, Cozzens has limited sympathy with the fanatical champions of social reform—what in *Ask Me Tomorrow* (1940) he called "the illiterate architects of the future" scratching for lice and making mistakes in arithmetic "as they tinkered with their millennium."[12] Cozzens prefers conserving traditional values, as they are reflected in the manners and mores of the élite, who enjoy wealth, privilege, and status. His is a fundamentally individualistic ethic suspicious of the morality of Howells's Christian socialism or the uncertain socialism of Sinclair Lewis. In *Men and Brethren*, for example, Cozzens undercuts the idealism of Wilber Quinn, who wants to combine Christianity with socialism by showing that the appeal to reason and good will never really persuades the masses to be altruistic. As the Reverend Mr. Cudlipp puts it: "Your friends downtown aren't getting anywhere, Wilber. They're sentimentalists. They don't believe in the doctrine of original sin. Realists are the only people who get things done. A realist does the best he can with things as they are. Don't waste your time trying to change things so you can do something. Do something, do your Christian duty, and in time you may hope things will change" (*MB*, 140). Cozzens was thus not understating his position when he told Malcolm Cowley, "I am more or less illiberal and strongly antipathetic to all political and social movements. I was brought up an Episcopalian, and where I live the landed gentry are Republican."[13]

The conservatism of Cozzens is a thorn in the side of many of his critics. He has been denounced as deficient in human sympathy; largely indifferent to the emotional sensibilities of ideological partisans; indifferent to passionate commitments of any kind; and out of touch with the Zeitgeist. Dwight Macdonald, Chester E. Eisinger, and Irving Howe have excoriated Cozzens for having appropriated "the role of an irritated spokesman for the values of a snobbish and soured rationalism that approaches 19th century American Know Nothingism." Howe dismisses the popularity of *By Love Possessed* by saying that "a civilization that finds its symbolic embodiment in Dwight David Eisenhower and its practical guide in John Foster Dulles has been well prepared for receiving the fruits of the Philosophy of Limit. It is a civilization that, in its naked and graceless undelusion, deserves as its laureate James Gould Cozzens—Novelist of the Republic."[14]

It is unfortunate that Cozzens should be the whipping boy of the liberal intelligentsia. He is certainly not a spokesman for the kinds of cultural mediocrity the Left is contemptuous of. Cozzens was pretty rough on the fuzzy-mindedness of some of the European social visionaries of the thirties—and with justice. But he is too intelligent, aggressive, and articulate to serve as an adequate symbol of the reactionary inanities of the fifties. And if his fiction suggests an irritating piety for the past to some radicals, it is well to remember that an articulate socialist, Allen Guttmann, has recently argued in *The Conservative Tradition in America* that the weakness of social democracy is that it has an insufficiently developed sense of the past.[15] And if Cozzens can look unemotionally on "the observable inequality of men in every known society," he at least does not assert, as Russell Kirk does in "Class, Manners, Beauty and the Shape of Modern Society," that "there *ought* to be inequality of condition in the world. For without inequality, there is no class; without class, no manners and no beauty; and then a people sink into public and private ugliness."[16] Cozzens, in fact, is a representative victim of the fate of the conservative novelist of manners neglected because the major periodicals of review and criticism are organs of what has been called the Liberal Establishment. As Harry John Mooney, Jr., has observed, a "formidable gulf" separates Cozzens from "a body of criticism written largely by men who assume that a certain reformist vitality and liberality of outlook are the *sine qua non* of the serious modern novel."[17]

The value of Cozzens's fiction is that, while he is a vigorous spokesman for social conservatism, his novels of manners reveal an accurate eye for detail, the power of bringing character to life, the talent for creating moral dramas out of our social experience, and an increasingly interesting style. *Guard of Honor* and *By Love Possessed* are two of the better books of a dull postwar period. Louis O. Coxe argued in 1958 that "this Puritanical, aristocratic, angular novelist is the best we have."[18] Whether or not this praise is excessive, Cozzens's novels of manners have earned him a reputation as a writer of power whom most critics have not acknowledged. As Frederick Bracher has argued, "the best of Cozzens's works are evidence that the traditional social novel, with its high seriousness and moral urgency, is still viable in a period of experiment and disorder."[19]

III

With the fiction of Louis Auchincloss I bring this study of major American novelists of manners to a close. Auchincloss is the rightful heir of the tradition as it has been handed down through the great European and American practitioners of the form. Auchincloss is not only conscious of the tradition but he has written extensively about it—in relation to the fiction of Proust, Trollope, Meredith, Thackeray, George Eliot, Mrs. Wharton, Marquand, James, and O'Hara. And because he has offered us an orientation toward his fiction by calling himself a "Jacobite"—that is, a follower of Henry James, many reviewers have concluded that it is enough to describe him as an imitator of the Master. Auchincloss calls himself a Jacobite "because so much of my lifetime's reading has been over the shoulder of Henry James." To read the criticism, letters, and fiction of James, Auchincloss has observed, "is to be conducted through the literature of his time, English, American, French and Russian, by a kindly guide of infinitely good manners, who is also infinitely discerning, tasteful and conscientious." James, for Auchincloss, has always been a "starting point," a "common denominator."[20] But Auchincloss has always, once started, gone his own way—often qualifying and contesting, as well as enlarging, the social insights of the nineteenth-century novelist of manners. His work includes *The Indifferent Children* (1947), *Sybil* (1952), *A Law for the Lion* (1953), *The Great World and Timothy Colt* (1956), *Venus in Sparta* (1958), *The Pursuit of the Prodigal* (1959), *The House of Five Talents* (1960), *Portrait in Brownstone* (1962), *The Rector of Justin* (1964), *The Embezzler* (1966), and *A World of Profit* (1968). He has also produced four volumes of short stories, two of literary criticism—*Reflections of a Jacobite* (1961) and *Pioneers and Caretakers* (1965)—and a pictorial biography, *Edith Wharton: A Woman in Her Time* (1971). Not all of his novels are novels of manners—he is fascinated by the unexhausted possibilities of the novel of character—and not all of his novels of manners are of equal interest. Nevertheless, his talents have developed so rapidly since 1960, his social and psychological insight has deepened so, and his formal designs are so fascinating that nearly every one of his books repays perusal.

The world brought to life in his novels of manners is the world of the metropolitan rich in New York City—particularly the lives of the lawyers, bankers, trust officers, corporation executives, and their wives and daughters. As a lawyer, Auchincloss knows them in their Park Avenue penthouse apartments and in their soberly dignified Wall Street offices. He sees the glitter and glamour of their world, its arrogant materialism and its unexpected generosities. He knows the rigidity of its conventions—just how far they can be bent, at what point they break—or break a character. He understands what happens to the idealistic men and the unfulfilled women of this world. And he is able to tell their stories with unusual sympathy. Rarely has Auchincloss ventured from this small but exclusive world because it is the world he knows best. From Henry James he learned the lesson that Edith Wharton would not: the lesson that she *must* be "tethered in native pastures, even if it reduces her to a backyard in New York."[21] The New York haut monde is Louis Auchincloss's backyard. His ten novels are his Austenean two inches of ivory.

IV

Auchincloss most nearly resembles James in the emphasis he gives to moral issues that grow out of the social lives of the very rich. Yet he differs from the Master in the informed analysis he is able to give to the nice problems of ethics in the legal profession—a command of the world of Wall Street brokers and bankers which James himself sorely regretted not having. *Venus in Sparta*, for example, balances the story of a trust officer who risks malfeasance by concealing evidence affecting the interpretation of a will with the story of a couple whose marriage ends in adultery, divorce, and a suicide. In *The Embezzler*, Guy Prime steals a large sum of money for reasons ultimately ambiguous. But his partner's affair with Prime's wife suggests that together they have robbed him of his capacity to function both as a broker and as a husband. In *The Great World and Timothy Colt*, an idealistic lawyer deliberately insults a client and refuses to apologize because his act has been a matter of conscience, not superficial bad manners. But when his wife, fearing that he will lose his long-sought partnership, compels him to apologize—to compromise his integrity, as he sees it—he enters the "great world" with a vengeance: he models his conduct on that of his amoral partner; he has an affair with another woman; and he conceals information in such a way as to neglect his trust. Colt draws back from utter disaster before the point of no return; but recovering his integrity costs him his brilliant legal career.

In some of his novels of manners Auchincloss explores the ambiguities of selfhood, affirming, finally, the freedom and autonomy of the human personality. I have already suggested the extent to which novelists of manners like Edith Wharton, John O'Hara, and J. P. Marquand—who have been profoundly influenced by the behaviorism of the naturalistic sciences—tend to believe that the personality is conditioned by the material environment and to recreate character through descriptions of houses, clothes, furniture, and the like. Auchincloss rejects this approach to characterization. For him, "character" exists independent of the web of the material environment that surrounds it. As Ida Trask Hartley observes, in describing the narrow gray limestone facade of Mr. Robbins's house—with its "grinning lions' heads and balconies for flowerpots supported by squatting ladies, and topped with a giant dormer studded with bull's-eye windows": "Nobody passing it today would believe that it had not been built by the most pushing parvenu. Yet I know how little the houses of that era sometimes expressed the souls of their occupants."[22]

In *A Law for the Lion*, Eloise Dilworth seeks to discover whether there is any real identity beneath the various roles she has played during her lifetime—the childish niece to her aunt and uncle, the submissive wife to her indifferent husband, the taken-for-granted mother to her children. Her search for an answer leads her to reject the meaningless manners and conventions of the social world she has been brought up in. But her losses are more than compensated for by her discovery that there is a real self beneath the functions imposed on her by her social existence. This kind of "Who am I?" theme is also developed in *Sybil*, *Portrait in Brownstone*, and *The House of Five Talents*. A variation on it is the "Who is he?" theme developed in *The Rector of Justin*. In this novel Frank Prescott, recently deceased headmaster of a preparatory school, is recreated through the differing recollections and impressions of several characters—the priggish young admirer, the irreverent daughter, the wife, the friends, the students, and alumni. What the novel suggests is that we can never know what Prescott was really like because none of the narrators knew the real Prescott—he presented a different side to each of them. It might well be asked whether there was any "real" Prescott behind his various masks. The answer is yes, but we can never know him except through his various biographers. Auchincloss's dramatic technique in this "conventional novel of character" creates a built-in ambiguity comparable to that of James's *The Awkward Age.*

Auchincloss's preoccupation with identity in fiction is based, I believe, on a question posed by James, in a conversation between Isabel Archer and Madame Merle in *The Portrait of a Lady*, about the "shell of circumstances" and the irreducible self: "What shall we call our 'self?'" Madame Merle asks Isabel. "Where does it begin? Where does it end? It overflows into everything that belongs to us—and then it flows back again. I know a large part of myself is in the clothes I choose to wear. I've a great respect for *things!* One's self—for other people—is one's expression of one's self; and one's house, one's furniture, one's garments, the books one reads, the company one keeps—these things are all expressive."[23] Auchincloss rejects the behaviorism of Madame Merle. The personality of Frank Prescott is never adequately expressed by the impressions of others, just as the irreducible "I" of Eloise Dilworth is never fully expressed by her furniture or the sum of her functions.

But to make this point is to oversimplify what is in fact a complex problem for Auchincloss as a creator of character. For in some of his novels, he is at great pains to show that society (with its misimpressions) and time (with its alteration of conventions) *do* impinge on the self which—for better or worse—is expressed through its various roles. For Eloise, Timothy Colt, Sybil Hilliard, Ida Hartley, and Augusta Millinder, the triumph of the personality over the roles imposed by the external world makes for a kind of limited victory of the self. But Auchincloss's world has its darker depths, and his novels by no means always end in such "moral triumphs." For Geraldine Brevoort in *Portrait*, for Michael Farrish in *Venus in Sparta*, and for Guy Prime in *The Embezzler*, the world is an arena of ever more burdensome responsibilities arising out of the illusory importance of caste and class.

For each, society offers only one role—complete with props—a role he cannot play. Michael Farrish, for example, is brought up to satisfy the social expectations of his mother. A Farrish leads a certain kind of life. So Michael is sent off to Averhill prep school, then to Harvard; he is taken into the Hudson River Trust Company; eventually he becomes a partner. He is slated to become director and chairman—all of this because it is expected of him; he is, after all, a Farrish. But Michael Farrish is unequipped for the role society has fashioned for him. He has no psychological armor against the bitch goddess success and the socially created myth of what manhood constitutes. And when a crisis occurs in his professional life and his marriage goes on the rocks, he tries to escape his social role by running away to Mexico.

The figure of the child fearing and expecting punishment for some failure to live up to the expectations of the adult world is a recurrent image in Auchincloss's fiction. Frequently he welcomes punishment as a relief—such is the burden of his guilt at not successfully playing his role. And if punishment does not come he often seeks to relieve his guilt through some suicidal or self-destructive act. Timothy Colt punishes himself, for abandoning his idealism, by courting his own professional destruction: he openly confesses a misprision which could never have been proved against him. Guy Prime invites the governmental inquiry into the stock exchange which leads to his own punishment. Geraldine Brevoort jumps from an eighth-story hotel room window. And Michael Farrish ends by drowning himself in the ocean. Such is the toll exacted of some of the characters in Auchincloss's fiction. It is not a tragic cost. None of his characters is of tragic importance. In fact, Auchincloss himself has conceded that "pathos has a bigger place than tragedy in the study of manners."[24] But it is a poignant cost to which, in the subtlety and insight of Auchincloss's characterization, this summary does inadequate justice.

V

The House of Five Talents (1960) and *Portrait in Brownstone* (1962) are the most interesting American novels of manners of the 1960s. Both are set in New York City; both deal with rich and "aristocratic" families during a period of several generations; both portray the emergence of a woman as the matriarch of the tribe (although one is an old maid); and both offer a bittersweet portrait of the manners and morals of the very rich. Opening at the death of Queen Victoria, *Portrait* focuses on the Denisons of Fifty-third Street from the turn of the century into the 1950s. Full of illuminating flashbacks, the novel is a social history of the brownstone era told from the point of view of Ida Trask Hartley, a passive and obedient child who matures into the leader of a large and refractory family. Auchincloss's narration of how she comes to manipulate, in her passive way, the children and grandchildren, the cousins and uncles and aunts of the tribe, is a truly impressive achievement, based, very probably, on the character of Martha Little in Edith Wharton's "Duration," published in *The World Over* (1936). Ida's emergence as the dominant force for unity, in a family disintegrating from external and internal pressures, is accompanied by a perceptive study of the changing manners and morals of the American aristocracy in New York. All shades of sexual behavior, for example, are reflected in the lives of Ida and her family. Ida has her first chaste kiss (the seal of her engagement) in the Egyptian Room of the Metropolitan Museum in 1911. One of the few meeting places for unchaperoned couples in her youth, this Metropolitan Museum setting serves a symbolic function comparable to the setting for Newland Archer and Ellen Olenska's last interview in *The Age of Innocence*—the room of Cesnola archaeological antiquities. That the manners and mores of Ida's youth have become archaeological curiosities is indicated by Ida's advising her daughter to try going to bed with her boyfriend before she decides whether or not to marry him. Dorcas, of course, takes her mother's advice. Such is the transition between the age of Victoria and the age of Dr. Kinsey.

Auchincloss's sense of the effect of time on the conventions

and attitudes that affect people's behavior has been shaped, I believe, by Mrs. Wharton's studies of Old New York. He knows,
as she and Proust knew, that "any society will apply all known
standards together or individually, or in any combination needed,
to include a maverick who happens to please or to exclude an
otherwise acceptable person who happens not to." And he knows
that society people are not the least conscious of their inconsis-
tency and that arbitrariness is the mark of their values. He also
knows that society "is not aware of changing its standards, for it
has no memory except for its own acts of condemnation, and for
these only so far as the individual condemned is concerned."[25]

One of embezzler Guy Prime's greatest resentments is that it
would do him no good to return to New York, after paying his
debt to society, because despite the greater tolerance of society,
its mind is made up: "The late Mrs. Edith Wharton, who was a
childhood friend of my mother's," Guy Prime tells us, "wrote a
very apt little story on this subject called 'Autres Temps.' It deals
with a wife who is cast out of New York society for eloping with
her lover and who comes back, a generation later, to find that the
doors of her erstwhile friends, who have accepted the same conduct in her own daughter, are still closed to her. The world,"
Guy Prime concludes, "is too busy to revise old judgments."[26]
(Mrs. Wharton's *The Mother's Recompense* also dramatizes this
irrationality in social attitudes.) Granville Hicks has suggested
that Auchincloss writes as if Proust had never written.[27] Auchincloss has learned a great deal, both from Proust and from Mrs.
Wharton. Guy Prime goes away to Panama when he gets out
of jail.

Portrait in Brownstone is also an *ubi sunt* lament for an older
New York now accessible only in *King's Notable New Yorkers*,
in old letters in Newport attics, and in the memories of those who
knew the face of New York before it began to change so rapidly.
But it is not a New York that anyone, particularly Auchincloss,
wishes to bring back. In a passage that might have come from
Mrs. Wharton's "A Little Girl's New York," Ida thinks:

As for the past where Derrick had first proposed to her, that quiet
brownstone past, with its fussiness and its quibbling and its love, how
was it possible to bring *that* back? And why, really, should she want

to? Was it not better to forget it altogether with its emotional tangle of stultifying family duties? Had it not forgotten itself? Where were the Denisons of Fifty-third Street, she wondered as she came out to the sunlight through Aunt Dagmar's heavy grilled doors. Uncle Philip's house at the corner was gone. A jewelry store occupied its site. Uncle Willie's had made way for a parking lot, and her father's was a nightclub, or perhaps worse. Everything in New York reminded one of the prevalent dust to which, almost immediately, it seemed, one was condemned to return. If one didn't seize that day, a contractor would. [*PB*, 243]

Such are the ravages of time on these Old New York families that at the end of *The Embezzler* the Prime house is torn down to make room for one of Mr. Moses's commuter parkways.

The House of Five Talents is the story of the rise of an American middle-class family from parvenu origins to aristocratic status during the period 1875–1948. It is the story of the five Millinder children who descend from one of the most ruthless robber barons of the age of Grant, and of their fortune and what became of it. In chronicling the history of the Millinder money, Auchincloss addresses himself to what he believes are some prevalent misconceptions about the relationship between wealth and American society. In the first place, although social mobility nowadays is a "clanging escalator," Auchincloss does not hold with the old myth that it takes only three generations from shirtsleeves to shirtsleeves. At the end of the novel, the twelve living grandchildren of old Julius Millinder have all multiplied their talents. All are rich. As Oswald, the family Communist, complains, "Why, they're spread all over the globe! I figure that it takes no less than a thousand human souls to wait on the old pirate's progeny!"[28] Another myth Auchincloss tries to deflate is the belief that the rich are really different from the economic middle and lower classes. Fitzgerald and O'Hara wrote a number of stories with the thesis that the very rich *are* different from you and me. Even Marquand conceded that "wealth beyond a certain point always created its own small world of unreality."[29] But for Auchincloss, this is a middle-class illusion; quantity of money does not qualitatively affect our essential humanity. For him, men are pretty much the same, however much money they have. A fortune may permit a choice of masks to don before the world, but little else. "There has always been the theory, embraced alike by Tory and Red," Augusta Millinder reflects, "that there is something actually different about the rich. But I wonder if this theory still exists." Her opinion is that the Millinders had about as much talent and beauty and capacity for life, among them, as most families. But none of them as individuals particularly excelled at anything: "None of us would really have stood out from the crowd without the money" (*HFT*, 10–11).

Told from Augusta's point of view, *The House of Five Talents* is a series of episodes illustrating the poignant effect of the money upon the members of the family. Gussie believes that money is intended to help people over their difficulties. And she summons her own huge fortune to rescue many of her relatives. But most often her good intentions end in disaster, the novel illustrating the triumph of money over love, compassion, affection, and honor. The failure of Gussie's engagement to Lancey Bell, the murderous rivalry between her mother Eliza and Aunt Daisy in the Victorian "social game," Lucius Hoyt's ruthless victory over his equally ruthless but incompetent father, the human failures of Ione and Lydig, the defalcations of Collier Haven, and Oswald's retreat into communism—all of these episodes illustrate the triumph of the power of money over a group of people who, Gussie insists, were "at all times simple, ordinary people, pursuing simple, ordinary tasks, who stood out from the crowd only in the imagination of those observers who fancied from reading the evening papers that tiaras and opera boxes made an organic difference. Perhaps that is my ultimate discovery of what the money meant," she concludes, "that it meant nothing at all, or, at any rate, very little" (*HFT*, 368).

At the same time, *The House of Five Talents* is the tragicomedy of an old maid who never married because she feared that her one suitor wanted her only for her money. A romantic goose who grows up reading Ouida and Marie Corelli (hidden in the wrappers of Henry James novels), Gussie Millinder thinks of life largely in terms of the romantic fiction she has read. When Lancey Bell begins to court her sister Cora, Gussie reflects: "It was a traditional part of the picture that the beau should treat the gawky young sister with an affectation of gallantry and that she should fall in love with him, and Lancey and I were faithful to our roles" (*HFT*, 48). Later, when Cora marries a foreign aristocrat and Lancey proposes to *her*, Gussie assumes that he is the fortune hunter of romantic fiction and she foolishly rejects him. But Gussie matures as she grows older. One of her mature perceptions is that people react to others largely in terms of stereotypes and that these stereotypes can be not merely lived with but even exploited. In her thirties she resents the fact that she is becoming an old maid because she dislikes the implications of the stereotype—implications brilliantly studied, incidentally, in Balzac's *La Vieille Fille* (1837) and in Edith Wharton's *Old New York: The Old Maid (The 'Fifties)* (1924). But Lucius Hoyt urges Gussie not to be afraid of labels and stereotypes, not to fear to *be* an old maid: "Be a great old maid! Be a magnificent old maid!" (*HFT*, 141). Ione also urges Gussie to give up her fear that people are interested in her only for her money: "We're all bits and pieces of our background, our tastes, our inheritances, even our clothes," she says in a passage reminiscent of Madame Merle's theory. "It's only natural for people to be curious because you're a Millinder and live in a big house. It's up to you to turn that curiosity into something better!" Ione teaches her that "the role of an old maid could be a far bigger one than I had ever imagined, that an old maid could reach the young because she was neutral in the conflict between generations and because she was the priestess at the shrine of tradition. An old maid, at least a rich one, could wear big jewelry and drive around in an antique town car and wear fussy clothes out of fashion and weep at the opera and threaten naughty street urchins with her stick; she could join the boards of clubs and charities and be as officious and bossy as she liked; she could insist on giving the family party on Christmas Eve; she could even, in her new, shrewd, noisy way, become the head of the remnants of the Millinders." In other words, she could become, for all her family, the "wonderful" person she yearned to be. "It was the simplest idea in the world," Gussie concedes, "yet it changed my life" (*HFT*, 216–17).

In becoming a magnificent and indomitable old maid, Gussie discovers that people are only too happy to treat her with the respect that such a conception of herself required. "Civilized life is a fancy-dress party," she reflects, "and everyone is encouraged to don a costume. It makes for color to have queens and cardinals about, and for enough color nobody minds doffing a hat. The illusion is created as much by him who performs the reverence as him to whom it is made. Both, after all, are members of the same cast" (*HFT*, 267). Gussie's costume is the pearl choker, the antiquated car, the faithful servants, the opera box, the rigid punctuality, and the respectful visits of submissive relatives. She *affects* a brilliant theatrical performance which old Aunt Daisy, a genuine anachronism from Newport days, really thinks it is still possible to live. Aunt Daisy will not talk on the telephone, go into a department store, attend the movies, or tolerate smoking, drinking, Democrats, short skirts, traffic, or taxes. She believes herself to be the incarnation of social standards formed in the days of *the* Mrs. Astor and she is not about to abandon them because of the changing times. Thus on opening night at the opera, when Gussie wishes to avoid publicity and suggests going in by a side door, Aunt Daisy refuses and insists on going in through the front foyer; it is what society expects of her: " 'Thank God, I can still do my duty!' was her indignant rejoinder as she and I descended from the tall old green Rolls-Royce, like two big dolled up, gaudy bugs, and made our slow way through the crowd of cameramen, our evening bags held resolutely up to cover our faces. The men shouted familiar but friendly greetings to Aunt Daisy like 'Go it, old girl!' and I was sure that behind her pursed lips and forward-looking stare her heart was beating with a fierce pride at so fitting a Nunc Dimittis" (*HFT*, 214).

What saves Augusta Millinder from ridicule is that she is conscious of the wonderful comedy inherent in living (as Aunt Daisy does) or playing (as she does) such arbitrary roles. Gussie never lets herself forget that hers is a role performed to satisfy, largely, other people's illusions. It is, as well, an act softening the hard reality of her life—the fact, for example, that she had only one proposal, never married, and was never loved by a man, as she believed, wholly for herself. Yet she has the wisdom to recognize that happiness may consist in electing the role other people cast her in. In accepting the obligation to dramatize the role, Augusta becomes, indeed, the magnificent, indomitable old maid.

Auchincloss has remarked that "the paralyzing effect of a class-conscious background is largely illusory." Nowadays people are not as "preoccupied with their exact social niche as writers like O'Hara, for example, suggest." Consequently, the novelist of manners may invest his form with a new dimension of psychology by showing that "the function of a character's background" may be "only his misconception of it. . . ."[30] This is the case with Charles Gray in *Point of No Return*; his return to Clyde has "the effect of psychoanalysis." Going back to Clyde frees him from the tyranny of ghosts which have haunted him since his youth. And this is the case with the representative Auchincloss hero. The real cause of his conflict is psychological, not social, pressure. The conventions of the aristocracy may be entirely a thing of the past, but if a man's self-image requires him to behave as if the obligations of caste are changeless and inflexible, he can do no other. This, according to Angelica, is Guy Prime's problem: he believes in the old myth of the splendor of the Prime family. "Guy saw his family as the readers of tabloids saw them, in tiaras and opera boxes. Like many people in the social world he preferred the account of a party in a gossip column to his own recollection of it" (*E*, 228). According to Angelica, the Primes were not a distinguished family. But such is Guy Prime's enslavement to this obsolete myth of their caste importance that his conduct is almost wholly determined by it. Thus the novel of manners passes over into the psychological novel: manners become the gestures by which characters, believing in the reality of their own theatrical pretense, frustrate and destroy themselves. One of the delights of Augusta Millinder is that she has no illusions about herself or about the "authority" of her class and the obligations imposed on her by it. Her sanity is reflected in her recognition that her role is both a charade and an anachronism; she caps her act, this old fossil, by bequeathing her fortune to an archaeological institute.

VI

In semipolitical literary criticism there are sometimes objections to the kind of people Cozzens and Auchincloss write about. It is sometimes said, for example, that the world of New York society people is somehow not as interesting as that of sharecroppers, boxers, or big game hunters. Granville Hicks has confessed this bias in remarking that "to many people, myself included, an Italian boy who robs a poor Jew is a more challenging subject than an upperclass New Yorker who misappropriates funds, and a bewildered intellectual in search of wholeness of spirit belongs more truly to our times than the aged headmaster of a fashionable preparatory school."[31]

But there is no necessary reason why this claim should be true. *The Assistant* and *Herzog* may be better novels than *The Embezzler* and *The Rector of Justin*. But their superiority has nothing to do with the subject matter or the "relevance" of these books—it has to do only with the greater artistry by which the novels of Bellow and Malamud are brought more vividly to life. In justifying the attention he gives to people like Guy Prime, Augusta Millinder, Ida Trask, and Frank Prescott, I find it instructive to remember Auchincloss's observation on the universality of Tolstoy's art: "What he understands is that if a human being is described completely, his class makes little difference. He becomes a human being on the printed page, and other humans, of whatever class, can recognize themselves in his portrait. The lesson of Tolstoy is precisely how little of life, not how much, the artist needs."[32]

His view of Proust also casts light on Auchincloss's choice of subject. In arguing that there has never been "so brilliant or so comprehensive a study of the social world" as that found in Proust, Auchincloss observes: "To him the differences between class and class are superficial. Snobbishness reigns on all levels, so why does it matter which level one selects to study? Why not, indeed, pick the highest level, particularly if one's own snobbishness is thus gratified? Society in Proust parades before us, having to represent not a segment of mankind, but something closer to mankind itself. It is the very boldness of Proust's assumption that his universe is *the* universe . . . that gives to his distorted picture a certain universal validity. It is his faith that a sufficiently careful study of each part will reveal the whole, that the analysis of a dinner party can be as illuminating as the analysis of a war. It is his glory that he very nearly convinces us."[33]

Without wishing to draw the parallel too closely, I submit that Auchincloss also sees that the differences between classes are superficial and that there is therefore no adequate reason why one should not deal with headmasters and lawyers, bankers and brokers, if they permit the kind of social analysis that illuminates our essential human predicament. The problem implicit in his choice is that of making us believe that his universe is—if not *the* universe—at least a *believable* universe and in describing his characters so fully and convincingly that we do not care about the class they belong to. It is Auchincloss's difficulty that, as good as most of his novels are, he does not always so convince us. But the limitation is one of the writer's talent, not of his material.

It is probably a mistake to think about Auchincloss's characters as belonging to a distinct "class." He does not believe that the United States is a classless society. But he does recognize that it is not possible for the contemporary American novelist of manners to write the kind of fiction produced by Howells, Wharton, and James. The increasing democratization of the United States, he argues in *Reflections of a Jacobite*, has resulted in a rearrangement of social attitudes, so that today "snobbishness is more between groups than classes, more between cliques than between rich and poor." "Surely there is a difference," he remarks, "between the feelings of the man who has not been asked to dinner and those of the man who has been thrown down the front stairs."[34]

Most of these groups, however (labor-capital, East-West, North-South, young-old, workers-intelligentsia), do not provide much for the would-be novelist of manners. "It is my simple thesis," Auchincloss has argued, "that the failure more generally to produce this kind of novel is not attributable to the decadence or escapism of mid-twentieth century writers, but rather to the increasingly classless nature of our society which does not lend itself to this kind of delineation. I do not mean by this that we are any duller than the Victorians, but simply that the most exciting and significant aspects of our civilization are no longer to be found in the distance and hostility between the social strata."[35] Consequently, like James, he has turned increasingly toward the inward lives of his characters in order to explain why, in this classless but cliquish society, people hang on to their snobbish ways as they do.

The divided career of Louis Auchincloss (as lawyer-novelist) and his indifference to sociological explanations of evil have led other critics to attack Auchincloss's social and moral criticism as fakery, and to claim that Auchincloss is captivated by the very social prejudices which are his subject. Robert M. Adams, for example, has ridiculed Auchincloss for writing, "like a latter-day Trollope, a pseudo-critique of commercialism which collapses docilely as soon as one perceives it is being launched from a platform provided by commercialism itself."[36] The assumption on which this statement is based—that the novelist must stand outside the world he seeks to criticize before his criticism can be authentic—is arrant nonsense. Auchincloss may be a conservative; he may not be interested in reform or in Old or New Left radicalism. But this fact in itself does not invalidate his critique of the limitations—moral and social—of the world he belongs to and describes. There is certainly adequate rational, theological, and moral justification for the claim that evil arises from selfish, dissipated, snobbish people as well as from economic or sociological causes.[37]

No politician, Auchincloss takes society, for literature, more or less as he finds it. But he is not guilty of what Edith Wharton called "the tendency not infrequent in novelists of manners—Balzac and Thackeray among them—to be dazzled by contact with the very society they satirize."[38] He is fascinated by the world he portrays: he loves the details of an estate settlement as much as Thackeray loved the stylish little supper parties of Mrs. Rawdon Crawley; he is as fascinated by the complexities of a corporation merger as Proust was by the intricacies of precedence; and he is as delighted by the eccentricities of the rich as Balzac was by the spectacle of miserly greed. But if Auchincloss loves his world, he is not taken in by it. Conscious of the moral and social incongruities between his world and the world of, say, Malamud, he is as disturbed as any reader of the *Partisan Review* that no matter how painstakingly Proust "underlines the dullness, the selfishness, and the fatuity of the Guermantes set, they remain to the end still invested with much of the glamour in which his imagination clothed them."[39]

But Auchincloss has no wish to idealize or glamorize his "aristocracy" or to claim for it a nostalgic virtue inconsistent with the known facts of New York City social life. Nor is he "hankering after any good old days." He has asked whether anyone would wish to return to "a New York where servants slept in unheated cubicles on the top of drafty brownstones, with an evening off every second week. . . ."[40] His love for the elegance and iniquity of this world is the love of an artist for his material, which is quite another thing from his feeling for it as a man. Every writer, he has observed, has two points of view "about the society in which he lives: that of a citizen and that of an artist. The latter is concerned only with the suitability of society as material for his art. Just as a liberal journalist may secretly rejoice at the rise of a Senator McCarthy because of the opportunity which it affords him to write brilliant and scathing denunciations of demagogues, so will the eye of the novelist of manners light up at the first glimpse of social injustice. For his books must depend for their life blood on contrast and are bound to lose both significance and popularity in a classless society."[41] Our awareness of the distinction between society as experienced and society as transformed in fiction ought to discourage us from condemning, as a reactionary, the novelist who insists on exploring inequities and ambiguities from inside the social citadel. Auchincloss's value is that he keeps alive a lively tradition in novels that are themselves vital proof of his considerable talent.

11

The Way We Live Now

The most exciting writers today, which is to say those writers nearest the happy condition of genius, are preoccupied with forms other than the novel of manners. There are a number of reasons why this should be so. One is the apparent homogeneity of the surfaces of American life. The observation of class differences in a mass society has apparently become more difficult and less interesting than it used to be, and many American novelists have turned elsewhere for their material. The common experience truly is the common experience, they seem to say. The way we live now, to borrow one of Trollope's titles, seems to be the way we all live. The image of American social life manufactured by television, movies, pulp fiction, and the press is that of bland middle-class affluence, of comfortable mediocrity, of easily disposable values. The media seem generally indifferent to the real pluralism of our national life, and we passively prefer to be indoctrinated in the belief that there are not any real social differences among us.

It does very little good to say that the image of a homogeneous America is distorted and that the novelist's job is to tell it like it is. We have a culture of poverty as well as a culture of affluence, but it does very little good to lecture our novelists on the need to portray the manners, the style, and the significance of these cultures if they are occupied elsewhere. The "invisible culture" of our ghettos and the continuous transformation of our metropolitan elites (Fitzgerald's café society," giving way to Russell Lynes's "Upper Bohemians" who have given way to Marylin Bender's "Beautiful People") matter very little if our novelists are unable to relate these phenomena to any conception of the social order. It matters very little that regional antagonism is about as intense as ever if our novelists are too much concerned with intensities of the private self. Though the signals of status are vaguer than before, we still *do* have social "classes." And although politics is complicated by generational attitudes, we *do* have a new radicalism and a neoconservatism emerging, complete with new personal styles, costumes, and manners. But it does very little good to point this out if our writers are thinking about something else.

What are our novelists thinking about? From a look at the current crop of novelists it is clear that many of them are thinking about themselves—which, in a way, is as it should be. But much of what we are asked to read today implicitly denies the reality of public values, of shared experience. If we think about the fiction of Hawkes, Nabokov, Purdy, or Paul Bowles, for example, it is a world that is oriented inward, reflecting the inner eye, the private vision, the subjective self. Alienated from the social order—even from the role of critic of that order—such writers create their visions out of dream, fantasy, and nightmare. To some extent this preoccupation is a continuation of the older metaphysical romance that Hawthorne, Melville, and Faulkner practiced. Sometimes, however, these interests manifest themselves in antinovels in which the sense of the world out there passing through measurable time is submerged in the design of metaphor and image, in the evocation of style as feeling, and in the demonstration of awareness as pictorial design. The locus of reality in such novels is not the outer world, as we experience it in society, but the subjective consciousness as expressed in the dream vision, the bad trip, the apocalyptic hallucination, the psychedelic freak-out. Perception, consciousness, feeling are the instruments by which the "exterior social reality" is sacrificed in the service of autistic myths and symbolism. The mind of the writer increasingly knows only itself, wards off intrusions from without, and projects itself only in design. The world outside, the world of society, the world of nature, the world of things, is denied. Between these and the authorial consciousness there is no mediation. Human nature evaporates as a norm for the understanding of character. The writer abandons the effort to penetrate the surfaces of the world in pursuit of meaning, for it has no meaning to him and cannot yield, by way of formal relationships, any feelings or emotions. Sometimes comically, sometimes tragically, he ponders the impassable abyss between man and society, wherein he finds himself the alien and stranger.

Many other novelists, however, are still interested in society as a field for fiction. Bellow, Updike, Ellison, and Mailer, for example, have gone a good way down the road that leads from lyrical autobiography to the social chronicle. But none of them, clearly, has gone as far as Marquand, O'Hara, Cozzens, or Auchincloss. To escape the rigidities of an apparently outworn tradition, each of them has experimented with forms other than the novel of manners. Though preoccupied with the same kinds of social concern that generate the novel of manners, Bellow's *The Adventures of Augie March* is a picaresque chronicle. Baldwin works the essay form and understandably shrill and hectoring "notes" which have all the intensity and social relevance of the novel of manners but not the form. Others have indulged the sociological essay, like Robert Penn Warren in *Segregation: The Inner Conflict of the South* (1956) and *Who Speaks For the Negro?* (1965). Stephen Birmingham has also moved from novels like *Young Mr. Keefe* and *Barbara Greer* to social histories of the upper class like *Our Crowd* (1961) and *The Right People* (1968). John Brooks has apparently given up fiction for social histories like *The Seven Fat Years: Chronicles of Wall Street* (1958), *The Fate of the Edsel and Other Business Ventures* (1963), and *The Great Leap: The Past Twenty-five Years in America* (1966). Wright Morris, Mary McCarthy, Herbert Gold, and Harvey Swados continue to write novels exploring social problems, but their positions are neither artistically nor ideologically very compelling.

All literary forms are of course subject to the same historical pressures I have already mentioned as bearing on the novel of manners. But they are also to some extent the consequence of our literary criticism, which for the past fifty years has periodically announced that the novel, the realistic-naturalistic novel (and *particularly* the novel of manners) is dead. The admonition to "make it new" is a noble one, and we owe to this proposition some of the most interesting examples of avant-garde experimentalism in the twentieth century. But when the idea gains currency that a whole genre is exhausted in the achievement of its first great example, writers whose genius may best find expression in traditional forms are driven toward the extremes of a futile, dead-end experimentalism—simply to be "inventive," to escape the charge of "imitation." The flowering and fulfillment of a great art, however, may arise in an already well-established literary tradition—witness Shakespeare's use of the formal conventions of the Renaissance drama. "If there were no names in the history of art except those belonging to the creators of new forms," as André Gide has observed, "there would be no culture. The very word implies a continuity, and therefore it calls for disciples, imitators and followers to make a living chain; in other words, a tradition."[1]

The usual admirable urgency to make it new largely motivates our writers today, and though many would do better to work in the traditional forms, much of the new experimentation *is* interesting. In the present situation, as Irving Howe has observed, there are "a great many new difficulties for the younger writers. New difficulties, which is also to say: new possibilities."[2] A particularly notable instance of new possibilities is illustrated in an essay called "Bringing the News," by Norman Podhoretz. Podhoretz asks whether it is not possible that some other literary form is taking over the job that the novel used to do. Podhoretz has in mind the magazine article. As editor of *Commentary*, he argues that our novelists move around much more "freely, intelligently, imaginatively and *creatively*" when they are not called upon to tell what they know through "the medium of an invented story." James Agee, Mary McCarthy, Elizabeth Hardwick, Randall Jarrell, Leslie Fiedler, and James Baldwin—he observes in "The Article as Art"—write discursive prose which is "richer, more imaginative, and fundamentally more honest" than their novels and stories. This is an unusual judgment—one I am not sure the indicated writers may wholly appreciate. It is the final reductio of Lionel Trilling's claim that the function of the novel has been preempted by the literature of sociology. It has one major difference, though: Trilling never claimed for sociology the accomplishment of art. But Podhoretz does not like "the idea that novel-writing is the only 'real' writing." For him, magazine journalism is not only "real" writing, it is a form of art. Thus he argues that Dwight Macdonald and Richard Rovere have "carried on a more exhaustive and accomplished investigation of our morals and manners than the bulk of contemporary fiction." What all of this suggests, of course, is that it is *issues* rather than art, the utility of *ideas* rather than the intrinsic value of the created form, that matters to Podhoretz. And in suggesting that "we may be looking in the wrong place for the achievements of the creative literary imagination when we look for them only where they were last seen—in novels and poems and plays," he is in effect inviting writers not merely to pause in their creative enterprises to write journalistic prose (criticism, reviews, autobiographical essays, and the like) but to think of this nonfiction as a primary mode of discourse, as the generic equivalent of the "established" literary art forms.[3] This invitation, in the current novel-is-dead atmosphere, has provided new fuel for contemporary experimentalism in prose; it has provoked a new urgency in scouting out new modes and possibilities for the novel of manners. Norman Mailer's recent work suggests one possibility.

Faced with the decline of interest in the novel, Mailer has tried to describe for himself what happened to fiction, where it "went wrong." In *Cannibals and Christians* (1966) he theorizes that two traditions have operated in the American novel since about 1900: the Genteel Tradition of the novel of manners, derived from Balzac, Tolstoy, and Zola; and the counter-tradition of Naturalism, which has portrayed the underside of American life during the process of rapid industrial and sociological change. Like Alfred Kazin, Mailer illustrates these two traditions in a contrast between Mrs. Wharton and Theodore Dreiser. Dreiser, according to Mailer, had "no manner, no eye for the deadly important manners of the rich, he was obliged to call a rich girl 'charming'; he could not make her charming when she spoke, as Fitzgerald could, and so he did not really prepare the army of his readers for what was ahead. His task was doubly difficult—it was required of him to give every upstart fresh strategy and tactics. No less than the secret sociology of society is what is needed by the upstart and that strategy Dreiser gave him. But tactics—the manners of the drawing room, the deaths and lives of the drawing room,

the cocktail party, the glorious tactics of the individual kill—
that was all beyond him."[4] Mrs. Wharton, with all the ideological
and literary strategy and tactics provided by her class, could do
what Dreiser could not. But neither she nor the other writers of
the Genteel Tradition who could do it, according to Mailer,
ever "went down into the pits to bring back the manner alive
of the change going on down there": "The gap in American letters continued, Upper-class writers like John Dos Passos made
brave efforts to go down and get the stuff and never quite got it,
mainly in Dos Passos's case because they lacked strategy for the
depths—manners may be sufficient to delineate the rich but one
needs a vision of society to comprehend the poor, and Dos Passos
had only revulsion and injustice, which is ultimately a manner."[5]

The effect of this dichotomy, according to Mailer, was that no
one ever wrote a comprehensive novel about the whole of American social experience. Each author made a separate peace and
was content to deal with only a fragment of the American experience. The social realism of Dreiser gave way to the moral
seriousness of Bellow in *Herzog*; and the Genteel Tradition of
the novel of manners, according to Mailer, gave way to the Camp
sensibility of Truman Capote and Terry Southern: "Camp is the
art which evolved out of the bankruptcy of the novel of manners.
It is the partial thesis of these twenty minutes [these remarks
were originally presented as a paper before the Modern Language and American Studies associations] that the pure novel of
manners had watered down from *The House of Mirth* to the
maudlin middle reaches of *The Rector of Justin*; had in fact gone
all the way down the pike from *The Ambassadors* to *By Love
Possessed*. So, one does not speak of the novel of manners any
longer—one is obliged to look at the documentary, *In Cold Blood*
—or one is obliged to look at satire" like Terry Southern's *The
Magic Christian*.[6]

These are interesting views on what has happened to the novel
of manners since the time of Mrs. Wharton. They are informed
with the authority of Mailer's personal style. But what Mailer
misses is exactly that comprehensiveness of social vision in, say,
Wharton's *Bunner Sisters*, that balanced subtlety and savagery
of *Melville Goodwin, U.S.A.* and *Sincerely, Willis Wayde*, the

imagination of disaster in novels like *Venus in Sparta* and *Guard of Honor*. They simply cannot be dismissed by talk of the bankruptcy of the form. But this is neither here nor there since Mailer *believes* that the form is bankrupt. Where, then, does it leave Mailer?

Since he believes that the novel is a failed form, for him it is no longer capable of touching significantly on the observed realities of the whole social situation, of bridging the gap between the heights and the depths, of shaping a comprehensive social vision out of the fragments of the national culture: "Literature then had failed. The work was done by the movies, by television. The consciousness of the masses and the culture of the land trudged through endless mud."[7]

The mark of what Mailer takes to be the failure of the novel is, I believe, stamped on his own work. After the dazzling success of *The Naked and the Dead* (1948) and the middling achievement of *Barbary Shore* (1951) and *The Deer Park* (1955), Mailer was ten years in producing another novel. It now appears that he has not permanently abandoned the form, but the existential fantasy of sexuality and murder in *An American Dream* (1965) and the parable of our national disgrace in *Why Are We in Vietnam?* (1967) serve only to reinforce the nagging suspicion that Literature as the Novel has failed him and that his major energies are being spent in movie-making or nonfiction equivalents like *Advertisements for Myself* (1959) and *The Presidential Papers* (1963). This view is not surprising at a time when reputable historians like Barbara Tuchman can suggest that because of "the decline of the contemporary novel" people are turning away from fiction to "the books of reality," to "the literature of actuality."[8]

Mailer's most recent books—*The Armies of the Night*, *Miami and The Siege of Chicago*, *Of a Fire on the Moon*, and *The Prisoner of Sex*—are attempts to write the literature of actuality, the so-called books of reality. Originally published in *Harper's* and *Commentary*, *The Armies of the Night*, an account of the anti-Vietnam War protest march on the Pentagon in October 1967, was intended to present a double perspective on the events it narrated; it was both a private impression and a public record; it tried to realize both modes of discourse implied in its subtitle: "History as a Novel, the Novel as History." What it constitutes is a desperate gamble to make it new by trying to turn the sow's ear of magazine journalism into the silk purse of art. In dramatizing himself in various radical postures—like charging the federal marshals at the Pentagon and getting arrested—Mailer placed himself at the center of an interesting historical event and then exploited it as the raw material for a nonfiction novel. It is a brilliant piece of journalism. What it succeeds in laying bare, though, is Mailer's growing exasperation with art as formal design created by the imagination. The image of the writer in his study is somehow less admirable than that of the writer as Self-Promoter and Publicity-Conscious Careerist parlaying himself into national attention by "provoking" history himself and then writing about it.

Mailer's self-advertisement in nonfiction novels, *his* substitute for the novel of manners, has been praised most consistently by Norman Podhoretz, who sees Mailer as engaged in the task of trying to discover, through a public experiment on himself, whether the American dream of success always costs a man his soul or whether he can make it big-time and come out of it still pure in spirit. The rise of a person like Mailer from literary obscurity to fame, from poverty to riches, from social obscurity to the top of the greasy pole—this is typically a concern of the novel of manners. Podhoretz considered writing a book about that kind of success story based on the career of Norman Mailer. Instead, he wrote it about himself. But such is his skepticism about the viability of the novel form that in writing *Making It* Podhoretz also chose the Tuchmanian "book of reality," the Capotean documentary, the Mailerean nonfiction novel of the dramatized self.

Making It (1967), like some of these other books I have mentioned, is also meant to be a modern nonfiction novel of manners. Written out of a distrust of the novel in the sixties and informed with the editor's belief that discursive prose can be the equal in art of the novel, *Making It* is a brilliant study of the spiritual costs of upward social mobility in the United States today. Not even Mailer succeeds more powerfully than Podhoretz in describing the omnipotence of Success, the bitch goddess whom nearly all

Americans worship. A confessional, it recounts The Rise of Norman Podhoretz from the lower-class slums to the luxury apartments of Manhattan, from a Brooklyn high school to Columbia and Clare College (Cambridge), and from obscurity to wealth, power, fame, and success as critic, author, and editor of *Commentary*. The process by which this brilliant boy of the slums made his entry into New York society—after shedding his T-shirt and red satin athletic jacket for conventional clothes, purifying his speech of the Brooklyn accent, abandoning the Jewish dietary taboos, and becoming a cultivated Columbia College gentleman—is a paradigm of the Horatio Alger myth. Podhoretz celebrates it because it made him understand the heterogeneity of the American society he was being invited to enter; he satirized it because, in offering to let him become "a facsimile WASP," American society tried to estrange him from the lower-class world he had been born into. Recorded with sensitivity and honesty, the story of Norman Podhoretz is revealed in the dangers to the life of the spirit in the process of upward social mobility, but it also affirms the possibility of coming through it more or less spiritually intact.

What principally dissatisfies about *Making It*, though, is the nagging suspicion that—like *In Cold Blood* and *The Armies of the Night*—it might have been permanently more interesting, as a work of art, had it been a novel. The structure is there, the personalities, the point of view, the social insights, the take-off from a private moral experience to an act of social criticism. (In fact, the "I" of the book is not really Podhoretz so much as a persona; the reviewers who attacked him for arrogance and egotism missed the point.) But like Mailer's self-advertisements, *Making It* is thin and two-dimensional. It distrusts the imagination, doubts the reality, autonomy, and the authority of the subjective self. What is going on, for Podhoretz, is *"out there,"* where society is; it is out there, centered in an Ontological Other, where everything after all is "really going on," where "history" is "being made."[9] And for Podhoretz the only way to apprehend it is through the idea-oriented activity of the reason, not through imagination. Quite a number of remarkable things can go on in the privacy of the imagination, however; it is not all happening out there. But to plunge into its murky depths is to be drawn into the realm of what Podhoretz has called "these irrepressible praters about aesthetic values."[10] And this attraction he resists. Having failed as a poet, his youthful ambition, Podhoretz seems determined not to fail as a novelist. And this, for the sake of American art, is too bad, because he might become a better novelist than editor, and he is a very good editor indeed. Besides, one has the feeling that his failures as a novelist might be more interesting than some of the modest successes I have discussed in this study. But we will never know what we are losing from the realm of art, so long as the novel-is-dead cliché continues current and writers like Mailer and Podhoretz avoid the really dangerous risks that take place in the realm of the imagination—where the private vision, through the creative act, is transformed into the public design of art.[11]

The American social experience of the 1960s was marked by public controversy and polemic unmatched in the 1950s. The Kennedy campaign in 1960 which brought the first Catholic president into the White House, the Cuban missile crisis and the Bay of Pigs invasion, the Kennedy assassinations, the invasion of the Dominican Republic, the escalations of the Indo-China war, the organization of radical protest groups, the spectacle of private citizens pitting themselves individually against the policies of the U.S. government, the civil rights protests, black militancy and its radical chic support, the assassination of Dr. Martin Luther King, the nearly annual summer riots somewhere, and the abdication of President Johnson—all of these events have made for impassioned feelings, public disorder in the universities and elsewhere, and a high degree of conscious concern about American society that are reminiscent of the 1930s. We have nothing at present like the "mass society" Irving Howe described as typical of the fifties—with its widespread social drift and passivity, the ready acceptance of manufactured opinion handed down from above, the reluctance to become committed or engaged in behalf of social causes, and so on.

Even so, we have not had a rejuvenation of the novel which attempts to dramatize the panorama of these new social tensions. We have, instead, as Mailer complained, a number of isolated milieux: the lower-class world of Old World Jews in Bellow and Bernard Malamud; the world of the upper-class New York

WASPs in Auchincloss; the fundamentalist territory of Flannery O'Connor's South; the Yankee backwaters of John Cheever; the beat underworld of Jack Kerouac; the Woodstock generation of Richard Fariña and Richard Brautigan; and the dreary exurbias of J. D. Salinger and John Updike. What these locales signify is the disintegration of what we like to look back upon as an older, coherent American social order, now fragmented by the forces of continuous change. In the process of this social fragmentation, there have not yet appeared any theories of society useful to the postwar novelist, any ideas which—transformed as sentiments and feelings—can be embodied and dramatized in fiction. Consequently, though we still acknowledge the persistence of the class structure, still detect the signs of class and status, still experience the influence of institutional structures on our manners, and are still surprised into recognition of the vestiges of ceremony and form in the public life, our novelists do not quite know what to make of it all. We are said to be beyond ideology. But until the intellectual community produces some viable ideas, some conceptual framework within which these diverse social phenomena can be organized and interpreted, what is happening in our time may not be wholly expressed by our novelists. And we will get more private symbolic romances, more disembodied antinovels, and more nonfiction novels.

But in the meantime, while we await fresh significant conventional instances of the form, it is worth taking stock of what the novel of manners has meant in the history of American fiction. In the first place, the novel of manners has offered our writers one of the most flexible and successful forms for the analysis and criticism of American society. Though the utopian romance has had its uses (in works like *A Traveler from Altruria* and *Looking Backward*), the novel of manners has been the principal medium for testing, imaginatively, the postulates of Jeffersonian and Jacksonian thought as they have been translated into the customs and conventions of a social organization in the process of more or less continuous change. It has also offered one of the major literary strategies for exploring—from a spectrum of felt ideologies —the pluralistic forms of American social experience in metropolis, city, town, and country. Generally it has been most often exploited as the means of embodying the conservative social vision. Cooper's very personal conception of American democracy in *Home As Found* and the Littlepage trilogy, the ambivalent piety for the past in James's *The Princess Casamassima* and Edith Wharton's *The Age of Innocence*, the nostalgia for lost forms in Marquand's *Women and Thomas Harrow*, and the pronounced distrust of radical social experiments in O'Hara's *From the Terrace* and Cozzens's *Ask Me Tomorrow*—all of these conservative works have sought to demonstrate, in one way or another, that society is most secure and men happiest when they can discover their identity in a relatively stable order where the forms and manners governing their social obligations are firmly established.

But the novel of manners had been equally useful as a genre for criticizing the rigidities of conservatism. Howells's democratic egalitarianism which gave way in *A Hazard of New Fortunes* to Christian socialism, the revolutionary tone of socialism in Sinclair Lewis's *Main Street*, Fitzgerald's quasi-socialistic assumptions in *This Side of Paradise* and the barely concealed radicalism of *Tender Is the Night* are all illustrations of a less than radical but nevertheless powerful aspiration for a more perfect social order based on a fairer distribution of the world's goods, on an openness of social intercourse among all our people, and on a genuine sense of human brotherhood. Thus the novel of manners in America is a treasury of some of the most valuable fictional treatments of the American social order—what it has been, is, and could be.

But beyond this achievement, which is purely historical, the novel of manners has also constituted a body of imaginative literature of a high, and occasionally a *very high*, artistic quality. Some of our greatest writers have worked within the form, and some of the great works of our literature are expressions of the genre. Novels of manners like James's *The American* and *The Portrait of a Lady*, Edith Wharton's *The House of Mirth* and *The Age of Innocence*, Fitzgerald's *The Great Gatsby*, Marquand's *The Late George Apley* and *Point of No Return*, and Auchincloss's *Portrait in Brownstone* suggest how brilliant the execution of this form may be. How rich a contribution to our pleasure they have made, how impoverished would our literature be without them. Far from being dead, the novel of manners is so flexible and elastic a form that I cannot help feeling sanguine for its future. There are too many unfulfilled possibilities for it, too many modes of social being as yet unexpressed in the novel, for our writers to give it up. We await only the reconstitution of our fragmented national culture and a new synthesis of social thought which, as dramatized idea, can bring into play the talents of our best novelists. Speed the day.

✖ Abbreviations

The Age of Innocence	*AI*
The American	*A*
The American Scene	*AS*
Appointment in Samarra	*APS*
Ask Me Tomorrow	*AMT*
B. F.'s Daughter	*BFD*
By Love Possessed	*BLP*
The Chainbearer	*C*
A Chance Acquaintance	*CA*
The Embezzler	*E*
From the Terrace	*FT*
The Gods Arrive	*GA*
The Great Gatsby	*GG*
Hawthorne	*H*
Home As Found	*HAF*
Homeward Bound	*HB*
The House of Five Talents	*HFT*
The House of Mirth	*HM*
Hudson River Bracketed	*HRB*
The Late George Apley	*LGA*
The Lockwood Concern	*LC*
Main Street	*MS*
Men and Brethren	*MB*
A Modern Instance	*MI*
The Pioneers	*P*
Point of No Return	*PNR*
Portrait in Brownstone	*PB*
The Portrait of a Lady	*PL*
A Rage to Live	*RL*
The Redskins	*R*

The Rise of Silas Lapham	*RSL*
Roderick Hudson	*RH*
Satanstoe	*S*
Ten North Frederick	*TNF*
Their Wedding Journey	*TWJ*
This Side of Paradise	*TSP*
Women and Tomas Harrow	*WTH*

❧ Notes

PREFACE

1. Howard Mumford Jones, *Jeffersonianism and the American Novel* (New York, 1966), p. 15.
2. Irving Howe, "Mass Society and Post-Modern Fiction," in *Recent American Fiction: Some Critical Views*, ed. Joseph J. Waldmeir (Boston, 1963), p. 7.
3. Henry James, "The Art of Fiction," in *The Future of the Novel: Essays on the Art of Fiction*, ed. Leon Edel (New York, 1956), p. 4.

CHAPTER 1

1. Lionel Trilling, "The Novel Alive or Dead," *A Gathering of Fugitives* (Boston, 1956), p. 125.
2. Harold Nicolson, "Is the Novel Dead?" *Observer*, 29 August 1954, cited in John O. McCormick, "The Novel and Society," *Jahrbuch für Amerikastudien* 1 (1956): 70.
3. Henry James, "The Future of the Novel," in *The Future of the Novel: Essays on the Art of Fiction*, ed. Leon Edel (New York, 1956), p. 40.
4. See particularly Trilling's "Manners, Morals, and the Novel" and "Art and Fortune" in his *The Liberal Imagination* (Garden City, N.Y., 1950); Richard Chase's *The American Novel and Its Tradition* (Garden City, N.Y., 1957); Marius Bewley's *The Eccentric Design* (London, 1959); John W. Aldridge's *After the Lost Generation* (New York, 1958) and *In Search of Heresy* (New York, 1956). These works touch on the general argument that the novel of manners never established itself in this country. For representative counterstatements, see David H. Hirsch's "Reality, Manners, and Mr. Trilling," *Sewanee Review* 72 (1964): 425; William Barrett's "American Fiction and American Values," *Partisan Review* 18 (1951): 681–90 (a reply to Barrett is Aldridge's "Manners and Values," *Partisan Review* 19 [1952]: 347); Delmore Schwartz's "The Duchess' Red Shoes," *Partisan Review* 20 (1953): 58; Hilton Kramer's "Unreal Radicalism," *Partisan Review* 23 (1956): 554; Arthur Mizener's "The Novel of Manners in America," *Kenyon Review* 12 (1950): 19; W. M. Frohock's *Strangers to This Ground: Cultural Diversity in Contemporary American Writing* (Dallas, 1961); and *The Living Novel: A Symposium*, ed. Granville Hicks (New York, 1957)—particularly John Brooks's "Some Notes on Writing One Kind of Novel," Ralph Ellison's "Society, Morality, and the Novel," Flannery O'Connor's "The Fiction Writer and His Country," and Hicks's "Introduction." For ancillary discussions of the argument, see Trilling's "William Dean Howells and the Roots of Modern Taste," in *The Opposing Self: Nine Essays in Criticism* (New York, 1955); Allen Tate's "What Is a Traditional Society?" in *Reason in Madness* (New York, 1941); David Riesman's *The Lonely Crowd* (Garden City, N.Y., 1953), together with Trilling's "Two Notes on David Riesman" in *A Gathering of Fugitives*; Ludwig Lewisohn's *Expression in America* (New York,

1932), p. 252; Louis Auchincloss's *Reflections of a Jacobite* (New York, 1961); Flannery O'Connor's *Mystery and Manners*, ed. Sally Fitzgerald and Robert Fitzgerald (New York, 1969); Charles C. Walcutt, "*Sister Carrie*: Naturalism or the Novel of Manners?" *Genre* 1 (1968): 76–85.

5. Trilling, "Manners, Morals, and the Novel," pp. 200–201.

6. Chase, *American Novel and Its Tradition*, pp. 157–59; Trilling, "Manners, Morals, and the Novel," p. 207.

7. Mark Schorer, "Foreword: Self and Society," in *Society and Self in the Novel: English Institute Essays, 1955* (New York, 1956), pp. viii–ix.

8. W. Witte, "The Sociological Approach to Literature," *Modern Language Review* 36 (1951): 87–88.

9. W. M. Frohock, *Strangers to This Ground*, p. 28.

10. James Fenimore Cooper, *Notions of the Americans, Picked Up by a Travelling Bachelor*, ed. Robert E. Spiller, 2 vols. (New York, 1963), 2:108–9.

11. Alexis de Tocqueville, *Democracy in America*, ed. Phillips Bradley, 2 vols. (New York, 1958), 2:229–30.

12. William Cullen Bryant, review of *Redwood* by Catherine M. Sedgwick, *North American Review* 20 (April 1825); reprinted in *William Cullen Bryant: Representative Selections*, ed. Tremaine McDowell (New York, 1935), pp. 182–83.

13. Ibid.

14. Horace Walpole, "*The Castle of Otranto*," in *Shorter Novels: Eighteenth Century*, ed. Philip Henderson (London, 1930), p. 102.

15. Chase, *American Novel and Its Tradition*, p. 13.

16. Clara Reeve, *The Progress of Romance*, Facsimile Text Society, ser. 1, vol. 4 (1785; reprint ed. New York, 1930), p. 111.

17. William Gilmore Simms, *The Yemassee: A Romance of Carolina*, ed. C. Hugh Holman (Boston, 1962), pp. 5–6.

18. Philip Rahv, "Fiction and the Criticism of Fiction," *Kenyon Review* 18 (1956): 285.

19. Irving Howe, "The Passing of a World," in *Twentieth Century Interpretations of "The Sound and the Fury,"* ed. Michael H. Cowan (Englewood Cliffs, N.J., 1968), p. 38.

20. William Gilmore Simms, *Views and Reviews in American Literature, History and Fiction: First Series*, ed. C. Hugh Holman (Cambridge, Mass., 1962), p. 259.

21. Nathaniel Hawthorne, *The Blithedale Romance* (Boston, 1876), p. vi.

22. Nathaniel Hawthorne, *The Marble Faun* (Boston, 1880), pp. vii–viii.

23. Henry James, *Hawthorne* (London, 1879), p. 43.

24. Ibid., pp. 43–44.

25. William Dean Howells, "James's *Hawthorne*," *Atlantic Monthly* 45 (February 1880): 284.

26. Henry James, *The Letters of Henry James*, ed. Percy Lubbock, 2 vols. (New York, 1920), 1:72.

27. Henry James, *The American Scene* (London, 1907), p. 12.

28. F. W. Dupee, *Henry James* (Garden City, N.Y., 1956), p. 238.

29. Edith Wharton, "The Great American Novel," *Yale Review*, n.s. 16 (1927): 649.

30. James Fenimore Cooper, *Home As Found*, ed. Lewis Leary (New York, 1961), p. xxviii.

CHAPTER 2

1. James Grossman, *James Fenimore Cooper* (n.p., 1949), p. 21.

2. Sir Walter Scott, *The Journal of Sir Walter Scott*, ed. J. G. Tait and W. M. Parker (Edinburgh, 1950), p. 144.

3. Sir Walter Scott, "General Preface," *Waverley* (Boston, 1857), p. 19.

4. Scott, "A Postscript, Which Should Have Been a Preface," *Waverley*, p. 367.

5. Nelson Bushnell, "Walter Scott's Advent as Novelist of Manners," *Studies in Scottish Literature* 1 (1963): 31.

6. Sir Walter Scott, *Miscellaneous Prose Works* (Edinburgh, 1834), 4:69.

7. Sir Walter Scott, *The Letters of Sir Walter Scott*, ed. H. J. C. Grierson (London, 1932–37), 2:445.

8. Ibid., 8:56.

9. Scott, *Journal of Sir Walter Scott*, p. 144.

10. Review of J. G. Lockhart's *Narrative of the Life of Sir Walter Scott, Bart.*, in *The Knickerbocker, or New York Monthly Magazine* 12 (1838): 363–64.

11. F. L. Pattee, "James Fenimore Cooper," *American Mercury* 4 (1925): 292–93.

12. James Fenimore Cooper, *The Works of J. Fenimore Cooper*, 32 vols. (New York, 1859–61), vol. 21, *Precaution* (1861), p. 379 (hereafter cited as *Works*).

13. James Fenimore Cooper, *The Letters and Journals of James Fenimore Cooper*, ed. James Franklin Beard (Cambridge, Mass., 1960), 1:44.

14. Leon Howard, "Introduction," *The Pioneers* by James Fenimore Cooper (New York, 1959), p. viii.

15. Cooper, *Works*, vol. 19, *The Pioneers; Or, The Sources of the Susquehanna: A Descriptive Tale*, p. 421.

16. James Fenimore Cooper, *Notions of the Americans, Picked Up by a Travelling Bachelor*, ed. Robert E. Spiller (New York, 1963), 1:155–56.

17. James Fenimore Cooper, *The American Democrat, or Hints on the Social and Civic Relations of the United States of America* (New York, 1956), pp. 43, 45, 80.

18. Cooper, *Works*, vol. 9, *Homeward Bound* (1860), p. 22.

19. Cooper, *Works*, vol. 8, "Preface," *Home As Found* (1860), p. vii.

20. "Introduction," *Home As Found* by James Fenimore Cooper, ed. Lewis Leary (New York, 1961), p. xxv.

21. See, for example, David M. Ellis, *Landlords and Farmers in the Hudson-Mohawk Region, 1790–1850* (Ithaca, N.Y., 1946); Edward P. Cheyney, *The Anti-Rent Agitation in the State of New York, 1839–1846* (Philadelphia, 1887); James W. Tuttleton, "The New England Character in Cooper's Social Novels," *Bulletin of the New York Public Library* 70 (1966): 305–17.

22. "Introduction," *Satanstoe* by James Fenimore Cooper, ed. Robert E. Spiller and Joseph D. Coppock (New York, 1937), p. x.

23. Cooper, *Works*, vol. 24, *Satanstoe* (1860), p. vi. *The Chainbearer* (1860), vol. 3, and *The Redskins, or Indian and Injin* (1860), vol. 23, are hereafter cited by abbreviation and page number in the text.

CHAPTER 3

1. Henry James to Elizabeth Boott, 10 December 1873, quoted in Nathalia Wright, *American Novelists in Italy* (Philadelphia, 1965), p. 201.

2. Henry James, "Four Meetings," in *The Portable Henry James*, ed. Morton D. Zabel (New York, 1951), p. 47.

3. Herbert Croly, "Henry James and His Countrymen," in *The Question of Henry James*, ed. F. W. Dupee (New York, 1945), p. 29.

4. Henry James, "Howells's 'Foregone Conclusion,'" *Nation*, 7 January 1875, pp. 12–13.

5. Henry James, *The Letters of Henry James*, ed. Percy Lubbock, 2 vols. (New York, 1920), 1:396.

6. Henry James, *French Poets and Novelists* (London, 1919), p. 220.

7. James, *Letters*, 1:316.

8. Quoted in Simon Nowell-Smith's *The Legend of the Master* (New York, 1948), p. 104.

9. Vernon L. Parrington, *The Beginnings of Critical Realism in America, 1860–1920* (New York, 1930); Van Wyck Brooks, *The Pilgrimage of Henry James* (New York, 1925).

10. William Troy, "The New Generation," in *Henry James: A Collection of Critical Essays*, ed. Leon Edel (Englewood Cliffs, N.J., 1963), p. 84.

11. Henry James, *The Notebooks of Henry James*, ed. F. O. Matthiessen and Kenneth B. Murdock (New York, 1961), p. 23.

12. Leon Edel, *Henry James*, vol. 2, *The Conquest of London: 1870–1881* (Philadelphia, 1962), p. 44.

13. Henry James, "A Bundle of Letters," *Tales* (London, 1962), 4:442.

14. Croly, "Henry James and His Countrymen," p. 30.

15. Ralph W. Emerson, "Manners," *Essays by Ralph Waldo Emerson* (New York, 1961), p. 361.

16. Richard Poirier has observed that "the failure of hope and ambition in *Roderick Hudson* have [*sic*] nothing to do with social status or with one's being an American" (*The Comic Sense of Henry James* [New York, 1967], p. 47). This is not precisely the case. Hudson's insignificance in the social scheme, his poverty, his flamboyant Americanism are precisely the qualities that make him so much less engaging a candidate for Christina's hand, in the eyes of the Cavaliere and Mrs. Light, than Prince Casamassima.

17. *Roderick Hudson* (New York, 1907), p. 101. All quotations from this novel are to the edition cited.

18. Oscar Cargill, *The Novels of Henry James* (New York, 1961), p. 37, n. 31.

19. Henry James, *The Art of the Novel: Critical Prefaces by Henry James*, ed. R. P. Blackmur (New York, 1934), pp. 15–17.

20. Ibid., p. 10.

21. James, *Letters*, 1:22.

22. Ibid., p. 69.

23. Ibid., p. 48.

24. Henry James, *The Selected Letters of Henry James*, ed. Leon Edel (New York, 1955), pp. 41, 50, 51.

25. Quoted in Edel's *Henry James: The Conquest of London*, p. 263.

26. James, *Notebooks of Henry James*, p. 24.

27. Cargill, *Novels of Henry James*, p. 45.

28. G. B. Fitch, "Emile Augier and the Intrusion-Plot," *Publications of the Modern Language Association* 63 (1948): 274–80.

29. Henry James, *The American* (New York, 1960), p. 19. For this novel I have preferred to use a reprint of the first edition rather than the New York edition, for its occasional greater picturesqueness of phrasing. All quotations from the novel are to the first edition.

30. Henry James, *Portraits of Places* (Boston, 1884), p. 75.

31. Irving Howe, "Henry James and the Millionaire," *Tomorrow* 9 (1950): 53.

32. John Kinnaird, "The Paradox of an American 'Identity,'" *Partisan Review* 25 (1958): 381.

33. James, *Selected Letters*, pp. 22–23.

34. Frederick J. Hoffman, "Freedom and Conscious Form: Henry James and the American Self," *Virginia Quarterly Review* 37 (1961): 275.

35. Henry James, review of *The French at Home* by Albert Rhodes (New York, 1875), in the *Nation*, 5 August 1875, p. 92.

36. I. M., "The American Colony in France," *Nation*, 18 April 1878, p. 258.

37. Ibid., p. 259.

38. William Dean Howells, *Through the Eye of the Needle* (New York, 1907), p. 63.

39. Henry James, *The American Scene* (New York, 1907), p. 24.

40. James, *Art of the Novel*, pp. 35–36.

41. Edel, *Henry James: The Conquest of London*, p. 249.

42. James, *Selected Letters*, pp. 68–69.

43. Henry James, *Hawthorne* (New York, 1966), p. 46.

44. Nathaniel Hawthorne, *The Complete Works of Nathaniel Hawthorne*, ed. G. P. Lathrop, 12 vols. (Boston, 1883), vol. 6, *The Marble Faun*, p. 15 (hereafter cited as *Works*).

45. Hawthorne, *Works*, vol. 5, *The Scarlet Letter*, p. 55.

46. Hawthorne, *Works*, vol. 3, *The House of Seven Gables*, p. 13.

47. Hawthorne, *Works*, vol. 5, *The Blithedale Romance*, pp. 321–22.

48. Nathaniel Hawthorne, *Twice-Told Tales* (Boston, 1900), p. liv; Jay Leyda, *The Melville Log* (New York, 1951), 1:406; Hawthorne, *Works*, vol. 5, *The Scarlet Letter*, pp. 56–57.

49. William Dean Howells, "James's *Hawthorne*," *Atlantic Monthly* 45 (February 1880):282–85; reprinted in *Discovery of a Genius: William Dean Howells and Henry James*, ed. Albert Mordell (New York, 1961), pp. 94, 96.

50. James, *Letters*, 1:71–74.

51. T. W. Higginson, "Henry James, Jr.," in *The Question of Henry James*, p. 2.

52. Henry James, *The Princess Casamassima*, 2 vols. (New York, 1908), 2:145–46.

53. Henry James, *Transatlantic Sketches* (Boston, 1900), pp. 17–18.

54. James, *American Scene*, pp. 10–11.

55. Quoted by Edel, *Henry James: The Conquest of London*, p. 277.

56. James, *Letters*, 1:124.

57. James, *Princess Casamassima*, 2:23.

58. James, *Letters*, 1:73.

59. Ibid., p. 31.

60. "James's *Portrait of a Lady*," *Nation*, 2 February 1882, pp. 102–3.

61. Edel, *Henry James: The Conquest of London*, p. 425.

62. Henry James, *The Portrait of a Lady*, 2 vols. (New York, 1908), 2:356, 164.

63. Christof Wegelin, *The Image of Europe in Henry James* (Dallas, 1958), p. 29.

64. Henry James, *The Question of Our Speech and the Lesson of Balzac: Two Lectures* (Boston, 1905), pp. 12, 36–37, 14, 51.

CHAPTER 4

1. Olov Fryckstedt, *In Quest of America: A Study of Howells' Early Development as a Novelist* (Upsala, 1958), pp. 38–39.

2. Henry Steele Commager, "The Return to Howells," in *The War of the Critics over William Dean Howells*, ed. Edwin H. Cady and David L. Frazier (Evanston, Ill., 1962), pp. 191–92.

3. Quoted in J. Henry Harper's *The House of Harper* (New York, 1912), p. 326.

4. William Dean Howells, *Life in Letters of William Dean Howells*, ed. Mildred Howells, 2 vols. (Garden City, N.Y., 1928), 1:162.

5. William Dean Howells, *Their Wedding Journey* (Boston, 1878), p. 2.

6. William Dean Howells to J. M. Comly, 31 March 1871, quoted in Fryckstedt, *In Quest of America*, p. 102.

7. Delmar Gross Cooke, *William Dean Howells: A Critical Study* (New York, 1922), p. 144.

8. Quoted in Van Wyck Brooks, *Howells: His Life and World* (New York, 1959), p. 76 n.; Henry Adams, "Howells's *Their Wedding Journey*," in *The War of the Critics over William Dean Howells*, p. 9.

9. Dorothy Dudley, *Dreiser and the Land of the Free* (New York, 1946), p. 143. Fryckstedt has persuasively noted, however, that Dreiser's emphasis on the couple's arguments suggests that he may have had *A Modern Instance* in mind.

10. William Dean Howells, *A Chance Acquaintance* (Boston, 1873), p. 242.

11. E. L. Godkin, *Life and Letters of Edwin Lawrence Godkin*, ed. Rollo Ogden, 2 vols. (New York, 1907), 1:307.

12. George N. Bennett, *William Dean Howells: The Development of a Novelist* (Norman, Okla., 1959), p. 21.

13. Edwin H. Cady, *The Road to Realism* (Syracuse, 1956), p. 183.

14. Thomas S. Perry, "William Dean Howells," *Century Magazine* 23 (1882): 683.

15. Henry James, *The Letters of Henry James*, ed. Percy Lubbock, 2 vols. (New York, 1920), 1:34.

16. Howells, *Life in Letters of William Dean Howells*, 1:174–75.

17. Bernard Smith, "Howells: The Genteel Radical," in *The War of the Critics over William Dean Howells*, p. 172; C. Hartley Grattan, "Howells: Ten Years After," in *The War of the Critics over William Dean Howells*, p. 159.

18. William Dean Howells, *Literary Friends and Acquaintance* (New York, 1900), p. 286.

19. Howells, *Life in Letters of William Dean Howells*, 1:210.

20. Ibid., pp. 232–33.

21. T. W. Higginson, "The Trick of Self-Deprecation," *The New World and the New Book: With Kindred Essays* (Boston, 1892), p. 211.

22. Quoted in Rudolf Kirk and Clara Kirk, *William Dean Howells* (New Haven, 1962), p. 210.

23. William Gibson, "Introduction," *A Modern Instance* by William Dean Howells (Boston, 1957), p. vii.

24. William Dean Howells, review of *Recollections of a Busy Life* by Horace Greeley, *Atlantic Monthly* 23 (February 1869): 261.

25. William Dean Howells, *A Modern Instance* (Boston, 1957), p. 18.

26. William Dean Howells, review of *A Passionate Pilgrim* by Henry James, *Atlantic Monthly* 35 (April 1875): 491.

27. Fryckstedt, *In Quest of America*, p. 226.

28. Richard Chase, *The American Novel and Its Tradition* (Garden City, N.Y., 1957), p. 159.

29. Fryckstedt, *In Quest of America*, p. 230.

30. William Dean Howells, "Editor's Easy Chair," *Harper's Magazine* 102 (1901): 318.

31. William Dean Howells, *Literature and Life* (New York, 1902), pp. 29–30.

32. Still, for some reason, Bennett insists that "it is not necessary to compress the novel into narrow limitations, to regard it as dealing merely with social life. It need not be viewed simply as a comedy of manners which somehow comes to be involved with a moral problem" (*William Dean Howells*, p. 150). This claim is equivalent to saying that *Moby-Dick* need not be seen as a symbolic romance about the pursuit of a white whale.

33. William Dean Howells, *The Rise of Silas Lapham*, ed. E. H. Cady (Boston, 1957), p. 24.

34. William Dean Howells, review of *Recollections of a Busy Life*, p. 260.

35. Alexander Harvey, *William Dean Howells: A Study of the Achievement of a Literary Artist* (New York, 1917), p. 120.

36. Constance Rourke, "The American," *The Question of Henry James* (New York, 1945), pp. 157–58.

37. T. W. Higginson, "Acts of Homage," *Book and Heart* (New York, 1897), p. 197.

38. Henry James, "A Letter to Mr. Howells," *North American Review* 195 (1912): 558–62.

39. William Dean Howells, "Equality as the Basis of Good Society," *Century Magazine* 51 (1895): 67.

CHAPTER 5

1. Edith Wharton, *A Backward Glance* (New York, 1934), p. 73.
2. Edith Wharton, *Hudson River Bracketed* (New York, 1929), p. 394.
3. Blake Nevius, *Edith Wharton: A Study of Her Fiction* (Berkeley, 1953), pp. 8–9.
4. Wharton, *A Backward Glance*, p. 144.
5. Henry James, *The Letters of Henry James*, ed. Percy Lubbock, 2 vols. (New York, 1920), 1:395–97. In Mrs. Wharton's view, however, as she observed in "Souvenirs du Bourget d'Outremer," "en effet, c'est seulement en ayant vu d'autres pays, étudié leurs moeurs, lu leurs livres, frequenté leurs habitants, que l'on peut situer son propre pays dans l'histoire de la civilisation" (*Revue Hebdomadaire*, 21 June 1936, p. 276).
6. Edith Wharton, "The Great American Novel," *Yale Review*, n.s. 16 (1927): 652.
7. Edith Wharton, *The House of Mirth* (New York, 1962), p. 303.
8. William Graham Sumner, *Folkways: A Study of the Sociological Importance of Usages, Manners, Customs, Mores, and Morals* (Boston, 1906), p. 156.
9. Edith Wharton, "Mr. Sturgis's 'Belchamber,'" *Bookman* 21 (May 1905): 309–10.
10. Erskine Steele, "Fiction and Social Ethics," *South Atlantic Quarterly* 5 (1906): 262.
11. Wharton, *A Backward Glance*, p. 207.
12. Northrop Frye, *Anatomy of Criticism* (Princeton, 1957), p. 38.
13. Louis Auchincloss, *Reflections of a Jacobite* (Boston, 1961), p. 144.
14. Wharton, *A Backward Glance*, p. 7.
15. Ibid., p. 369.
16. Edith Wharton, *The Age of Innocence* (New York, 1920), p. 42.
17. Wharton, *A Backward Glance*, pp. 21–22.
18. Edith Wharton, "A Little Girl's New York," *Harper's* 176 (March 1938): 357.
19. Edith Wharton, *French Ways and Their Meaning* (New York, 1919), p. 97.
20. Wharton, *Hudson River Bracketed*, p. 354.
21. Edith Wharton, *The Writing of Fiction* (New York, 1925), p. 10.
22. James, *Letters of Henry James*, 2:282–85.
23. Wharton, *A Backward Glance*, p. 190.
24. Wharton, *Writing of Fiction*, pp. 13–14.
25. Edith Wharton, *The Gods Arrive* (New York, 1932), p. 273.
26. Wharton, *Writing of Fiction*, p. 156.
27. Ibid., p. 21.

28. Wharton, *A Backward Glance*, p. 191.

29. E. K. Brown, "Edith Wharton," *Études anglaises* 2 (1938): 19.

30. Arthur Mizener, *The Sense of Life in the Modern Novel* (Boston, 1964), pp. 267–68.

31. Saul Bellow, "Where Do We Go from Here: The Future of Fiction," *Saul Bellow and the Critics*, ed. Irving Malin (New York, 1967), p. 220.

32. Edith Wharton, "A Cycle of Reviewing," *Spectator*, 3 November 1928, supplement, pp. 44–45.

33. Hamlin Garland, *Crumbling Idols* (New York, 1894), p. 43.

34. One evidence of this possibility is Allen Guttmann's recent criticism, from a socialist slant, of liberal philosophies because they are almost totally oriented toward the future. His argument is that ignorance of the past, for state planners, is "socially dysfunctional" but that knowledge of the traditions of Western civilization can be not only instrumentally instructive in helping us to understand the present and the future but *humanely* instructive as well. "The problem for social democracy," he observes, "is not only to assure everyone the material basis for a good life but also to expand, preserve, and make available for all men the diverse, priceless achievements of the past as well as the present" (*The Conservative Tradition in America* [New York, 1967], pp. 176–80). Mrs. Wharton would hardly have sympathized with Professor Guttmann's epigram: "Socialism with a sense of the past is the name of my desire." But the conservative attitude toward the past, rendered dramatically in fiction, suggests how humanely instructive to contemporary liberalism a view like hers can be.

CHAPTER 6

1. Sinclair Lewis, *The Man from Main Street: Selected Essays and Other Writings, 1904–1950*, ed. Harry E. Maule and Melville H. Cane (New York, 1953), p. 173.

2. Sinclair Lewis, "Introduction," in *The Good Old Days: A History of American Morals and Manners as Seen through the Sears, Roebuck Catalogs 1905 to the Present* by David L. Cohn (New York, 1940), p. viii.

3. Sinclair Lewis, *The Man from Main Street*, p. 187.

4. Stephen S. Conroy, "Sinclair Lewis's Sociological Imagination," *American Literature* 42 (1970): 348.

5. Mark Schorer, *Sinclair Lewis: An American Life* (New York, 1961), p. 268.

6. Sinclair Lewis, *From Main Street to Stockholm: Letters of Sinclair Lewis, 1919–1930*, ed. Harrison Smith (New York, 1952), p. 21.

7. Leonard Bacon, "Yale '09," *Saturday Review of Literature*, 4 February 1939, p. 13.

8. Chauncey Brewster Tinker, "Sinclair Lewis: A Few Reminiscences," *Yale Alumni Magazine* (June 1952), p. 10.

9. Grace Hegger Lewis, *With Love from Gracie* (New York, 1955), p. 60.

10. Sinclair Lewis, *Free Air* (New York, 1919), pp. 55, 66–67.

11. T. K. Whipple, "Sinclair Lewis," *Spokesmen* (Berkeley, 1963), p. 223.

12. Sinclair Lewis, *From Main Street to Stockholm*, p. 10.

13. Maxwell Geismar, "Sinclair Lewis," *The Last of the Provincials* (Boston, 1947), pp. 82–83.

14. Schorer, *Sinclair Lewis*, p. 271.

15. Ibid., p. 272.

16. Harlan Hatcher, *Creating the Modern American Novel* (New York, 1935), p. 115.

17. Sinclair Lewis, *The Man from Main Street*, p. 214. James also debunked

the village-paradise myth in observing that "manners are a help in life—a help not only to avoid certain vices, but to bear with certain virtues"—like neighborliness and busybody "helpfulness." Yet American villagers and townspeople "have not that assistance, and we wonder what it is that saves them, their nerves or their temper or their lives or their breakable objects—what it is that holds them or their hearthstones together." With "so little of the *margin* supplied by manners," our American good humor, patience, and forebearance are all that constitute one's security against the invasion of privacy (Henry James, "The Manners of American Women," *Harper's Bazaar* 41 [1907]: 647–48).

18. Meredith Nicholson, *A Hoosier Chronicle* (Boston, 1912), p. 606.

19. Sinclair Lewis, *Main Street* (New York, 1920), p. 264. All quotations from *Main Street* are to the edition cited.

20. Not only subjects but also stylistic effects Lewis derived from Mrs. Wharton. In her broad satires, for example, she ridiculed preposterous social views by pinning grotesque names on those who held them—Ora Prance Chettle, Norma Hatch, Eldorada Tooker, and Indiana Frusk, for example. Lewis liked the comic effect of these names and filled his own novels with scores of them—Almus Pickergill, Rippleton Holabird, T. Cholmondeley Frink, Sara Hetwiggin Butts, and so on. On the ground of verisimilitude Lewis may deserve to be criticized for using such preposterous names. But in all probability he found them somewhere. He was nearly sued by a George F. Babbitt of Boston, it is worth remembering, and Grace Hegger Lewis observed in 1951: "I cannot pass a forgotten back-road cemetery without exploring it for rare and wondrous names as Hal and I used to do" (*With Love from Gracie*, p. 106).

21. Whipple, "Sinclair Lewis," p. 256.

22. Meredith Nicholson, *The Valley of Democracy* (New York, 1919), p. 56.

23. Ibid., pp. 54–55.

24. Stow Persons, "The Americanization of the Immigrant," *Foreign Influences in American Life* (Princeton, 1944), p. 42.

25. Sinclair Lewis, *The Man from Main Street*, pp. 276–77.

26. Schorer, *Sinclair Lewis*, p. 301.

27. August Derleth, *Three Literary Men: A Memoir of Sinclair Lewis, Sherwood Anderson, and Edgar Lee Masters* (New York, 1963), pp. 12–13.

28. Grace Lewis, *With Love from Gracie*, p. 119.

29. H. L. Mencken, "Consolation," in *Sinclair Lewis: A Collection of Critical Essays*, ed. Mark Schorer (Englewood Cliffs, N.J., 1962), p. 18.

30. Meredith Nicholson, "Let Main Street Alone," *The Man in the Street* (New York, 1921), pp. 9–10.

31. Hatcher, *Creating the Modern American Novel*, p. 120.

32. Schorer, *Sinclair Lewis*, p. 435.

33. F. Scott Fitzgerald, *The Letters of F. Scott Fitzgerald*, ed. Andrew Turnbull (New York, 1963), p. 467.

34. Grace Lewis, *With Love from Gracie*, p. 23.

35. Sinclair Lewis, *From Main Street to Stockholm*, pp. 203, 212.

36. Schorer, *Sinclair Lewis*, p. 312.

37. Ibid., p. 347.

CHAPTER 7

1. *New York World Telegram*, 26 December 1940; quoted by J. F. Powers, "Dealer in Diamonds and Rhinestones," in *F. Scott Fitzgerald: The Man and His Work*, ed. Alfred Kazin (New York, 1962), p. 183 (hereafter this anthology is cited as *FSF*).

2. Weller Embler, "F. Scott Fitzgerald and the Future," *FSF*, p. 215.

3. "Power without Glory," *Times Literary Supplement*, 20 January 1950, p. 40.

4. William Goldhurst, *F. Scott Fitzgerald and His Contemporaries* (New York and Cleveland, 1963), p. 228.

5. Arthur Mizener, *The Far Side of Paradise* (New York, 1959), p. xxi.

6. Quoted in ibid., p. 109.

7. Malcolm Cowley, "Third Act and Epilogue," *FSF*, p. 148.

8. F. Scott Fitzgerald, *The Letters of F. Scott Fitzgerald*, ed. Andrew Turnbull (New York, 1963), p. 251.

9. Frederick Lewis Allen, "The Revolution in Manners and Morals," *Only Yesterday* (New York, 1959), pp. 61–86.

10. Henry Dan Piper, *F. Scott Fitzgerald: A Critical Portrait* (New York, 1965), p. 74.

11. John O'Hara, "In Memory of Scott Fitzgerald: II—Certain Aspects," *New Republic* 104 (1941): 311.

12. Arthur Mizener, "The Poet of Borrowed Time," *FSF*, p. 23.

13. F. Scott Fitzgerald, *This Side of Paradise* (New York, 1920), p. 299.

14. John W. Aldridge, "Fitzgerald: The Horror and the Vision of Paradise," *F. Scott Fitzgerald: A Collection of Critical Essays*, ed. Arthur Mizener (Englewood Cliffs, N.J., 1963), p. 32.

15. F. Scott Fitzgerald, *The Crack-Up*, ed. Edmund Wilson (New York, 1945), pp. 14–15.

16. Piper, *F. Scott Fitzgerald*, pp. 60–61. See also Mrs. Frank Learned, *The Etiquette of New York Today* (New York, 1906), pp. 284–86.

17. Quoted in Piper, *F. Scott Fitzgerald*, p. 227.

18. Fitzgerald, *The Crack-Up*, p. 87.

19. Ibid.

20. Ibid., p. 18.

21. Ibid., p. 15.

22. Ibid., p. 27. Fitzgerald's reference reminds us that Emily Price Post was a novelist of manners first and an authority on etiquette later. An Old New Yorker like Edith Wharton, Mrs. Post plied the international novel of manners in *The Flight of the Moth* (1904) and *Purple Linen* (1906). Asked by her publishers to write a book on polite manners, she responded with *Etiquette: In Society, in Business, in Politics, and at Home* (1922). Defining society as "an association of gentle-folk, of which good form in speech, charm of manner, knowledge of the social amenities, and instinctive consideration for the feelings of others" is typical, Mrs. Post brought her manual to life by inventing fictional persons (like the Richan Vulgars, Mr. and Mrs. Gotta Crust, the Worldlys, the Gildings, and "that odious Hector Newman") in order to dramatize comically the correct form for introductions, teas, balls and dances, dress, weddings, and so on. Since 1922—in the course of one million copies and ninety-nine editions—*Etiquette* has changed markedly. But though it is now less prescriptive, more a general guide to modern life, it still fails adequately to acknowledge the revolution in manners and morals which has taken place since Fitzgerald's time.

23. Fitzgerald, *The Crack-Up*, pp. 21–22.

24. "Mr. Grundy," " 'Polite Society,' " *Atlantic Monthly* 125 (May 1920): 606–12.

25. Katherine Fullerton Gerould, "Reflections of a Grundy Cousin," *Atlantic Monthly* 126 (August 1920): 160.

26. John F. Carter, "These Wild Young People—by One of Them," *Atlantic Monthly* 126 (September 1920): 301, 304.

27. [A Last Year's Débutante], "Good-Bye, Dear Mr. Grundy," *Atlantic Monthly* 126 (November 1920): 642–46.

28. Cornelia James Cannon, "Can Our Civilization Maintain Itself?" *Atlantic Monthly* 126 (November 1920): 633–36.
29. Fitzgerald, *The Crack-Up*, p. 15.
30. Mizener, *Far Side of Paradise*, p. 111.
31. Andrews Wanning, "Fitzgerald and His Brethren," *FSF*, p. 161.
32. Fitzgerald, *Letters*, p. 277.
33. Andrew Turnbull, *Scott Fitzgerald: A Biography* (New York, 1962), p. 150.
34. Fitzgerald, *The Crack-Up*, p. 190.
35. Fitzgerald, *Letters*, p. 484.
36. Quoted in Mizener, *Far Side of Paradise*, pp. 171–72.
37. Fitzgerald, *Letters*, p. 465.
38. F. Scott Fitzgerald, quoted in *The Great Gatsby: A Study*, ed. Frederick J. Hoffman (New York, 1962), p. 167.
39. Fitzgerald, *Letters*, p. 163.
40. Ibid., p. 166.
41. Ibid., p. 179.
42. Henry James, *The Art of the Novel* (New York, 1934), p. 22.
43. The connection with Petronian satire is also interesting on stylistic grounds. It was possible in classical times—according to the theory of the separation of literary styles—to assert that realism in style, as in the feast of Trimalchio, was the appropriate mode of comedy. Yet in the work of Fitzgerald, the elements of realism in the portrait of Gatsby bear a freight of tragedy. The reason for this, as Erich Auerbach has pointed out in *Mimesis* (1953), is that the modern novelist of manners refuses to be restrained by an arbitrary separation of styles which asserts that realism is appropriate to comedy and heightened rhetoric for tragedy. The neoclassical comedy of manners is of course realistic and comic because it relies on the classical separation of styles. But the novel of manners may very well manifest itself as tragedy or pathos in a style appropriately heightened to suit the material and to convey the emotional intensity and significance of the action.
44. F. Scott Fitzgerald, *The Great Gatsby* (New York, 1925), pp. 13, 48, 154.
45. Ibid., pp. 79, 89, 49.
46. Quoted in Turnbull, *Scott Fitzgerald*, p. 150.
47. Fitzgerald, *Letters*, pp. 289–90.
48. Ibid. See Richard Lehan's discussion of Spengler in *F. Scott Fitzgerald and the Craft of Fiction* (Carbondale, Ill., 1966), pp. 30–36, but note Robert Sklar's objection that Fitzgerald's source in *The Great Gatsby* for these ideas of social disintegration could not have been Spengler (*F. Scott Fitzgerald: The Last Laocoön* [New York, 1967], p. 135). In his notebook, Fitzgerald planned to treat satirically in one of his tales the "recurrent idea in America about an education that would leave out history and the past, that should be a sort of equipment for aerial adventure, weighed down by none of the stowaways of inheritance or tradition" (*The Crack-Up*, p. 109). Here, of course, he was looking at the figure in Edith Wharton's carpet. Although they have money and Lily Bart does not, like Lily, Tom and Daisy have no "centre of early pieties, of grave endearing traditions" to which their hearts may revert for strength, purpose, and moral order.
49. Goldhurst, *F. Scott Fitzgerald*, p. 183.
50. Quoted in Turnbull, *Scott Fitzgerald*, p. 543.
51. Fitzgerald, *Letters*, p. 79.
52. Fitzgerald, *The Crack-Up*, p. 308.
53. Fitzgerald, *Letters*, p. 509.
54. Ibid., p. 363.

55. Fitzgerald, *The Crack-Up*, p. 310.

56. Mizener, *Far Side of Paradise*, p. 200. Fitzgerald once confessed half seriously to Margaret Chanler that he had three ambitions in life: "To write the best and clearest prose of the twentieth century, to remain faithful to Zelda and to become an intimate friend of Mrs. Wharton. Mrs. Chanler's response was the same that her friend Edith might have made: 'As to your first ambition, I hope you attain it. As to your second, it is too personal for me to comment on. But as to your third, young man, you'll have to cut down on your drinking'" (Louis Auchincloss, *Reflections of a Jacobite* [Boston, 1961], p. 26).

57. Fitzgerald, *The Crack-Up*, p. 309.

58. Gilbert Seldes, "Spring Flight," *Dial* 79 (1925): 163.

59. Quoted in Andrew Turnbull's *Scott Fitzgerald* (New York, 1962), pp. 277–78.

60. Lionel Trilling, "F. Scott Fitzgerald," *FSF*, p. 199. Compare Harry Levin's observation that "for Fitzgerald the rich were different—not quantitatively, because they had more money, but qualitatively, because he had a novelistic interest in manners and morals" ("Observations on the Style of Ernest Hemingway," *Ernest Hemingway: A Collection of Critical Essays*, ed. Robert P. Weeks [Englewood Cliffs, N.J., 1962], p. 85). For hard-to-deny evidence that money makes a difference, see George G. Kirstein's *The Rich: Are They Different?* (Boston, 1968), Arnold M. Rose's *The Power Structure* (New York, 1967), and G. William Dornhoff's *Who Rules America?* (Englewood Cliffs, N.J., 1967).

61. Fitzgerald, *The Crack-Up*, p. 77.

62. Fitzgerald, *Letters*, p. 3.

63. Ibid., p. 436.

64. John Peale Bishop, "The Missing All," *Virginia Quarterly Review* 12 (1937): 115.

65. Fitzgerald, *Letters*, p. 349.

66. Trilling, "F. Scott Fitzgerald," *FSF*, p. 200.

67. Piper, *F. Scott Fitzgerald*, p. 158.

68. Fitzgerald, *Letters*, p. 311.

69. Ibid., p. 36.

70. Kenneth Eble, *F. Scott Fitzgerald* (New York, 1963), p. 97.

71. Lionel Trilling, "F. Scott Fitzgerald," *FSF*, pp. 202–3.

72. Arthur Mizener, "The Novel of Manners in America," *Kenyon Review* 12 (1950): 19.

CHAPTER 8

1. John O'Hara, *My Turn* (New York, 1967), p. 55.

2. Virginia Woolf, *Mr. Bennett and Mrs. Brown* (London, 1924), pp. 17–19.

3. Edith Wharton, *The Writing of Fiction* (New York, 1925), pp. 6–7.

4. Edith Wharton, "The Great American Novel," *Yale Review*, n.s. 16 (1927): 652.

5. O'Hara, *My Turn*, p. 55.

6. Lewis Nichols, "Interview with John O'Hara," *New York Times Book Review*, 27 November 1955, p. 26.

7. René Wellek and Austin Warren, *Theory of Literature* (New York, 1956), pp. 210–11.

8. John O'Hara, *Sweet and Sour* (New York, 1956), pp. 149–50.

9. Ibid., pp. 155–56.

10. Ibid., p. 119.

11. F. Scott Fitzgerald, *The Letters of F. Scott Fitzgerald*, ed. Andrew Turnbull (New York, 1963), p. 560.

12. John O'Hara, "Foreword," *Appointment in Samarra* (New York, 1934), p. xix.

13. O'Hara, *Sweet and Sour*, pp. 82–85.

14. Ibid., pp. 155–56.

15. Louis Auchincloss, "Marquand and O'Hara: The Novel of Manners," *Nation*, 19 November 1960, pp. 383–88.

16. O'Hara, *My Turn*, p. 90.

17. O'Hara, *Sweet and Sour*, pp. 155–56.

18. Ibid.

19. Ibid., pp. 83–85.

20. O'Hara has been a fairly severe critic of writers about the life of society in America, but he thought so well of Louis Kronenberger's *Company Manners* (1954), a cultural inquiry into American life, that he felt that he had been scooped in his *own* plan to publish a factual study of American manners (*Sweet and Sour*, p. 101). Kronenberger's *A Month of Sundays* (1961), incidentally, is a comic novel of manners set in a mental institution.

21. Arthur Mizener, "Afterword," *Appointment in Samarra* by John O'Hara (New York, 1945), p. 211.

22. John O'Hara, *Ten North Frederick* (New York, 1955), p. 110; *From the Terrace* (New York, 1958), p. 20; and *A Rage to Live* (New York, 1949), p. 89. All quotations from these novels are from the first editions.

23. Norman Podhoretz, "Gibbsville and New Leeds: The America of John O'Hara and Mary McCarthy," *Commentary* 21 (1956): 270.

24. Chester E. Eisinger, *Fiction of the Forties* (Chicago, 1965), p. 289.

25. O'Hara, *My Turn*, p. 58.

26. Ibid., pp. 133–34.

27. John Portz, "John O'Hara Up to Now," *College English* 16 (1955): 493–99, 513.

28. O'Hara, *My Turn*, p. 134.

29. Rollene Waterman, "Appt. with O'Hara," *Saturday Review*, 29 November 1958, p. 15.

30. Delmore Schwartz, "Smile and Grin, Relax and Collapse," *Partisan Review* 17 (1950): 294.

31. Still, it is probably an exaggeration to say, as Mizener does, that O'Hara is "an Irishman who ate his heart out because he did not belong to what passed for society in the hard-coal region of Pennsylvania" ("The Novel in America," *Perspectives*, no. 15 [Spring 1956], p. 136).

32. O'Hara, *My Turn*, pp. 67–68.

33. Ibid.

34. John O'Hara, *The Lockwood Concern* (New York, 1965), pp. 116–18.

35. Edmund Wilson, "The Boys in the Back Room: John O'Hara," *Classics and Commercials* (New York, 1950), p. 23.

36. Brendan Gill, "The O'Hara Report and the Wit of Miss McCarthy," *New Yorker*, 20 August 1949, p. 64.

37. John O'Hara, *Elizabeth Appleton* (New York, 1963), p. 299.

38. Podhoretz, "Gibbsville and New Leeds," p. 270.

39. Leslie Fiedler, "An Old Pro at Work," *New Republic*, 9 January 1956, p. 17.

CHAPTER 9

1. Clifton Fadiman, "Introduction," *Thirty Years* by John P. Marquand (New York, 1954), p. xi.

2. Leo Gurko, "The High-Level Formula of J. P. Marquand," *American Scholar* 21 (1952): 443.

3. Quoted in Mark Schorer, *Sinclair Lewis: An American Life* (New York, 1961), p. 780.

4. Marquand, *Thirty Years*, p. 349.

5. Chester E. Eisinger, *Fiction of the Forties* (Chicago, 1965), p. 14.

6. Edward Wagenknecht, *The Cavalcade of the American Novel* (New York, 1952), p. 439.

7. C. Hugh Holman, *John P. Marquand* (Minneapolis, 1965), p. 7.

8. Firman Houghton and Ruth Whitman, "J. P. Marquand Speaking," *Cosmopolitan* 147 (August 1959): 48.

9. Harvey Breit, *The Writer Observed* (Cleveland and New York, 1956), p. 47.

10. Houghton and Whitman, "J. P. Marquand Speaking," p. 50.

11. Alfred Kazin, "John P. Marquand and the American Failure," *Atlantic* 202 (November 1958): 153; Gurko, "High-Level Formula of J. P. Marquand," *passim*.

12. Houghton and Whitman, "J. P. Marquand Speaking," p. 50.

13. Nathan Glick, "Marquand's Vanishing American Aristocracy: Good Manners and the Good Life," *Commentary* 9 (1950): 435. The only full-length study of Marquand as a novelist of manners is Robert O. Johnson's "John P. Marquand and the Novel of Manners" (Ph.D. diss., University of Washington, 1964).

14. "Spruce Street Boy," *Time*, 7 March 1949, p. 105.

15. Roger Butterfield, "John P. Marquand: America's Famous Novelist of Manners . . . ," *Life*, 31 July 1944, pp. 69, 72.

16. Henry Dwight Sedgwick, *In Praise of Gentlemen* (Boston, 1935), p. 195.

17. "Spruce Street Boy," p. 109.

18. Edward Weeks, "John P. Marquand," *Atlantic* 206 (October 1960): 74; John P. Marquand, "Apley, Wickford Point and Pulham: My Early Struggles," *Atlantic* 198 (September 1956): 72.

19. M. A. DeWolfe Howe, ed., *Barrett Wendell and His Letters* (Boston, 1924), p. 145.

20. Oliver Wendell Holmes, *Elsie Venner* (New York, 1961), pp. 15–19.

21. See also Oliver Wendell Holmes, *The Autocrat of the Breakfast Table* (Boston and New York, 1892), pp. 20–23. For a witty discussion of the ethos of the Boston area, see Cleveland Amory's *The Proper Bostonians* (New York, 1947).

22. Marquand, "Apley, Wickford Point and Pulham," p. 72.

23. Ibid.

24. John P. Marquand, *The Late George Apley* (Boston, 1937), p. 7. All quotations from Marquand's novels are taken from the first editions.

25. John P. Marquand, *Timothy Dexter Revisited* (Boston, 1960), p. 24.

26. Marquand, *Thirty Years*, p. 11.

27. Ibid., p. 21.

28. Houghton and Whitman, "J. P. Marquand Speaking," p. 50.

29. Marquand, "Apley, Wickford Point and Pulham," p. 72.

30. Marquand, *Thirty Years*, p. 20.

31. Marquand, "Apley, Wickford Point and Pulham, p. 72.

32. Ibid., p. 71.

33. "Spruce Street Boy," p. 105.

34. John P. Marquand, *Point of No Return* (Boston, 1949), p. 464.

35. Holman, *John P. Marquand*, p. 24.

36. Mark Twain, *Letters from the Earth*, ed. Bernard DeVoto (New York, 1962), p. 156.

37. Louis Auchincloss, "Marquand and O'Hara: The Novel of Manners," *Nation*, 19 November 1960, p. 386.

38. John P. Marquand, *B. F.'s Daughter* (Boston, 1946), pp. 257, 254.

39. John P. Marquand, *Women and Thomas Harrow* (Boston, 1958), pp. 43–44.

40. "Spruce Street Boy," pp. 110, 113.

41. Compare Marquand's observation, "Frankly, I submit that human nature is about the same whatever the environment" ("Apley, Wickford Point and Pulham," p. 74) with Lloyd Warner's claim that modern man is very little different from an Australian aborigine: "Despite obvious differences, the fundamental core of life of each is very much the same" (*American Life: Dream and Reality* [Chicago, 1953], p. viii).

42. W. Lloyd Warner and Paul S. Lunt, *The Social Life of a Modern Community* (New Haven, 1941), quoted in Granville Hicks, "Marquand of Newburyport," *Harper's* 200 (April 1950): 102.

43. Warner, *American Life*, p. vii.

44. Randall Jarrell, " 'Very Graceful Are the Uses of Culture,' " *Harper's* 209 (November 1954): 94.

45. Hicks, "Marquand of Newburyport," p. 102. Perhaps a more balanced estimate of Marquand's achievement in this novel is Max Lerner's observation that "Marquand's insights into the nuances of the social hierarchy of Newburyport, in his *Point of No Return*, form a necessary supplement to the factual picture that Warner gives of the class structure of the same town" (*America as a Civilization* [New York, 1957], p. 533).

46. Houghton and Whitman, "J. P. Marquand Speaking," p. 48.

47. Glick, "Marquand's Vanishing American Aristocracy," p. 441.

48. Charles Gray, then, as Marquand later observed, "sees that he has passed the point of no return and might as well accept it." But when the play version was produced on Broadway in 1951, the producer Paul Osborn was disturbed by Marquand's clear implication that "the game in many ways is not worth the candle." So to make the play more palatable, Osborn had Charles "show a kind of revolt by refusing to join the Hawthorn Hill Country Club as the boss requests. This makes the play seem to mean that 'the game may be worth the candle if you learn to walk erect.' " This ending understandably annoyed Marquand. Cf Henry Hewes, "Mr. Marquand Turns a Point," *Saturday Review*, 26 January 1952, p. 22.

49. Houghton and Whitman, "J. P. Marquand Speaking," p. 50.

50. John P. Marquand, "Introduction," *Vanity Fair* by William Makepeace Thackeray (New York, 1959), p. xv.

51. Kazin, "John P. Marquand," p. 156.

52. Ellen Glasgow, *The Sheltered Life* (Garden City, N.Y., 1932), p. 295.

53. Kazin, "John P. Marquand," p. 154.

54. Herschel Brickell, "Miss Glasgow and Mr. Marquand," *Virginia Quarterly Review* 17 (1941): 405.

CHAPTER 10

1. John Brooks, "Some Notes on Writing One Kind of Novel," in *The Living Novel: A Symposium*, ed. Granville Hicks (New York, 1962), pp. 52–56.

2. "Spruce Street Boy," *Time*, 7 March 1949, p. 113.

3. Zechariah Chafee, Jr., "The Just and the Unjust," *Harvard Law Review* 56 (1943): 833–36.

4. Malcolm Cowley, "The World of Arthur Winner, Jr.," *New York Times Book Review*, 25 August 1957, p. 1.

5. Frederick Bracher, *The Novels of James Gould Cozzens* (New York, 1959), p. 94.

6. James Gould Cozzens, *By Love Possessed* (New York, 1957), pp. 544–45.

7. James Gould Cozzens, *The Last Adam* (New York, 1933), pp. 11–12.

8. Harry John Mooney, Jr., *James Gould Cozzens: Novelist of Intellect* (Pittsburgh, 1963), p. 7.

9. James Gould Cozzens, *Confusion* (New York, 1924), pp. 92–93.

10. James Gould Cozzens, *Guard of Honor* (New York, 1948), p. 534.

11. James Gould Cozzens, *Men and Brethren* (New York, 1936), p. 93.

12. James Gould Cozzens, *Ask Me Tomorrow* (New York, 1940), p. 149.

13. Cowley, "The World of Arthur Winner, Jr.," p. 1.

14. Irving Howe, "James Gould Cozzens: Novelist of the Republic," *New Republic*, 20 January 1958, pp. 17, 19.

15. Allen Guttmann, *The Conservative Tradition in America* (New York, 1967), p. 179.

16. Russell Kirk, *The Intemperate Professor* (Baton Rouge, La., 1965), p. 152 [italics added].

17. Mooney, *James Gould Cozzens*, p. 164.

18. Louis O. Coxe, "A High Place," *Critique* 1 (1958): 50.

19. Bracher, *The Novels of James Gould Cozzens*, p. 20.

20. Louis Auchincloss, *Reflections of a Jacobite* (Boston, 1961), pp. vii–viii.

21. Henry James, *The Letters of Henry James*, ed. Percy Lubbock, 2 vols. (New York, 1920), 1:396.

22. Louis Auchincloss, *Portrait in Brownstone* (Boston, 1962), p. 76.

23. Henry James, *The Portrait of a Lady*, 2 vols. (New York, 1951), 1:287–88.

24. Auchincloss, *Reflections of a Jacobite*, p. 144.

25. Ibid., pp. 107–8, 110.

26. Louis Auchincloss, *The Embezzler* (New York, 1965), p. 6.

27. Granville Hicks, "A Bad Legend in His Lifetime," *Saturday Review*, 5 February 1966, p. 36.

28. Louis Auchincloss, *The House of Five Talents* (Boston, 1960), p. 355.

29. John P. Marquand, *Sincerely, Willis Wayde* (New York, 1955), p. 20.

30. Auchincloss, *Reflections of a Jacobite*, pp. 147–48.

31. Hicks, "A Bad Legend," pp. 35–36.

32. Auchincloss, *Reflections of a Jacobite*, p. 163.

33. Ibid., p. 111.

34. Ibid., pp. 148–49.

35. Ibid., p. 142.

36. Robert M. Adams, "Saturday Night and Sunday Morning," *New York Review of Books*, 9 July 1964, p. 15.

37. Auchincloss, *Reflections of a Jacobite*, p. 8.

38. Edith Wharton, *A Backward Glance* (New York, 1934), p. 325.

39. Auchincloss, *Reflections of a Jacobite*, pp. 104–5.

40. Ibid., pp. 139–40.

41. Ibid., p. 140.

CHAPTER 11

1. Quoted in Van Wyck Brooks, *The Writer in America* (New York, 1953), p. 51.

2. Irving Howe, "Mass Society and Post-Modern Fiction," in *Recent American Fiction*, ed. Joseph J. Waldmeir (Boston, 1963), p. 8.

3. Norman Podhoretz, *Doings and Undoings: The Fifties and After in American Writing* (New York, 1964), pp. 129, 3, 131, 8.

4. Norman Mailer, *Cannibals and Christians* (New York, 1967), pp. 97–98.

5. Ibid., p. 98.

6. Ibid., p. 101.

7. Ibid., p. 102.

8. Barbara Tuchman, "The Historian's Opportunity," *Saturday Review*, 25 February 1967, p. 27.

9. Norman Podhoretz, *Making It* (New York, 1967), p. 262.

10. Ibid., p. 355.

11. Readers may find it interesting to note that, since my remarks were written, Mr. Podhoretz has changed his ground considerably. He has abandoned the view of literature as an instrument in the service of ideas in favor of an affirmation of the autonomy of imaginative literature. This recantation is contained in his essay "Repentance and a Stand": "It was not for the better, it was for the worse, that I, a critic, refused to regard literature as an end in itself. For in practicing criticism without the license of that belief, I was fostering the growth of a vulgar idea of the relevance of literature and thereby helping to subvert both the general understanding of what the autonomy of literature truly means and the general esteem for the literary mode and the virtues distinctive to it—to it alone and to no other mode of expression or public discourse" (*Commentary* 52 [1971]:4).

✖ Index